C0-AUB-149

Teach Yourself VISUALLY™
Quicken® 2001

by Elaine Marmel

Visual

From
maranGraphics™

&

IDG Books Worldwide, Inc.
An International Data Group Company
Foster City, CA • Indianapolis • Chicago • New York

Teach Yourself VISUALLY™ Quicken® 2001

Published by
IDG Books Worldwide, Inc.
An International Data Group Company
919 E. Hillsdale Blvd., Suite 300
Foster City, CA 94404
www.idgbooks.com (IDG Books Worldwide Web Site)

Original Text and Original Illustrations Copyright © 2001 IDG Books Worldwide, Inc.
Design and certain of the illustrations Copyright © 1991-2000 maranGraphics, Inc.
                                    5755 Coopers Avenue
                                    Mississauga, Ontario, Canada
                                    L4Z 1R9

All rights reserved. No part of this book, including interior design, cover design,
and icons, may be reproduced or transmitted in any form, by any means (electronic,
photocopying, recording, or otherwise) without prior written permission of the publisher.

Library of Congress Control Number: 00-107560

ISBN: 0-7645-3526-9

Printed in the United States of America
10 9 8 7 6 5 4 3 2 1

1K/RU/RR/QQ/IN

Distributed in the United States by IDG Books Worldwide, Inc.

Distributed by CDG Books Canada Inc. for Canada; by Transworld Publishers Limited in the
United Kingdom; by IDG Norge Books for Norway; by IDG Sweden Books for Sweden; by
IDG Books Australia Publishing Corporation Pty. Ltd. for Australia and New Zealand; by
TransQuest Publishers Pte Ltd. for Singapore, Malaysia, Thailand, Indonesia, and Hong Kong;
by Gotop Information Inc. for Taiwan; by ICG Muse, Inc. for Japan; by Intersoft for South
Africa; by Eyrolles for France; by International Thomson Publishing for Germany, Austria and
Switzerland; by Distribuidora Cuspide for Argentina; by LR International for Brazil; by Galileo
Libros for Chile; by Ediciones ZETA S.C.R. Ltda. for Peru; by WS Computer Publishing
Corporation, Inc., for the Philippines; by Contemporanea de Ediciones for Venezuela; by
Express Computer Distributors for the Caribbean and West Indies; by Micronesia Media
Distributor, Inc. for Micronesia; by Chips Computadoras S.A. de C.V. for Mexico; by Editorial
Norma de Panama S.A. for Panama; by American Bookshops for Finland.

For corporate orders, please call maranGraphics at 800-469-6616.

For general information on IDG Books Worldwide's books in the U.S., please call our
Consumer Customer Service department at 800-762-2974. For reseller information, including
discounts and premium sales, please call our Reseller Customer Service department at
800-434-3422.

For information on where to purchase IDG Books Worldwide's books outside the U.S., please
contact our International Sales department at 317-572-3993 or fax 317-572-4002.

For consumer information on foreign language translations, please contact our Customer
Service department at 1-800-434-3422, fax 317-572-4002, or e-mail rights@idgbooks.com.

For information on licensing foreign or domestic rights, please phone 1-650-653-7098.

For sales inquiries and special prices for bulk quantities, please contact our Order Services
department at 800-434-3422 or write to the address above.

For information on using IDG Books Worldwide's books in the classroom or for ordering
examination copies, please contact our Educational Sales department at 800-434-2086 or fax
317-572-4005.

For press review copies, author interviews, or other publicity information, please contact our
Public Relations department at 650-653-7000 or fax 650-653-7500.

For authorization to photocopy items for corporate, personal, or educational use, please
contact Copyright Clearance Center, 222 Rosewood Drive, Danvers, MA 01923, or fax
978-750-4470.

Screen shots displayed in this book are based on pre-released software and are subject to change.

LIMIT OF LIABILITY/DISCLAIMER OF WARRANTY: THE PUBLISHER AND AUTHOR
HAVE USED THEIR BEST EFFORTS IN PREPARING THIS BOOK. THE PUBLISHER
AND AUTHOR MAKE NO REPRESENTATIONS OR WARRANTIES WITH RESPECT TO
THE ACCURACY OR COMPLETENESS OF THE CONTENTS OF THIS BOOK AND
SPECIFICALLY DISCLAIM ANY IMPLIED WARRANTIES OF MERCHANTABILITY OR
FITNESS FOR A PARTICULAR PURPOSE. THERE ARE NO WARRANTIES WHICH
EXTEND BEYOND THE DESCRIPTIONS CONTAINED IN THIS PARAGRAPH. NO
WARRANTY MAY BE CREATED OR EXTENDED BY SALES REPRESENTATIVES OR
WRITTEN SALES MATERIALS. THE ACCURACY AND COMPLETENESS OF THE
INFORMATION PROVIDED HEREIN AND THE OPINIONS STATED HEREIN ARE NOT
GUARANTEED OR WARRANTED TO PRODUCE ANY PARTICULAR RESULTS, AND
THE ADVICE AND STRATEGIES CONTAINED HEREIN MAY NOT BE SUITABLE FOR
EVERY INDIVIDUAL. NEITHER THE PUBLISHER NOR AUTHOR SHALL BE LIABLE
FOR ANY LOSS OF PROFIT OR ANY OTHER COMMERCIAL DAMAGES, INCLUDING
BUT NOT LIMITED TO SPECIAL, INCIDENTAL, CONSEQUENTIAL, OR OTHER
DAMAGES.

Trademark Acknowledgments

The IDG Books Worldwide logo is a registered trademark, under exclusive license
from International Data Group, Inc. The Visual logo, Teach Yourself VISUALLY,
Master VISUALLY, Simplified, and related trade dress are trademarks of IDG Books
Worldwide, Inc., and may not be used without written permission. Quicken is a
registered trademark of Intuit Inc. The maranGraphics logo is a trademark of
maranGraphics Inc. All other trademarks are the property of their respective
owners. IDG Books Worldwide, Inc. and maranGraphics Inc. are not associated
with any product or vendor mentioned in this book.

**FOR PURPOSES OF ILLUSTRATING THE CONCEPTS AND TECHNIQUES
DESCRIBED IN THIS BOOK, THE AUTHOR HAS CREATED VARIOUS
NAMES, COMPANY NAMES, MAILING ADDRESSES, E-MAIL
ADDRESSES AND PHONE NUMBERS, ALL OF WHICH ARE FICTITIOUS.
ANY RESEMBLANCE OF THESE FICTITIOUS NAMES, COMPANY
NAMES, MAILING ADDRESSES, E-MAIL ADDRESSES AND PHONE
NUMBERS TO ANY ACTUAL PERSON, COMPANY AND/OR
ORGANIZATION IS UNINTENTIONAL AND PURELY COINCIDENTAL.**

Permissions

maranGraphics

Certain of the Illustrations are Copyright 1992-2000 maranGraphics
Inc., and are used with maranGraphics' permission.

is a registered trademark under exclusive
license to IDG Books Worldwide, Inc.
from International Data Group, Inc.

U.S. Corporate Sales	U.S. Trade Sales
Contact maranGraphics at (800) 469-6616 or Fax (905) 890-9434.	Contact IDG Books at (800) 434-3422 or (650) 655-3000.

ABOUT IDG BOOKS WORLDWIDE

Welcome to the world of IDG Books Worldwide.

IDG Books Worldwide, Inc., is a subsidiary of International Data Group, the world's largest publisher of computer-related information and the leading global provider of information services on information technology. IDG was founded more than 30 years ago by Patrick J. McGovern and now employs more than 9,000 people worldwide. IDG publishes more than 290 computer publications in over 75 countries. More than 90 million people read one or more IDG publications each month.

Launched in 1990, IDG Books Worldwide is today the #1 publisher of best-selling computer books in the United States. We are proud to have received eight awards from the Computer Press Association in recognition of editorial excellence and three from Computer Currents' First Annual Readers' Choice Awards. Our best-selling *...For Dummies®* series has more than 50 million copies in print with translations in 31 languages. IDG Books Worldwide, through a joint venture with IDG's Hi-Tech Beijing, became the first U.S. publisher to publish a computer book in the People's Republic of China. In record time, IDG Books Worldwide has become the first choice for millions of readers around the world who want to learn how to better manage their businesses.

Our mission is simple: Every one of our books is designed to bring extra value and skill-building instructions to the reader. Our books are written by experts who understand and care about our readers. The knowledge base of our editorial staff comes from years of experience in publishing, education, and journalism — experience we use to produce books to carry us into the new millennium. In short, we care about books, so we attract the best people. We devote special attention to details such as audience, interior design, use of icons, and illustrations. And because we use an efficient process of authoring, editing, and desktop publishing our books electronically, we can spend more time ensuring superior content and less time on the technicalities of making books.

You can count on our commitment to deliver high-quality books at competitive prices on topics you want to read about. At IDG Books Worldwide, we continue in the IDG tradition of delivering quality for more than 30 years. You'll find no better book on a subject than one from IDG Books Worldwide.

John Kilcullen
Chairman and CEO
IDG Books Worldwide, Inc.

*Eighth Annual
Computer Press
Awards ≥1992*

*Ninth Annual
Computer Press
Awards ≥1993*

*Tenth Annual
Computer Press
Awards ≥1994*

*Eleventh Annual
Computer Press
Awards ≥1995*

IDG is the world's leading IT media, research and exposition company. Founded in 1964, IDG had 1997 revenues of $2.05 billion and has more than 9,000 employees worldwide. IDG offers the widest range of media options that reach IT buyers in 75 countries representing 95% of worldwide IT spending. IDG's diverse product and services portfolio spans six key areas including print publishing, online publishing, expositions and conferences, market research, education and training, and global marketing services. More than 90 million people read one or more of IDG's 290 magazines and newspapers, including IDG's leading global brands — Computerworld, PC World, Network World, Macworld and the Channel World family of publications. IDG Books Worldwide is one of the fastest-growing computer book publishers in the world, with more than 700 titles in 36 languages. The "...For Dummies®" series alone has more than 50 million copies in print. IDG offers online users the largest network of technology-specific Web sites around the world through IDG.net (http://www.idg.net), which comprises more than 225 targeted Web sites in 55 countries worldwide. International Data Corporation (IDC) is the world's largest provider of information technology data, analysis and consulting, with research centers in over 41 countries and more than 400 research analysts worldwide. IDG World Expo is a leading producer of more than 168 globally branded conferences and expositions in 35 countries including E3 (Electronic Entertainment Expo), Macworld Expo, ComNet, Windows World Expo, ICE (Internet Commerce Expo), Agenda, DEMO, and Spotlight. IDG's training subsidiary, ExecuTrain, is the world's largest computer training company, with more than 230 locations worldwide and 785 training courses. IDG Marketing Services helps industry-leading IT companies build international brand recognition by developing global integrated marketing programs via IDG's print, online and exposition products worldwide. Further information about the company can be found at www.idg.com.   1/26/00

maranGraphics is a family-run business
located near Toronto, Canada.

At **maranGraphics**, we believe in producing great computer books — one book at a time.

maranGraphics has been producing high-technology products for over 25 years, which enables us to offer the computer book community a unique communication process.

Our computer books use an integrated communication process, which is very different from the approach used in other computer books. Each spread is, in essence, a flow chart — the text and screen shots are totally incorporated into the layout of the spread. Introductory text and helpful tips complete the learning experience.

maranGraphics' approach encourages the left and right sides of the brain to work together, resulting in faster orientation and greater memory retention.

Above all, we are very proud of the handcrafted nature of our books. Our carefully-chosen writers are experts in their fields, and spend countless hours researching and organizing the content for each topic. Our artists rebuild every screen shot to provide the best clarity possible, making our screen shots the most precise and easiest to read in the

industry. We strive for perfection, and believe that the time spent handcrafting each element results in the best computer books money can buy.

Thank you for purchasing this book. We hope you enjoy it!

Sincerely,

Robert Maran
President
maranGraphics
Rob@maran.com
www.maran.com
www.idgbooks.com/visual

CREDITS

Acquisitions, Editorial, and Media Development

Project Editor
Maureen Spears

Acquisitions Editor
Martine Edwards

Associate Project Coordinator
Lindsay Sandman

Copy Editors
Christine Berman, Tim Borek

Technical Editor
Lee Musick

Editorial Manager
Mary Corder

Media Development Manager
Rich Graves

Editorial Assistants
Amanda Foxworth, Candace Nicholson,
Sarah Shupert

Production

Book Design
maranGraphics Inc.

Project Coordinator
Maridee Ennis

Layout
Joe Bucki, Barry Offringa, Kristin Pickett

Editorial Graphics Production
Ronda David-Burroughs, Craig Dearing, Dave Gregory,
Mark Harris, Jill Johnson

Proofreaders
Laura Albert, Sally Burton, Marianne Santy,
Charles Spencer

Indexer
York Production Services, Inc.

ACKNOWLEDGMENTS

General and Administrative

IDG Books Worldwide, Inc.: John Kilcullen, CEO; Bill Barry, President and COO; John Ball, Executive VP, Operations & Administration; John Harris, CFO

IDG Books Technology Publishing Group: Richard Swadley, Senior Vice President and Publisher; Mary Bednarek, Vice President and Publisher; Walter R. Bruce III, Vice President and Publisher; Joseph Wikert, Vice President and Publisher; Mary C. Corder, Editorial Director; Andy Cummings, Publishing Director, General User Group; Barry Pruett, Publishing Director

IDG Books Manufacturing: Ivor Parker, Vice President, Manufacturing

IDG Books Marketing: John Helmus, Assistant Vice President, Director of Marketing

IDG Books Online Management: Brenda McLaughlin, Executive Vice President, Chief Internet Officer; Gary Millrood, Executive Vice President of Business Development, Sales and Marketing

IDG Books Packaging: Marc J. Mikulich, Vice President, Brand Strategy and Research

IDG Books Production for Branded Press: Debbie Stailey, Production Director

IDG Books Sales: Roland Elgey, Senior Vice President, Sales and Marketing; Michael Violano, Vice President, International Sales and Sub Rights

The publisher would like to give special thanks to Patrick J. McGovern,
without whom this book would not have been possible.

ABOUT THE AUTHOR

Elaine Marmel received her black-belt in book writing years ago. She earned her undergraduate degree from the University of Cincinnati (by way of Oxford, Ohio, Chicago, Illinois and Jerusalem, Israel). She earned her MBA from Cornell University.

Her three cats, Cato, Watson, and Buddy assist in her literary endeavors by alternately acting as paper weights, monitoring doors (as in "You're a better door than a window, since I can't see through you"), and bringing nutritious treats (lizards) right to her office door-step. She has authored a gazillion books and writes articles for three computer magazines.

AUTHOR'S ACKNOWLEDGMENTS

The author would like to acknowledge that the people at IDG Books Worldwide have been extremely kind to her, especially Maureen Spears, her Project Editor and Martine Edwards, her Acquisitions Editor. The author would also like to thank the Technical Editor, Lee Musick, for his competent, salient observations, and his great sense of humor. Thanks also to the graphics team, especially Ronda David-Burroughs for her creative art work and IDGB production staff for their hard work and long hours.

AUTHOR DEDICATION

I would like to dedicate this book to my mother, Susan Marmel.

TABLE OF CONTENTS

Chapter 1

STARTING QUICKEN THE FIRST TIME

Chapter 2

ENTER CHECKBOOK TRANSACTIONS

Chapter 3

BALANCE YOUR CHECKING ACCOUNT

Chapter 4

AUTOMATE TRANSACTIONS

TABLE OF CONTENTS

Chapter 5

TRACK CREDIT CARD DEBT

Chapter 6

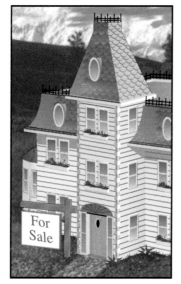

MANAGE YOUR PROPERTY

Chapter 7

TRACK INVESTMENTS

Chapter 8

QUICKEN AND TAXES

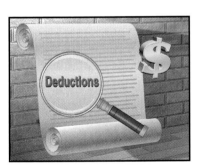

TABLE OF CONTENTS

Chapter 9

PLAN FOR THE FUTURE

Chapter 10

PROTECT YOUR INFORMATION

Chapter 11

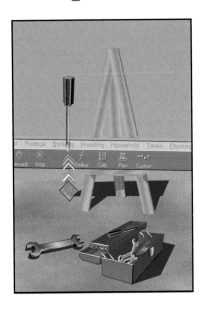

CHAPTER 1

Starting Quicken the First Time

Are you ready to start using Quicken? In this chapter, you learn to set up a bank account and an Internet connection, and you become familiar with Quicken's terminology.

INTRODUCING QUICKEN

Quicken is a personal financial management program that helps you in a variety of ways. With Quicken, you can track and pay bills, balance your checkbook, budget, track your spending for tax purposes, manage your investments, determine if you can afford to buy a home, and plan for college educations or retirement.

TRACK TAX DEDUCTIONS

In Quicken, every time you write a check or record a deposit, you assign the transaction to a category. Quicken allows you to assign categories to lines on your income tax return. By categorizing your spending and relating your spending to tax return lines, Quicken's reports on categories make preparing your income tax return easier.

PRINT CHECKS

If you write a lot of checks, printing them in Quicken saves you time. Although printed checks are more expensive, you may feel that the time and effort you save makes the expense worthwhile.

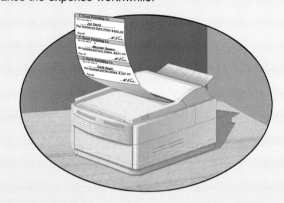

TRACK CREDIT CARDS

Help yourself stay out of credit card debt by tracking your credit card purchases as you make them. Many credit card companies enable you to download your transactions (daily, if you want) directly into Quicken to avoid time-consuming typing.

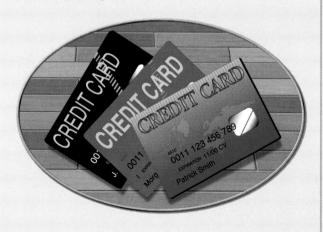

MANAGE YOUR MONEY AND YOUR PROPERTY

You can set up a budget easily in Quicken and then produce reports and graphs that help you identify how well you are sticking to your budget. You can also track assets (things you *own*) and liabilities (things you *owe*) in Quicken to help you get a clear picture of your personal net worth (the difference between what you own and what you owe).

BUDGET

	Budgeted	Spent
Telephone	$90.00	$86.89
Groceries	$75.00	$57.03
Insurance	$18.70	$18.70
Entertainment	$60.00	$35.00
Gas	$60.00	$52.48
Water	$50.00	$40.87
Electric	$60.00	$47.34

PLAN FOR THE FUTURE

Quicken contains five financial calculators that help you make mortgage-refinancing decisions, calculate loan payments or balances, project how much you will accumulate from saving, plan for your retirement, and figure out how much to save to finance a college education.

FOLLOW YOUR INVESTMENTS

Set up investment accounts in Quicken and download quotes from the Internet to update your portfolio's value daily. Some brokerage firms enable you to download investment transactions directly into Quicken. You can even "watch" stocks that you do not own.

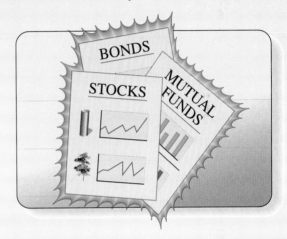

PAY BILLS AND BANK ONLINE

If your bank supports electronic banking and bill paying, you save time by paying bills electronically in Quicken. You record the check to pay the bill in Quicken and then send a message to your bank to pay the bill or to transfer the funds electronically from your account to the vendor's account. You also can transfer funds electronically between your checking and savings accounts and get your bank statements electronically.

WHEN TO START

When you set up an account, Quicken asks you for the ending balance on your last bank statement. Enter all checks you have written and deposits you have made since that statement. That is the "quick and dirty" way to start — but your first year of using Quicken, it will not contain enough information to help you do your taxes or evaluate your budget. Consider entering everything that has happened since the beginning of this year if you start using Quicken before July 1.

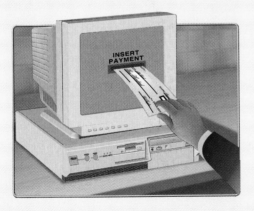

SET UP YOUR FIRST BANK ACCOUNT

The first time you open the program after installation, Quicken helps you set up a bank account.

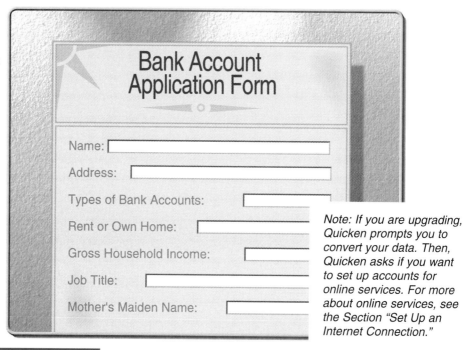

Bank Account Application Form

Name:

Address:

Types of Bank Accounts:

Rent or Own Home:

Gross Household Income:

Job Title:

Mother's Maiden Name:

Note: If you are upgrading, Quicken prompts you to convert your data. Then, Quicken asks if you want to set up accounts for online services. For more about online services, see the Section "Set Up an Internet Connection."

SET UP YOUR FIRST BANK ACCOUNT

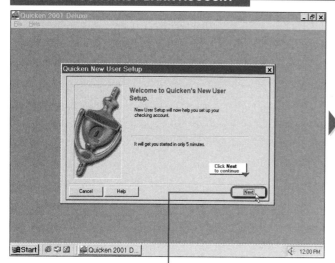

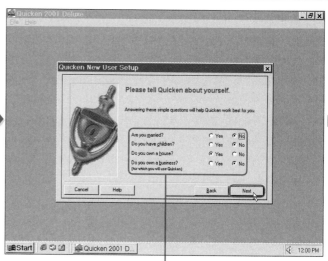

1 Double-click the **Quicken 2001 Deluxe** icon on your Desktop to start Quicken.

■ The New User Setup dialog box appears.

2 Click **Next**.

■ Quicken asks for some personal information about you.

3 Click **Yes** to all appropriate questions (○ changes to ◉).

4 Click **Next**.

Why does Quicken ask me for personal information?

The answers you type determine the categories Quicken automatically sets up for you. Quicken has standard categories that it sets up no matter how you answer the questions. In addition, it sets up extra categories for any question answered with a "Yes."

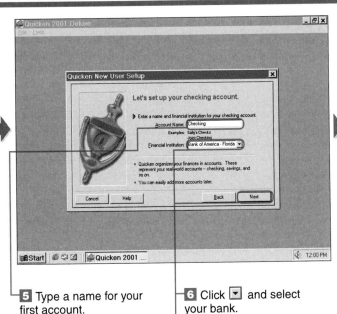

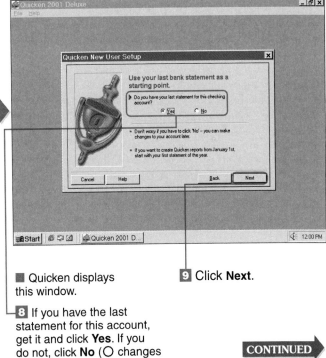

5 Type a name for your first account.

6 Click ▼ and select your bank.

Note: If you do not see your bank listed, leave the box blank.

7 Click **Next**.

■ Quicken displays this window.

8 If you have the last statement for this account, get it and click **Yes**. If you do not, click **No** (○ changes to ◉).

9 Click **Next**.

CONTINUED

SET UP YOUR FIRST BANK ACCOUNT

It does not matter whether you have your last bank statement. If you have the statement, Quicken uses the numbers you supply as the opening balance. If you do not have the statement, Quicken sets up your bank account with an opening balance of $0.00.

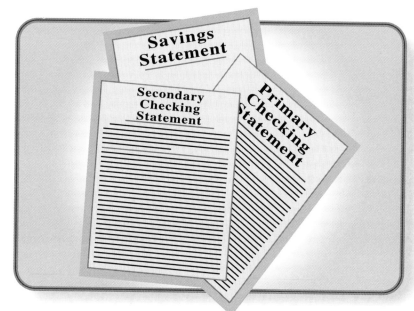

SET UP YOUR FIRST BANK ACCOUNT (CONTINUED)

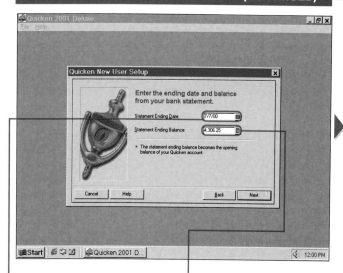

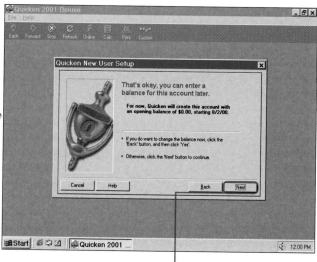

■ If you indicated that you have your last bank statement, Quicken displays a statement set up window.

10 Type the ending date that appears on your statement in the Statement Ending Date box.

11 Type the ending balance that appears on your statement in the Statement Ending Balance box.

■ If you indicated that you do not have your last bank statement, Quicken displays a window showing an opening balance of $0.00.

12 Click **Next**.

**If I do not have my statement
handy but want to get started,
what should I do?**

You do not need to go find your
bank statement right now; instead,
Quicken sets up your account with
a starting balance of $0.00. Later,
when you have your bank
statement, you can simply edit the
starting balance amount.

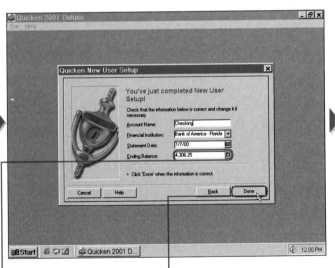

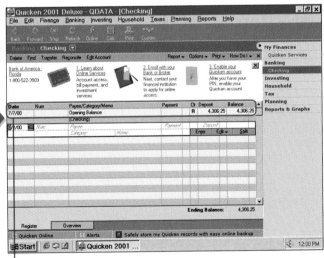

■ Quicken displays a
summary window.

■ If you supplied balance
information, Quicken
includes the balance in the
Ending Balance box.

*Note: If you did not type balance
information, Quicken displays
$0.00 as the amount.*

13 Click **Done**.

■ Quicken displays your
account register, including
an opening balance entry.

*Note: If you did not type
balance information, the amount
will be $0.00*

EXPLORE THE QUICKEN WINDOW

The Quicken window contains elements that
help you navigate the program.

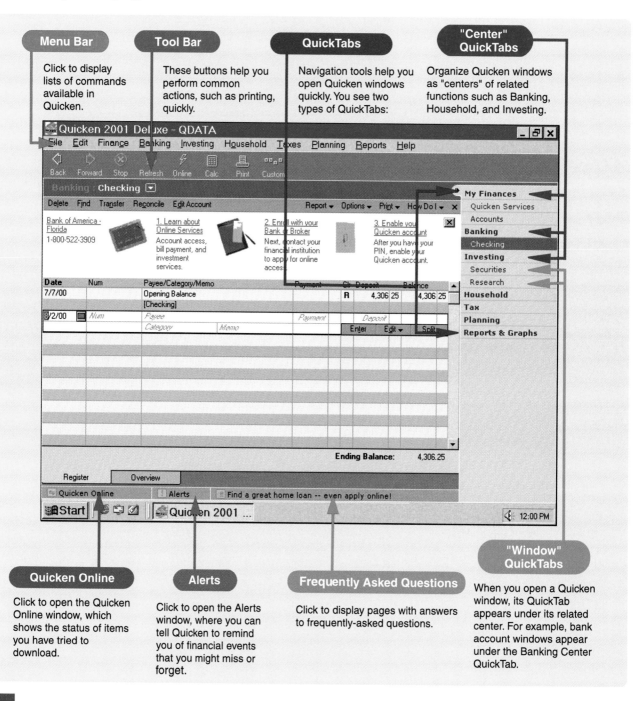

Menu Bar

Click to display
lists of commands
available in
Quicken.

Tool Bar

These buttons help you
perform common
actions, such as printing,
quickly.

QuickTabs

Navigation tools help you
open Quicken windows
quickly. You see two
types of QuickTabs:

**"Center"
QuickTabs**

Organize Quicken windows
as "centers" of related
functions such as Banking,
Household, and Investing.

Quicken Online

Click to open the Quicken
Online window, which
shows the status of items
you have tried to
download.

Alerts

Click to open the Alerts
window, where you can
tell Quicken to remind
you of financial events
that you might miss or
forget.

Frequently Asked Questions

Click to display pages with answers
to frequently-asked questions.

**"Window"
QuickTabs**

When you open a Quicken
window, its QuickTab
appears under its related
center. For example, bank
account windows appear
under the Banking Center
QuickTab.

Centers are QuickTabs (see the Section "Explore the Quicken Window") that show related information. You can use *links* to quickly "jump" to other Quicken features or to an Internet site. When you click a link on a QuickTab for a center, Quicken adds a QuickTab below the center for the feature window.

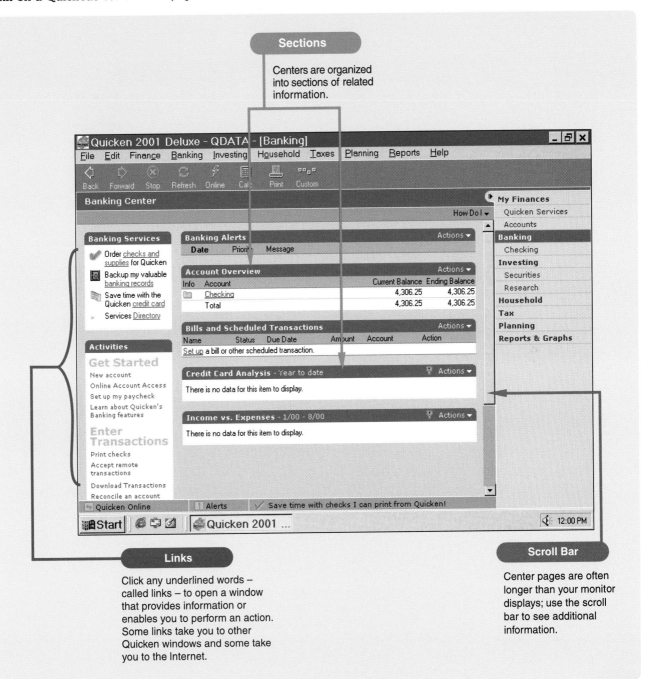

Sections

Centers are organized into sections of related information.

Links

Click any underlined words – called links – to open a window that provides information or enables you to perform an action. Some links take you to other Quicken windows and some take you to the Internet.

Scroll Bar

Center pages are often longer than your monitor displays; use the scroll bar to see additional information.

WORK WITH QUICKTABS

QuickTabs are navigational tools that allow you to quickly open frequently used windows. Quicken has two kinds of QuickTabs: Center QuickTabs and Window QuickTabs.

WORK WITH QUICKTABS

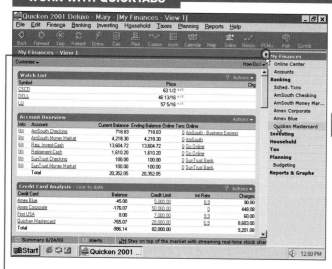

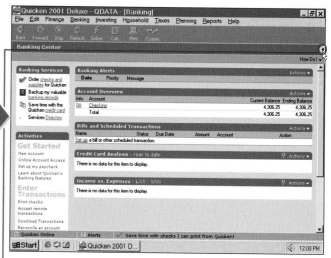

HIDE QUICK TABS

1 Click the QuickTab handle ◄ on the left side of the My Finances QuickTab.

■ Quicken hides all QuickTabs.

2 Click the QuickTab handle again to redisplay QuickTabs.

I rarely use the Taxes Center. Can I close it?

No. You cannot close any of the Center QuickTabs.

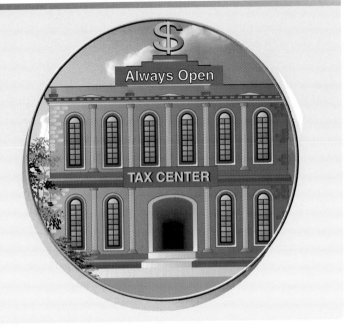

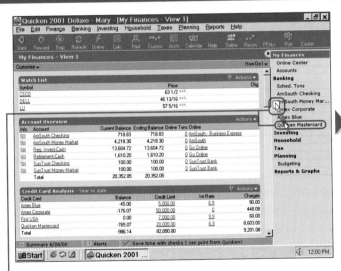

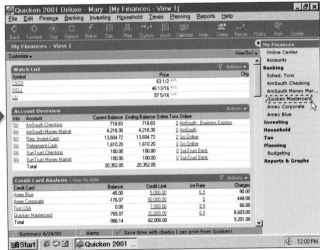

MOVE A QUICK TAB

1 Point ▷ at the window QuickTab you want to move.

2 Click and drag the QuickTab to a new location.

■ As you drag, Quicken adds a □ to ▷.

■ When you release the mouse button, Quicken places the QuickTab at the ▷ location.

Note: You cannot move Center QuickTabs.

CONTINUED ▶

WORK WITH QUICKTABS

You can switch the side
of the screen on which
QuickTabs appear or
close window QuickTabs
altogether.

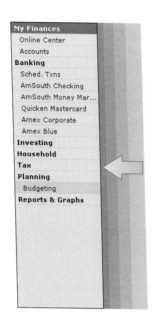

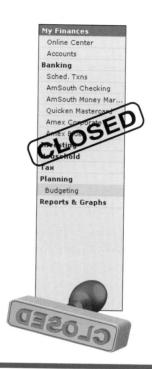

WORK WITH QUICKTABS (CONTINUED)

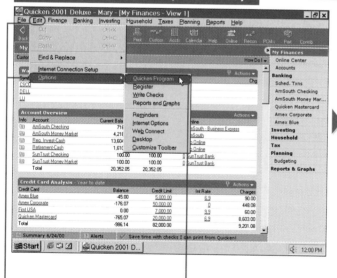

MOVE THE QUICKTAB LOCATION

-1 Click **Edit**.

-2 Select **Options**.

3 Click **Quicken Program**.

■ You see the QuickTabs
tab of the General Options
dialog box.

-4 Select the position of the
QuickTab (○ changes to ◉).

-5 Click **OK**.

I just noticed that some opened "window" QuickTabs — mostly reports — are no longer visible. Where did they go, and how do I get to them?

Notice the scroll bar on the outside edge of the QuickTabs. It appears as you open more and more "window" QuickTabs. Use it to scroll down and see the additional windows.

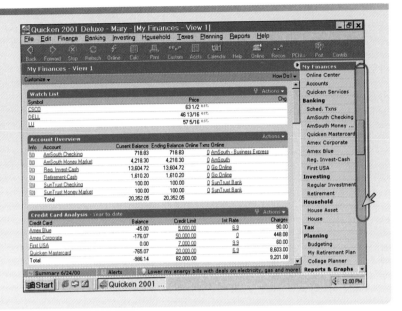

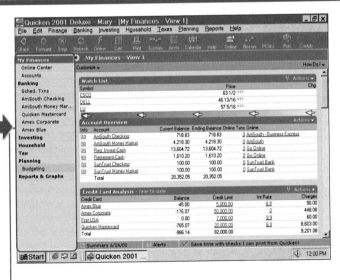

■ Quicken moves the QuickTabs to the other side of the window.

Note: You can use a shortcut to move the tabs back. Right-click My Finances and click either QuickTabs on Right or QuickTabs on Left.

■ In this example, the QuickTabs moves from the right to the left side of the screen.

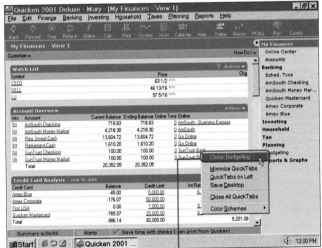

CLOSE A WINDOW QUICKTAB

1 Right-click the QuickTab you want to close.

2 Click **Close** from the shortcut menu that pops up.

USING THE HELP INDEX

You can use Quicken's
Help Index to locate Help
topics of interest.

USING THE HELP INDEX

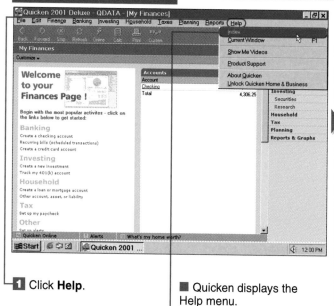

1 Click **Help**.

■ Quicken displays the
Help menu.

2 Click **Index**.

■ Quicken displays the Help
Topics Index tab, showing
major topics and indented
subtopics.

3 Type a few letters of a
topic that interests you.

■ Quicken highlights a topic
that matches your typing.

4 Click **Display**.

What do the underlined words signify?

Underlined words are *links* to additional help topics on related subjects. Click one, and you see help for that topic.

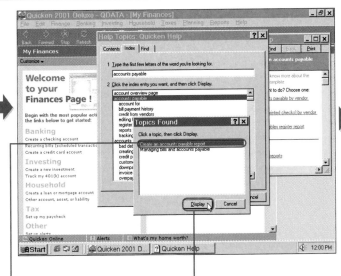

■ If you display a major topic, the Topics Found window appears.

5 Select a topic and click **Display**.

■ Quicken displays a Help window.

■ You can click a link to view a different help topic.

■ You can click **Index** to redisplay the Help Index.

6 Click ☒ to exit the Help window.

OTHER WAYS TO GET HELP

There are several
different ways to get
help if you need
assistance in Quicken.

OTHER WAYS TO GET HELP

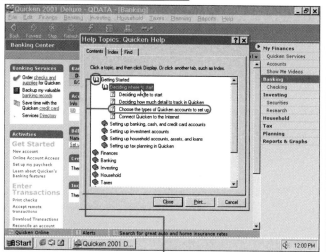

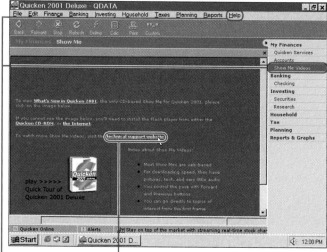

USING THE F1 FUNCTION

1 Press **F1**.

■ Quicken displays the
Help Topics window.

2 Double-click ◈ to see
more topics (◈ changes to 🔊).

■ The topic and its question
mark icon 🔲 displays.

3 Double-click a topic to
display it.

VIEW SHOW ME VIDEOS

1 Click **Help**.

2 Click **Show Me Videos**.

■ Quicken displays the
Show Me window.

*Note: Most Show Me videos are
stored on the Internet.*

3 Click the **technical
support website** link.

■ Quicken connects to the
Internet where you click a
link to download a video.

18

I used Quicken 2000 and there were Show Me Videos on the CD. Are there any Show Me videos on the Quicken 2001 CD?

You can find the "What's New in Quicken 2001" video on the CD.

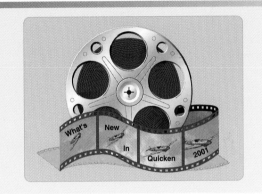

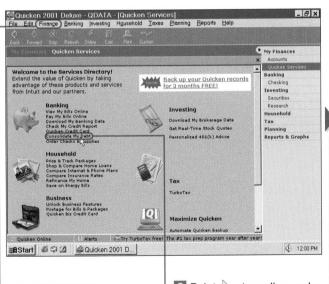

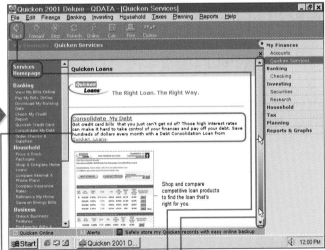

QUICKEN SERVICES

1 Click **Finance**.

2 Click **Quicken Services**.

■ Quicken displays the Quicken Services Directory window.

3 Point 🖑 at any line under a heading. These lines are links.

4 Click a link.

■ Quicken displays information about the link that you clicked. The Services Directory appears on the left.

5 Use the scroll bar to see more of the Services Directory.

6 Click the **Services Homepage** link or the **Back** button on the toolbar to redisplay the Quicken Services Directory page.

Quicken gives you access to Web-based and telephone support. On the Web, you can view frequently-asked questions and even make product suggestions.

OTHER WAYS TO GET HELP (CONTINUED)

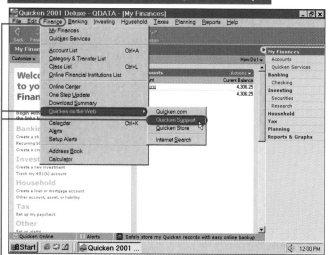

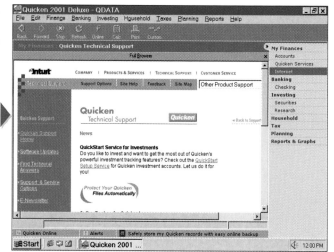

USING WEB-BASED SUPPORT

1 Click **Finance**.

2 Click **Quicken on the Web**.

3 Click **Quicken Support**.

■ Quicken displays a message indicating that you are going to connect to the Internet.

4 Click **OK**.

■ Quicken connects to the Internet and displays the Quicken Technical Support Web page.

5 Click a link on the page to see more information on a topic.

Note: You cannot view the Web page if you have not set up your Internet connection in Quicken. See the Section "Set Up an Internet Connection."

What happens if I click the Go to Web button in the Product Support dialog box?

Quicken displays the same window as the one you see when you click **Finance,** then **Quicken on the Web**, and **Quicken Support**.

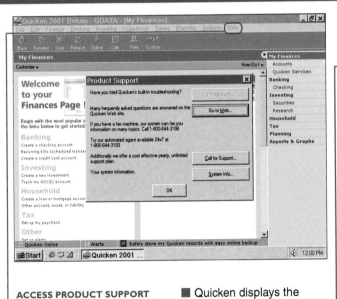

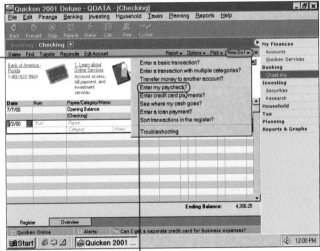

ACCESS PRODUCT SUPPORT

1 Click **Help**.

2 Click **Product Support**.

■ Quicken displays the Product Support dialog box.

ASK QUESTIONS ABOUT THE WINDOW YOU ARE VIEWING

1 In any window, click **How Do I**.

■ Quicken displays a menu of questions related to the window.

2 Click a question to display its Help topic.

VIEW AND CHANGE ACCOUNT INFORMATION

Suppose you want to change your account name, or you close an account? Quicken allows you to change your account information.

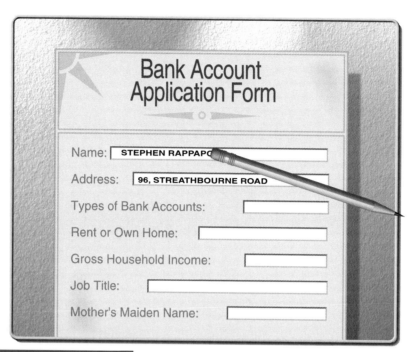

Bank Account
Application Form

Name: STEPHEN RAPPAPO

Address: 96, STREATHBOURNE ROAD

Types of Bank Accounts:

Rent or Own Home:

Gross Household Income:

Job Title:

Mother's Maiden Name:

VIEW AND CHANGE ACCOUNT INFORMATION

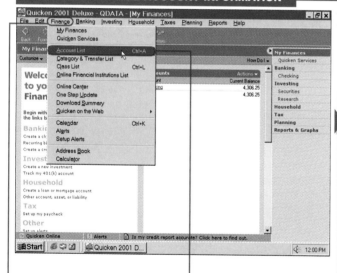

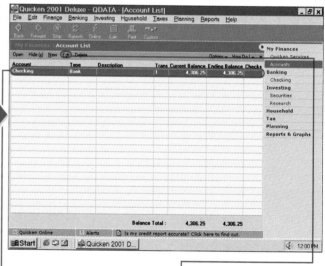

1 Click **Finance**.

2 Click **Account List**.

*Note: You can press **Ctrl-A** to display the Account List.*

■ Quicken displays the list of accounts you defined.

3 Click the account you want to edit.

4 Click **Edit**.

I have closed a bank account. Should I delete it?

You can hide the account instead of deleting it. That way, if you need it, you can redisplay it.

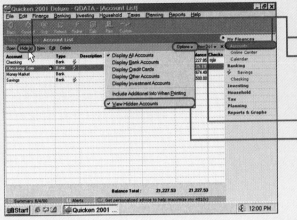

To hide the account:

1 Click the account in the Account List.

2 Click **Hide (x)**.

■ The Account is hidden.

To view again:

1 Click **Options**.

2 Click **View Hidden Accounts**.

■ Hidden accounts contain a "hand" icon.

■ To unhide the account, click it in the Account List and click **Hide (x)** again. The hand disappears.

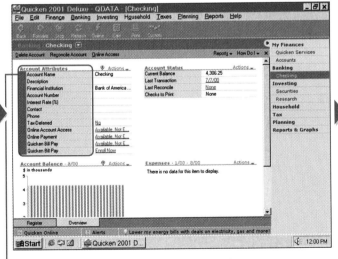

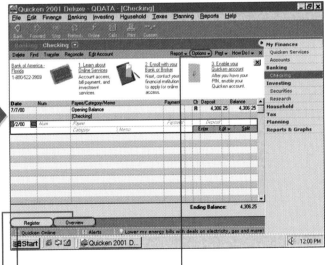

5 Make changes to the Account Attributes fields by clicking next to a field and typing in it.

6 Press **Enter** to save your typing.

■ You can use the register for this account by clicking the Register tab.

■ To edit the account again, click the Overview tab.

■ To view more of your register, you can hide the icons along the top. **Click Options** and then click **View Register Only**.

SET UP ADDITIONAL ACCOUNTS

You can create a variety of banking and cash accounts to track your finances. With Quicken, you can track credit card debt, investments, the value of your home, your mortgage, and more.

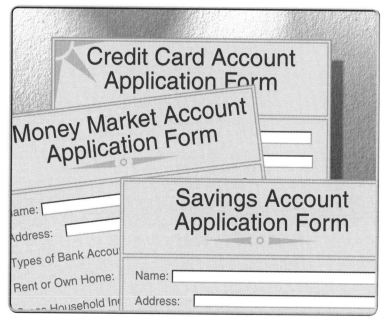

SET UP ADDITIONAL ACCOUNTS

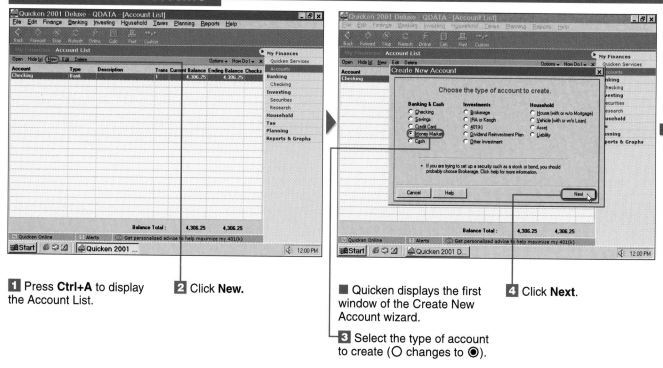

1 Press **Ctrl+A** to display the Account List.

2 Click **New.**

■ Quicken displays the first window of the Create New Account wizard.

3 Select the type of account to create (O changes to ⊙).

4 Click **Next.**

Do I see the same screens for every type of account I create?

Yes and No. This Section shows the screens that you see for Cash and Bank accounts using the New Account Wizard. You see different screens when you create investment accounts and household accounts.

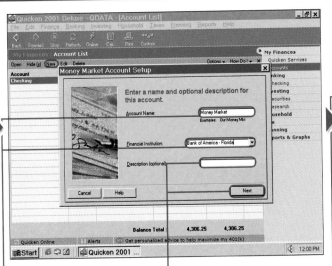

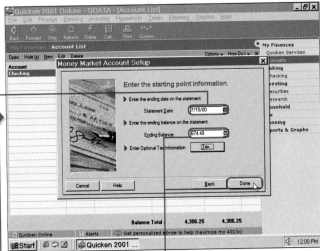

■ Quicken displays an account setup window

5 Type a name for the account.

6 Click ▼ and select your bank from the drop down menu.

Note: If you do not see your bank listed, leave the box blank.

■ You can type a description of the account for future reference.

7 Click **Next**.

■ Quicken displays a window asking for the statement date and ending balance.

8 Type the ending date that appears on the statement in the Statement Date box.

9 Type the ending balance that appears on the statement in the Ending Balance box.

10 Click **Done**.

■ Quicken redisplays the Account List.

UNDERSTANDING CATEGORIES

You can organize similar tranactions into groups using Quicken *categories*.

WHAT ARE CATEGORIES?

Every time you record a transaction in Quicken, you do so for a reason. Perhaps you are paying your telephone bill or recording your paycheck. In both cases, you can assign each transaction to a *category*. Quicken uses categories to group transactions of a similar nature. You use two basic kinds of categories: income categories and expense categories. You might have income categories for your salary, interest income, and dividend income. You might have expense categories for utilities, medical expenses, and lawn care.

HOW DO YOU KNOW WHAT CATEGORY TO USE?

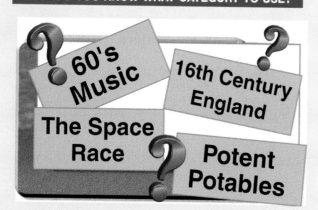

When you start Quicken for the first time, Quicken automatically sets up a list of categories. You can view the Category List and make changes to it — even delete categories that do not apply to you. For example, if you do not pay state income tax, you do not need that category.

USE ONE CATEGORY FOR SIMILAR EXPENSES

It is perfectly acceptable to assign your electric bill, gas bill, telephone bill, and water bill to one category called Utilities. You can easily find out how much you spend on utilities by reporting on the Utility category. If you ever want to know how much you paid for electricity in a year, you can find out by reporting on how much you paid to the electric company.

Categories

Inventors	16th Century England	Potent Potables
Thomas Edison	*	*
Alexander Graham Bell	*	*
Benjamin Franklin	*	*
Eli Whitney	*	*

CATEGORIES AND TAXES

Be sure to assign categories to any tax-related income or expenses. This can include: investment interest, charitable contributions, medical and dental expenses, state and local income taxes, real estate and personal property taxes, home mortgage interest and points, casualty and theft losses, moving expenses, and unreimbursed employee expenses. Because Quicken lets you assign categories to lines on your income tax return, you can easily prepare your tax return by using Quicken's tax reports (see Chapter 8 for more information on Quicken and Taxes).

Local Taxes

Medical

Mortgage Interest

Theft

ADD A CATEGORY

If Quicken's established category list does not contain a category you want to use, you can add one to the list. Remember, you can associate a category with a line on a tax form if the category affects your tax liability. By assigning categories to tax forms, you make preparing your taxes much easier.

ADD A CATEGORY

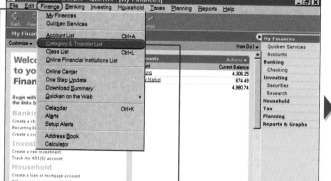

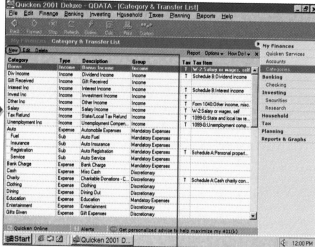

1 Click **Finance**.

2 Click **Category & Transfer List**.

■ Quicken displays the Category & Transfer List window.

3 Click **New**.

What is a category group?

A category group is a way to group categories together for reporting and budgeting. Quicken sets up three default category groups: Discretionary, Income, and Mandatory Expenses; you can make your own category groups.

Discretionary
Income
Mandatory

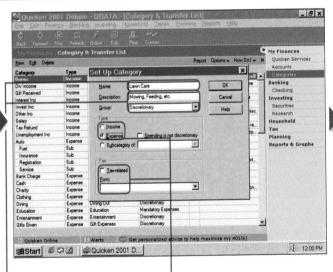

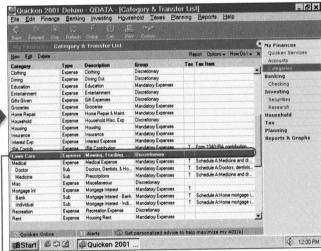

◼ Quicken displays the Set Up Category dialog box.

4 Type a category name.

◼ You can type a description and group for your category.

5 Identify the category as income or expense (○ changes to ◉).

◼ If the category is tax related, click the Tax-related box (☐ changes to ☑) and select a tax form (see Chapter 8 to select a form).

◼ When you click **OK,** your category appears in the Category & Transfer List.

EDIT A CATEGORY

Instead of adding categories, you can change an established category.

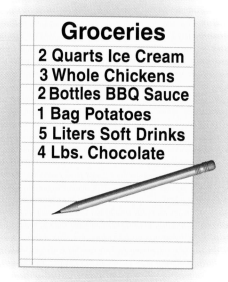

Groceries
2 Quarts Ice Cream
3 Whole Chickens
2 Bottles BBQ Sauce
1 Bag Potatoes
5 Liters Soft Drinks
4 Lbs. Chocolate

EDIT A CATEGORY

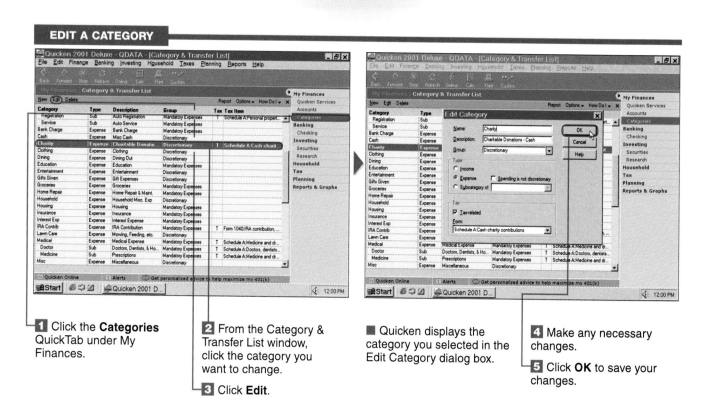

1 Click the **Categories** QuickTab under My Finances.

2 From the Category & Transfer List window, click the category you want to change.

3 Click **Edit**.

■ Quicken displays the category you selected in the Edit Category dialog box.

4 Make any necessary changes.

5 Click **OK** to save your changes.

DELETE A CATEGORY

The default Category & Transfer List that Quicken creates contains many categories that you may never use. You can delete them.

Note: If you delete a category after using it, Quicken deletes the category, but leaves the transaction. You see these types of transactions grouped under "Uncategorized" on your reports.

DELETE A CATEGORY

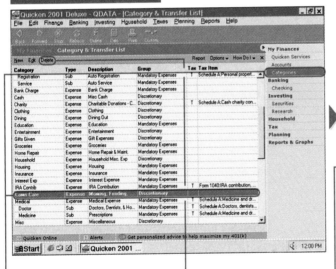

1 Click the **Categories** QuickTab under My Finances.

2 From the Category & Transfer List window, click the category you want to delete.

3 Click **Delete**.

■ Quicken displays the Delete Category dialog box.

4 Click **OK**.

■ Quicken deletes the category.

■ You can change the category of existing transactions by clicking **Replace Category** (○ changes to ⊙) and selecting another category. Quicken deletes the original category from the list.

SET UP AN INTERNET CONNECTION

To use any of Quicken's online capabilities, you must tell Quicken how you connect to the Internet and what browser you use. This task shows how to set up a dial-up connection and Internet Explorer 5.

If you do not use Internet Explorer 5, you can still use Quicken's online features, but some features will not be available because Quicken was optimized to work with Internet Explorer 4.0 or higher.

SET UP AN INTERNET CONNECTION

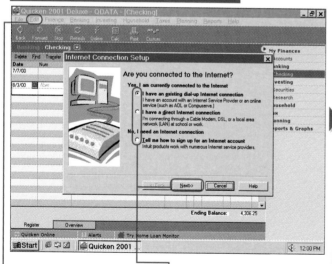

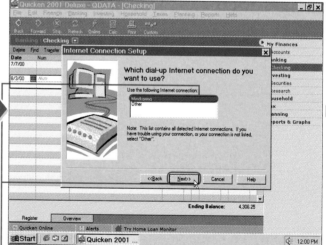

1 Click **Edit**.

2 Click **Internet Connection Setup**.

■ Quicken displays the Internet Connection Profile Manager window.

3 Click **Modify**.

■ Quicken asks if you are connected to the Internet.

4 Click an option.

5 Click **Next**.

6 Select a dial-up connection.

7 Click **Next**.

8 Click **Next**.

■ A message appears explaining that you need a browser to use Quicken's online features.

What's the purpose of the Internet Connection Profile Manager?

Many people have more than one Internet connection. You might use a dial-up connection on the road, a cable modem at home, and a LAN connection at work. Using the Profile Manager, you can define all your connections and then simply choose the connection you want to use. To define additional connections, click **New** in Step 3 and supply a connection name; then follow the rest of the steps. To select a connection to use, follow Steps 1 and 2. Then, in the Profile Manager window, highlight the connection you want to use and click **OK**.

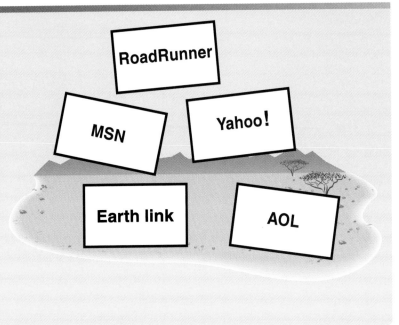

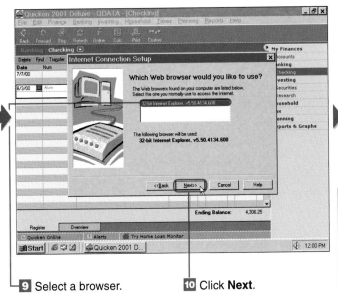

9 Select a browser.

10 Click **Next**.

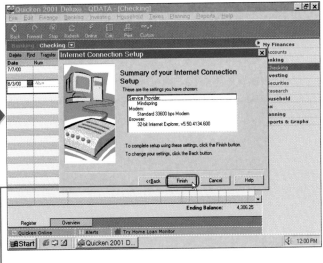

■ Quicken displays a summary of your choices.

11 Click **Finish**.

■ Quicken configures your connection and redisplays the Profile Manager window.

■ You can click **OK** to use the connection you just created.

QUICKEN ON THE ROAD

Do you spend lots of time on the road? Would you like to be able to keep up with your expenses in Quicken? You can use one of two methods: Quicken's Web Entry, a web-based tool, or Pocket Quicken, a version of Quicken that runs on handheld computers such as the Palm Pilot.

POCKET QUICKEN

Pocket Quicken is an application produced by Landware Software (www.landware.com) that works on Palm and Workpad handheld computers. With Pocket Quicken, you carry your account balances with you at all times. Using Pocket Quicken, you can enter transactions while you are away. When you return and synchronize your handheld with your desktop computer, Pocket Quicken transactions load into Quicken.

USING WEBENTRY

If you do not have a handheld computer but you have a notebook computer, you can use WebEntry. Register with Intuit to send your Account List, your Category & Transfer List, and your Class List to Quicken.com (no account numbers are stored on the Web). Using your browser, visit www.quicken.com and click the link to WebEntry. After you sign in, enter transactions. When you return to your desktop computer, click Finance and then One Step Update to download the web-stored transactions into Quicken.

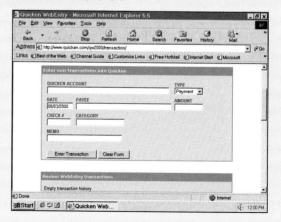

CHECK ONLINE FINANCIAL INSTITUTIONS

Online, you can pay bills, download banking, transactions, credit card transactions, and stock quotes.

Note: Some financial institutes might not support online banking. Check with your bank to see if they support online activities.

CHECK ONLINE FINANCIAL INSTITUTIONS

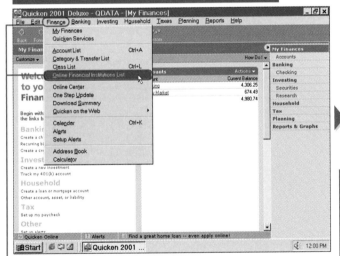

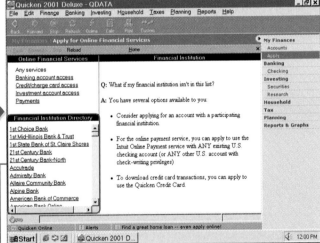

■1 Click **Finance**.

■2 Click **Online Financial Institutions List**.

■ Quicken prompts you to connect to the Internet.

■ After connecting, Quicken displays the Apply for Online Financial Services Web page, which shows, by default, all institutions that offer any services.

Note: To limit the institutions you see, click a link under Online Financial Services.

■3 Find your financial institution and click its link to learn how to apply.

■ If your institution does not appear, Intuit itself may be able to provide bill payment and credit card monitoring solutions for you.

ENABLE A BANK ACCOUNT FOR ONLINE USE

After you apply to your bank for online banking privileges, they send you some information that you use to set up a Quicken account for PC Banking.

ENABLE A BANK ACCOUNT FOR ONLINE USE

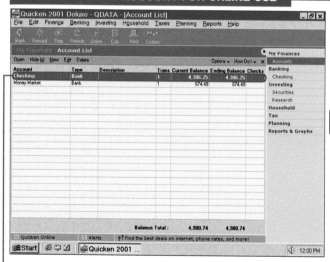

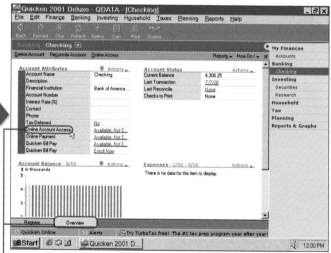

1 Press **Ctrl+A** to display the Account List

2 Double-click the account.

■ Quicken displays the account register.

3 Click the **Overview** tab.

4 Click **Online Account Access.**

■ Quicken connects to the Internet to collect information. Then, Quicken displays the Select Financial Institution window.

What if my bank does not offer online bill payment?

You can sign up to use the online bill payment service provided by Intuit. It works with all financial institutions as long as the account has check writing privileges. Select Intuit Online Payment in the Financial Institutions List window.

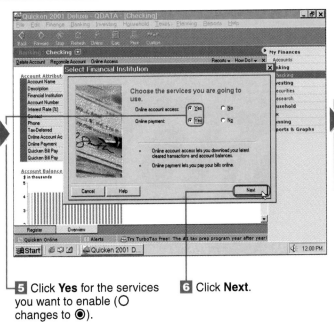

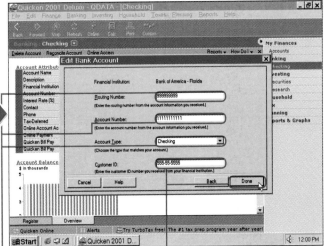

5 Click **Yes** for the services you want to enable (○ changes to ⦿).

6 Click **Next**.

7 Type your bank's routing number.

8 Type your bank account number.

9 Click ▼ and select Checking, Savings, Money Market or Line of Credit.

10 Type the customer ID number your bank provides.

11 Click **Done** to display a service agreement information box.

12 Read the box and click **OK** to redisplay the register.

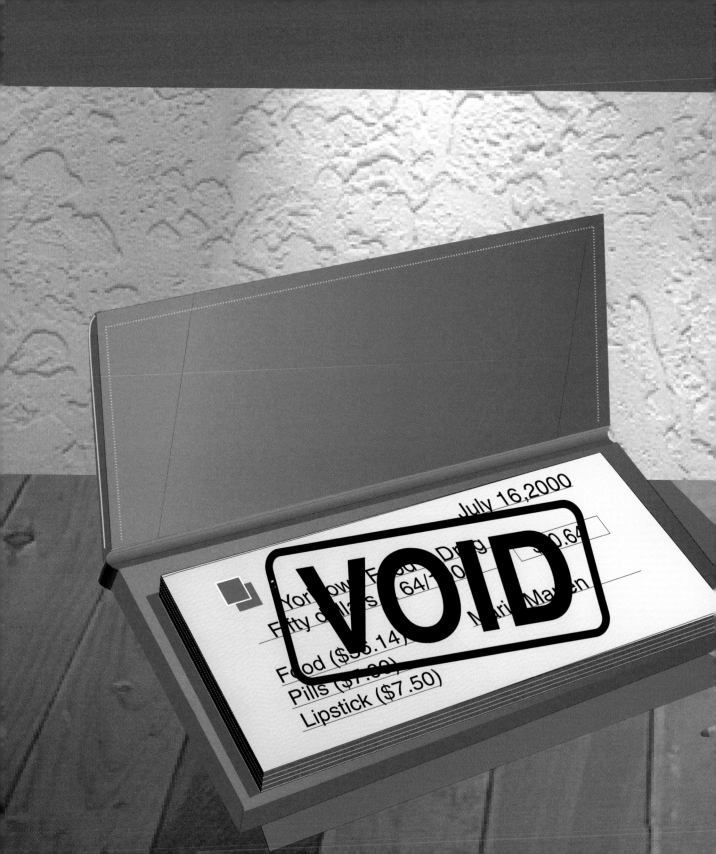

CHAPTER 2

Enter Checkbook Transactions

Are you wondering how to enter checkbook transactions like checks and deposits? Or do you want to know how to void a check you have written? This chapter shows you how.

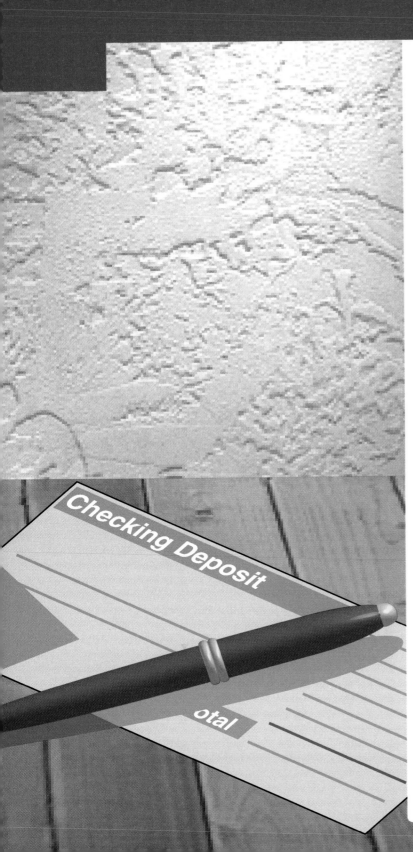

You can record a variety of transactions in Quicken's electronic check register allowing you to manage and track the balance of your checking account.

You can double-click the QuickEntry icon on your Desktop and follow the instructions in this Section to quickly enter transactions.

ENTER A TRANSACTION IN THE REGISTER

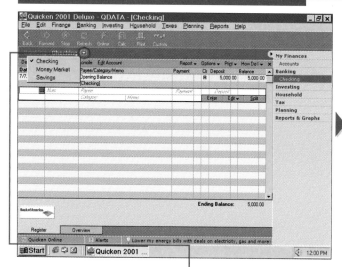

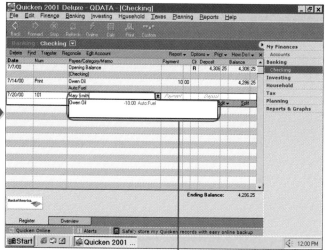

1 Open an account.

Note: If you do not see the account QuickTab, press Ctrl+A to open the Account List and double-click the account.

■ To switch accounts, you can click ▾ and select the account you want from the drop-down menu.

■ You can change the transaction date by pressing the ⊞ or ⊟ keys on your keyboard to add or subtract days.

2 Press Tab to move into the Num field and select a transaction type.

■ Quicken automatically displays a list of transaction types you can enter.

3 Press Tab. In the Payee field, type the name of the payee.

■ Quicken displays the last 2,000 payees; select one, and Quicken fills in your last transaction to that payee.

How do I choose the correct type of transaction to enter in a check register?

If you enable PC Banking and Bill paying for more than one account, you can choose from eight different types of transactions:

Select **ATM** to record an automatic teller machine withdrawal or deposit.

Select **Print Check** to record a check that you want to print.

Select **Online Transfer** to move money between accounts both in Quicken and at your bank.

Select **Next Check Num** to record an already-written check.

Select **EFT** to record electronic funds transfer transaction.

Select **Deposit** to add money to your account.

Select **Send Online Payment** to record a bill you want to pay electronically.

Select **Transfer** to move money between accounts.

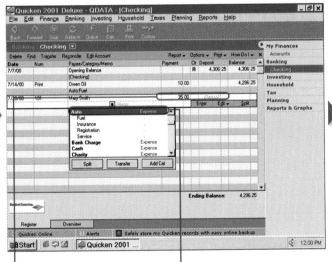

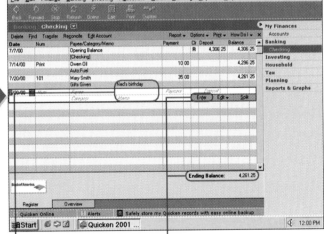

4 Press Tab and type an amount in the Payment field or the Deposit field.

Note: The insertion point automatically jumps to the Payment field or the Deposit field based on your entry in the Num field.

■ Press Tab to move into the Category field and select a category from the list Quicken displays.

■ You can type a reason for writing your check by pressing Tab and typing it in the Memo field.

Note: If you print the check, the text you type in the Memo field prints in the Memo block on your check.

5 Press (or click) **Enter** to save the transaction.

■ Quicken updates the Ending Balance in the register.

RECORD A CHECK IN THE WRITE CHECKS WINDOW

In addition to register windows, Quicken contains a window that looks like the actual check. Use Quicken's Write Checks window to write checks only if you intend to print the check, because you cannot assign a check number to a check in this window.

Note: Any text you type in the Memo field in the Write Checks window prints in the Memo block on your check.

RECORD A CHECK IN THE WRITE CHECKS WINDOW

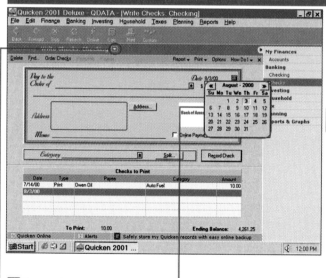

1 Press **Ctrl+W** to open the Write Checks window.

2 Click ▼ to select an account.

■ If you need to pre- or post-date a check, you can click 🗐 to display a calendar and change the check date.

3 Type the name of the Payee on the Pay to the Order of line.

4 Press Tab, type the dollar amount of the check, and press Tab again.

■ Quicken fills in the dollar amount in words.

■ If you type an address, you can mail the check in an envelope with a window.

Note: To store addresses in Quicken, see Chapter 6.

Can I assign one check to more than one category?

Yes. Click the **Split** button. For details on filling in the Split window that appears, see the Section "Assign a Check to Several Categories."

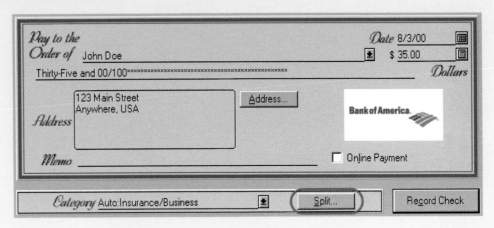

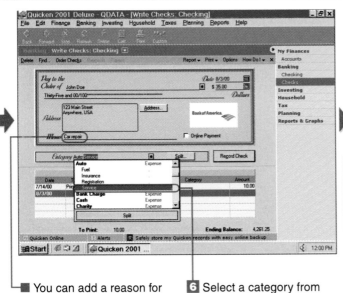

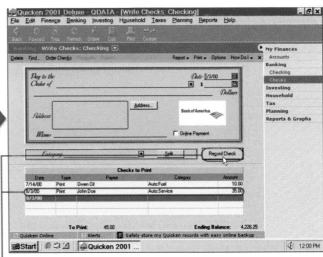

■ You can add a reason for writing the check by pressing Tab and typing it in the Memo field.

5 Press Tab to move into the Category field.

6 Select a category from the list Quicken displays.

7 Click the **Record Check** button to save the check.

■ You see an entry for the saved check at the bottom of the window.

■ To view or edit the check, click the entry, and the check details appear in the window.

■ To start a new check, press Page Down key.

ASSIGN A CHECK TO SEVERAL CATEGORIES

Quicken allows you to split a check among several categories so that you can accurately track your expenses even when you write only one check.

For example, you might write one check at the grocery store for a combination of food, pharmacy items, and cosmetics.

ASSIGN A CHECK TO SEVERAL CATEGORIES

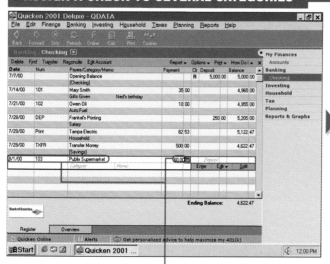

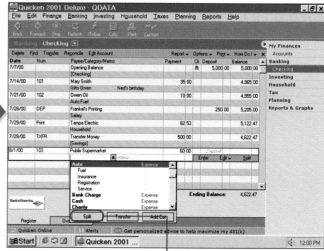

1 From the Banking QuickTab, click the account into which you want to record the transaction.

*Note: If you do not see the account, press **Ctrl+A**, and then double-click the account.*

2 Type the date, transaction type, and Payee. Press Tab to move between fields.

■ You can type the amount or let Quicken calculate the total of the split check.

3 Press Tab to move into the Category field.

■ Quicken automatically opens the Category List.

4 Click the **Split** button that appears at bottom of the list.

■ The Split Transaction window appears.

What do I do if I supplied an amount for the check in the register before opening the Split Transaction window and the amounts of my splits are not equal to the check amount I supplied?

You see the difference in the Split Transaction window. You can do one of two things. Click the **Adjust** button in the Split Transaction window to change the amount you typed in the check register before opening the Split Transaction window to equal the sum of the splits. Or, change one or more of the amounts in the Split Transaction window so that the split amounts are equal to the amount you typed in the check register prior to opening the Split Transaction window.

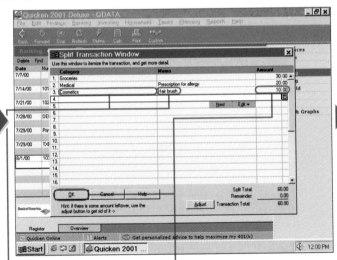

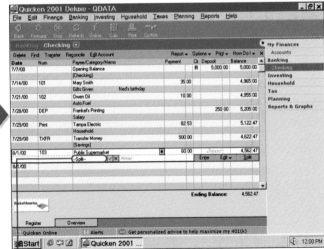

5 Type the first category to which you want to assign the check.

■ You can type a description of this portion of the expense in the Memo field.

6 Press `Tab` and type an amount.

7 Repeat Steps 5 through 6 until you have distributed the entire amount of the check.

8 Click **OK** to save the split information.

■ When Quicken displays the transaction in the register, the category reads `--Split--`.

CREATE ONLINE PAYEES

If you want to be able to pay bills online, you need to set up online payees.

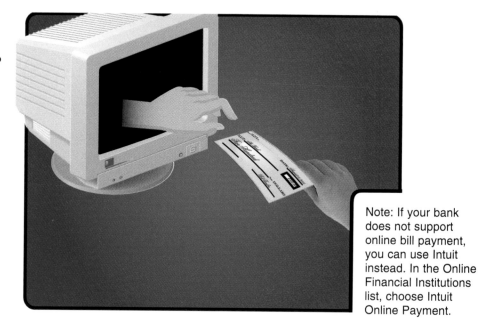

Note: If your bank does not support online bill payment, you can use Intuit instead. In the Online Financial Institutions list, choose Intuit Online Payment.

CREATE ONLINE PAYEES

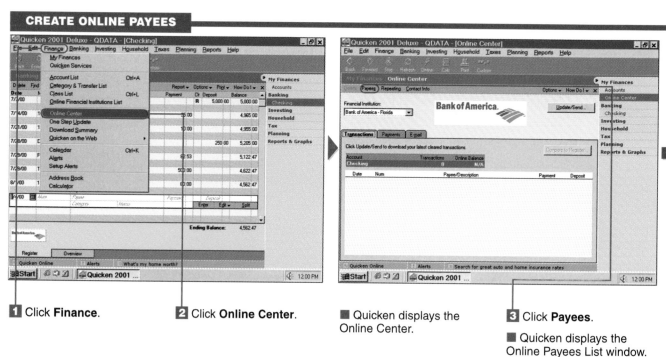

1 Click **Finance**.

2 Click **Online Center**.

■ Quicken displays the Online Center.

3 Click **Payees**.

■ Quicken displays the Online Payees List window.

How do I edit or delete an online payee?

From the Online Payee List window, select the payee in question and click either **Edit** or **Delete**. If you click **Edit**, Quicken displays the payee's information in the same window where you entered it originally. You can change everything except the payee's name. If you click **Delete**, Quicken displays a message asking if you are sure you want to delete the payee.

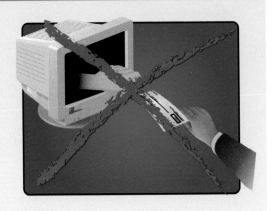

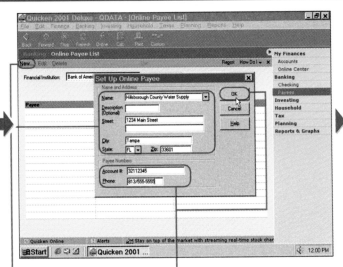

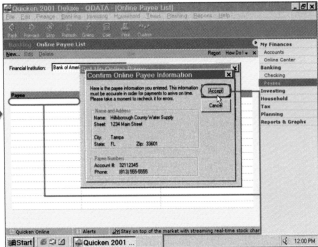

4 Click **New**.

■ Quicken displays the Set Up Online Payee window.

5 Type the payee's information in the Name and Address boxes.

6 Type your account number with the payee and the payee's phone number in the Payee Number boxes.

7 Click **OK**.

■ Quicken displays the Confirm Online Payee Information window so that you can verify your information.

8 Click **Accept**.

■ The payee appears in your Online Payee List window.

WHEN DOES MONEY LEAVE AN ACCOUNT?

The money leaves your account based on the lead time that your bank requires and the method that your bank uses to process online payments.

WHAT IS LEAD TIME?

Lead time is the number of business days between when you send an online payment instruction and when the payee receives the payment. Lead times appear in the Online Payee List and are determined by the payment model that your bank and the payee use. Check with your bank to determine whether the money leaves your account in one of the four following ways: one to four days before the payment is delivered; the day the payment is processed for delivery; the day the payment is delivered; or the day the payment (EFT or paper check) clears your account.

PERIODICALLY REVIEW LEAD TIMES

Occasionally, payee lead times change. For example, a payee might become able to receive an EFT payment, which reduces the lead time from four to two business days. Each time you connect to your bank, Quicken downloads new lead time information. To avoid paying too late or too early, review your Online Payee List occasionally to determine whether the lead time for a vendor has altered.

CHECK PAYMENT MODEL

If the payee cannot receive an EFT payment, your bank actually produces a paper check for the payment and mails the payment to the payee using standard U.S. mail. To accommodate the extra time needed to deliver a payment using this payment model, this type of transaction usually has a lead time of four business days.

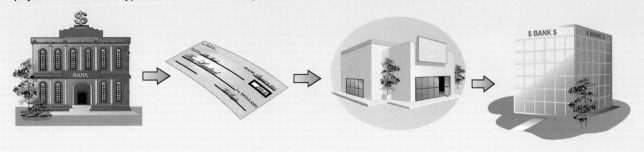

EFT PAYMENT MODEL

If the payee can receive an *electronic funds transfer* (EFT) payment, then typically your bank transfers the money directly from your account to the payee's account. This type of transaction usually has a lead time of one or two business days.

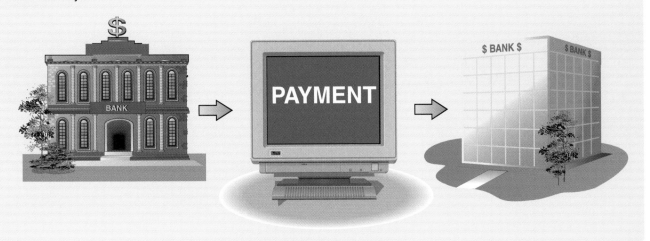

ENTER BILLS TO PAY ONLINE

When you receive a
bill you want to pay
online, you must enter
it as an *online bill*.

ENTER BILLS TO PAY ONLINE

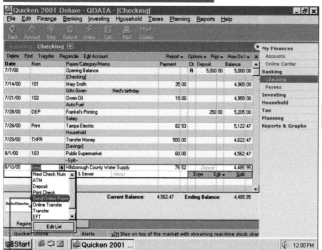

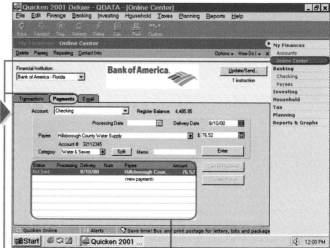

1 Enter the bill in the Num
field and click **Send Online
Payment** (see the section,
"Enter a Transaction in the
Register").

■ Quicken stores the
transaction as an online bill
waiting to be paid.

2 Click the **Online Center**
QuickTab.

■ Quicken displays the
Online Center.

3 Click the **Payments** tab.

■ You see a list of online
payments waiting to be sent
to your bank.

*Note: You can enter online bills
from this tab. Click the <**new
payment**> line at the bottom of
the window and type the Payee, etc.*

PAY BILLS ONLINE

After you enter bills to pay online in Quicken, you must send an electronic message to your bank, instructing it to pay the bill on the date you specify. Check marks appear next to each instruction.

You can pay some but not all of your bills. Do not send instructions for those bills that you do not want to pay. You can avoid sending an instruction by clicking the check mark next to it to remove it.

PAY BILLS ONLINE

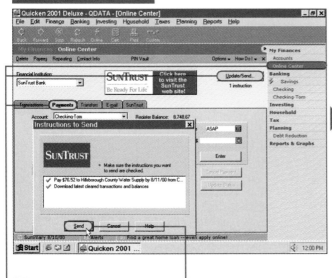

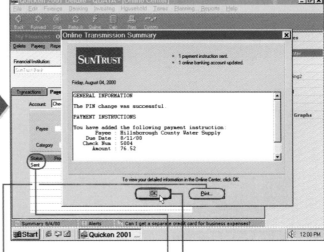

1 Click **Online Center**.

2 Click the **Payments** tab.

3 Click **Update/Send**.

■ Quicken displays the Instructions to Send window, with check marks next to each update action.

4 Click **Send**.

Note: If you are prompted to change the PIN number, type the number your bank sent you. Then, type and retype your new PIN number.

■ Quicken connects with your bank after transmitting, and displays the Online Transmission Summary window.

■ You can click **Print** to print the contents of the window.

5 Click **OK** to close the window.

■ The status of the transactions on the Payments tab changes to Sent. In your register, you see a lightning bolt next to each transaction.

VOID A TRANSACTION

Occasionally, you must need to void a check that you wrote but decided not to give to the payee. You can void the transaction in Quicken.

When you void a check, Quicken keeps a record of the check number but removes all monetary information related to the check.

VOID A TRANSACTION

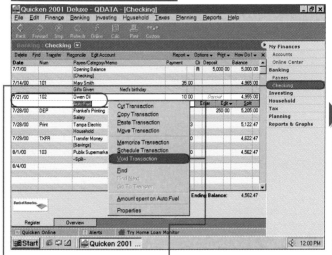

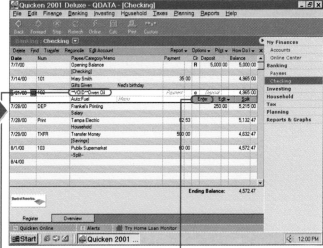

1 Click the QuickTab of the account register containing the transaction you want to void.

*Note: If you do not see the QuickTab, press **Ctrl+A** to open the Account List and double-click the account.*

2 Right-click anywhere on the transaction you want to void.

■ A shortcut menu displays.

3 Select **Void Transaction**.

■ Quicken sets the value of the transaction to $0.00 and voids the transaction.

4 Click or press **Enter** to save the changes.

*Note: Quicken automatically marks voided transactions as cleared. Note the **c** in the Clr column of the voided transaction.*

DELETE A TRANSACTION

You can delete a transaction in Quicken. Think of deleting a transaction as "destroying the evidence." Deleting a transaction removes it completely from your register.

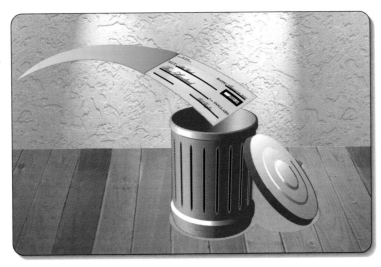

You will have *no* record of the transaction if you delete it, so make sure that you really do not need it before deleting.

DELETE A TRANSACTION

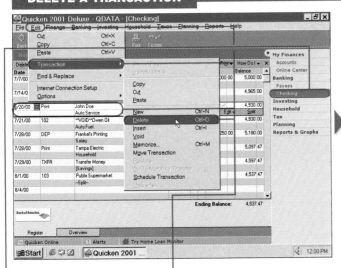

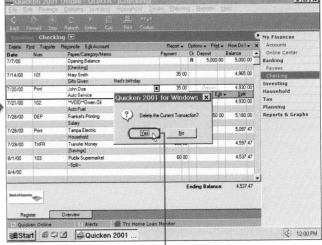

1 Click the QuickTab of the account register that contains the transaction you need to delete.

*Note: If you do not see the QuickTab, press **Ctrl+A** to open the Account List and double-click the account.*

2 Click anywhere on the transaction you want to delete (example: **John Doe**).

3 Click **Edit**.

4 Click **Transaction**.

5 Click **Delete**.

■ Alternatively, you can press **Ctrl+D** to delete the transaction.

■ Quicken asks you to confirm that you want to delete the transaction.

6 Click **Yes**.

*Note: Clicking **Yes** permanently deletes the transaction and it cannot be retrieved.*

■ Quicken permanently removes the transaction from the register.

CANCEL ONLINE PAYMENTS

You can cancel an online payment instruction if the bank has not yet followed your instruction and made the payment. Suppose, for example, that you make a mistake while entering online payments. If you sent the instruction, you must send another instruction to cancel the payment.

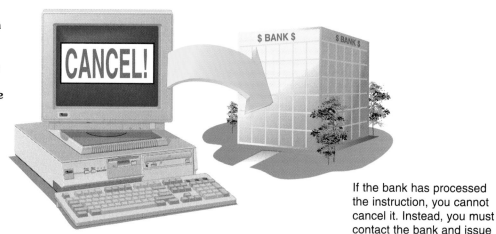

If the bank has processed the instruction, you cannot cancel it. Instead, you must contact the bank and issue a stop payment.

CANCEL ONLINE PAYMENTS

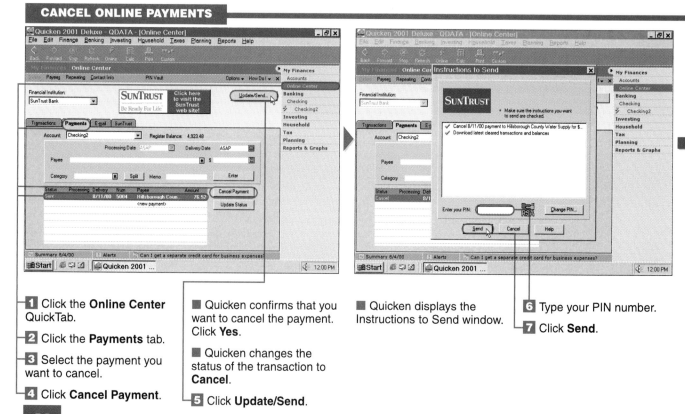

1 Click the **Online Center** QuickTab.

2 Click the **Payments** tab.

3 Select the payment you want to cancel.

4 Click **Cancel Payment**.

■ Quicken confirms that you want to cancel the payment. Click **Yes**.

■ Quicken changes the status of the transaction to **Cancel**.

5 Click **Update/Send**.

■ Quicken displays the Instructions to Send window.

6 Type your PIN number.

7 Click **Send**.

I mistakenly entered an online bill but I have not sent the instruction to pay it yet. How do I fix my mistake?

If you have not sent the instruction to pay the bill, you can simply edit the transaction or delete it from your register.

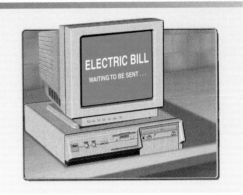

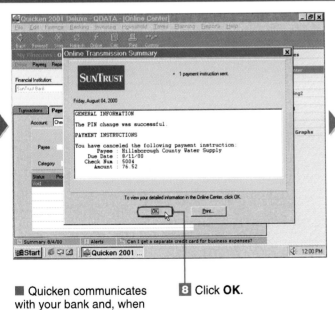

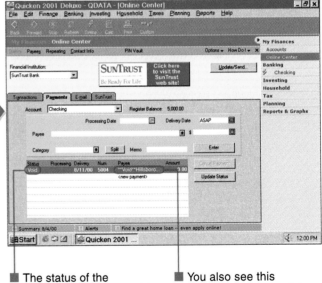

■ Quicken communicates with your bank and, when finished, displays the Online Transmission Summary.

8 Click **OK**.

■ The status of the transaction changes to Void in the Payments window.

■ You also see this transaction in your register with a Payee of ****VOID****.

SET UP A REPEATING ONLINE PAYMENT

You can set up a repeating payment and send the instruction to your bank. Suppose that you make the same payment every time to the same vendor — like your rent. You do not need to enter the transaction every time that you want to pay it.

SET UP A REPEATING ONLINE PAYMENT

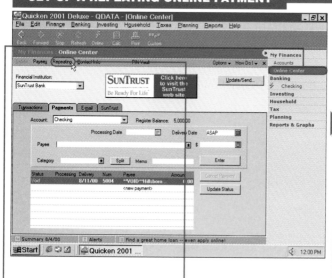

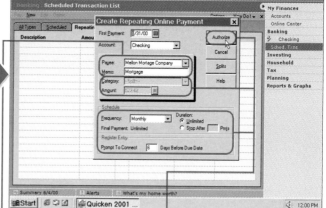

1 Click the **Online Center** QuickTab.

Note: If you do not see the Online Center Quicktab, see the Section "Create Online Payees" to display it.

2 Click **Repeating**.

■ Quicken opens the Scheduled Transaction List and displays the Create Repeating Online Payment window.

3 Type the payee's name and a memo.

4 Select a category and type the amount.

5 Set frequency, duration, and prompt information for the payment.

6 Click **Authorize** to save the transaction.

Do I need to set up a payee for a repeating payment?

Yes. However, if you do not set up the payee before you create the repeating transaction, Quicken walks you through the payee setup when you type the payee's name in the Create Repeating Online Payment window.

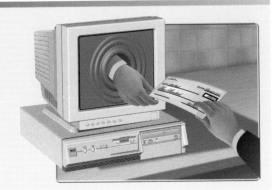

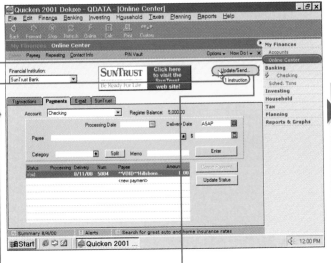

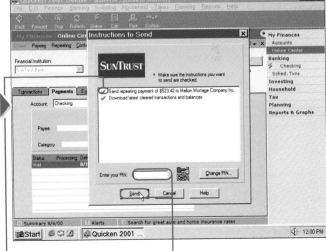

7 Click the **Online Center** QuickTab.

■ Quicken indicates that you have at least one instruction to send.

8 Click **Update/Send**.

■ Quicken displays the Instructions to Send window.

9 Look for a check mark next to the repeating payment instruction; if no check appears, click the instruction to mark it.

10 Type your PIN.

11 Click **Send**.

■ Quicken sends the instruction to your bank, adds it your register, and displays the Online Transmission Summary.

CANCEL A REPEATING ONLINE PAYMENT

You can eliminate a repeating online payment. If you have not transmitted instructions for a repeating payment, you can simply delete the transaction in the Scheduled Transaction List (see the section, "Schedule Transactions" in Chapter 4). However, if you sent a payment instruction to the bank, you must send an instruction to the bank to delete it.

If you want to cancel a single online repeating payment, use the instructions in the section, "Cancel Online Payments."

CANCEL A REPEATING ONLINE PAYMENT

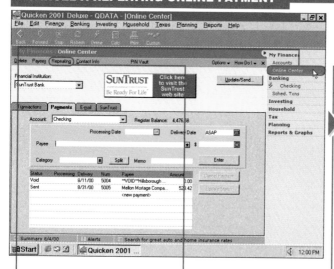

1 Click the **Online Center** QuickTab.

Note: If you do not see the Online Center QuickTab, see the Section "Create Online Payees" to display it.

2 Click **Repeating**.

■ Quicken opens the Scheduled Transaction List.

3 Select the payment you want to delete.

4 Click **Delete**.

■ Quicken confirms your request.

5 Click **Delete**.

■ Quicken changes the Type to Rept-Cancel and stores an instruction to send to your bank.

When I try to enter an online payment, I see a message stating that it is too late to enter the payment with the date I am using; then Quicken automatically changes the date. Why?

Quicken calculates the due date for the payment based on the lead time required to complete the transaction.

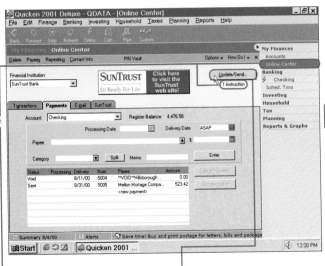

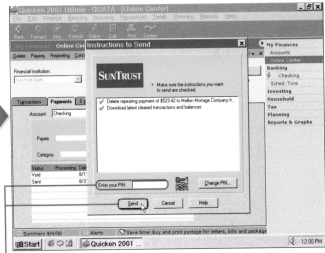

6 Click the **Online Center** QuickTab.

■ Quicken indicates that you have at least one instruction to send.

7 Click **Update/Send**.

■ Quicken displays the Instructions to Send window with the instruction to delete the repeating payment.

8 Type your PIN.

9 Click **Send**.

■ Quicken sends the instruction to your bank and displays the Online Transmission Summary.

■ Quicken also deletes the transaction from the Scheduled Transaction List and voids the transaction in your register.

CHECK THE STATUS OF AN ONLINE PAYMENT

You can check the status of any online payment. Suppose, for example, that you receive a transmission error while sending instructions and you are not sure of the status of a transaction. Quicken lets you check.

CHECK THE STATUS OF AN ONLINE PAYMENT

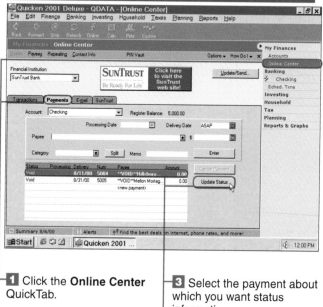

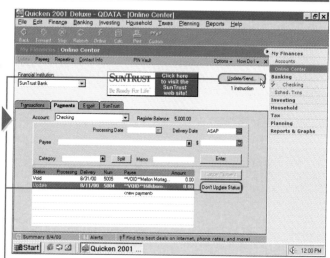

1 Click the **Online Center** QuickTab.

2 Click the **Payments** tab.

3 Select the payment about which you want status information.

4 Click **Update Status**.

■ The button text changes to "Don't Update Status" and adds an instruction to send to the bank.

5 Click **Update/Send**.

■ The Instructions to Send window appears.

6 Type your PIN and click **Send**.

■ Quicken contacts the bank. The Online Transmission Summary window appears.

7 Click **OK** to close the window.

You can e-mail your bank a question about either your account or a particular payment. You do not need to call the bank.

E-mail

$ BANK $ $ BANK $

ASK THE BANK A QUESTION

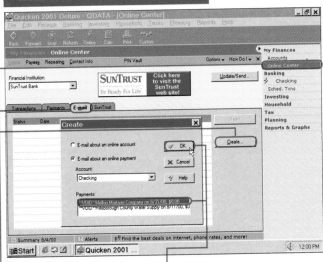

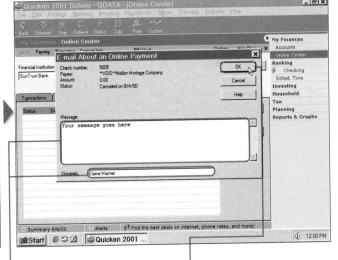

1 Click the **Online Center** QuickTab.

2 Click the **E-mail** tab.

3 Click **Create**.

■ Quicken displays the Create dialog box.

4 Describe what you want to ask the bank. If appropriate, highlight a payment.

5 Click **OK**.

■ Quicken displays a window in which you can type an e-mail message.

6 Type your message.

7 Sign your message.

8 Click **OK**.

9 Click **Update/Send**.

■ Quicken sends the e-mail.

Note: To delete the e-mail, you can select it and click **Delete** in the Online Center.

TRANSFER MONEY BETWEEN ACCOUNTS

If you have more than one bank account, you can easily transfer money between them.

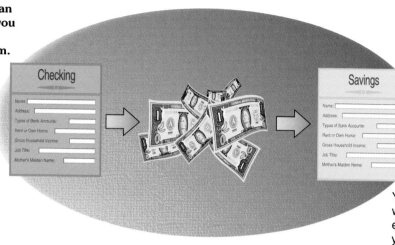

You can view any register while transferring money, even if the register that you are viewing is not involved in the transfer.

TRANSFER MONEY BETWEEN ACCOUNTS

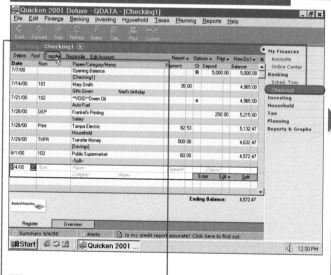

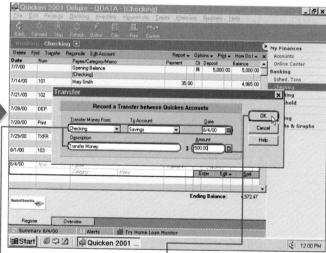

1 Under the Banking QuickTab, click the account containing the money you want to transfer.

*Note: If you do not see the account listed under the Banking QuickTab, press **Ctrl+A** to open the Account List window; then double-click the account.*

2 Click **Transfer**.

■ Quicken displays the Transfer dialog box.

3 You can change the Transfer Money From, To Account, Date, or Description information.

*Note: You can create the To account by selecting **Create New Account** from the To Account list.*

4 In the Amount field, type the amount to transfer.

5 Click **OK**.

What is the difference between using the Transfer dialog box or choosing the Transfer transaction in a register?

It is simply a matter of personal preference. You certainly can use the Transfer transaction in a register. When you tab into the Category field, Quicken displays all the other accounts you have created, but you will not see any categories. Simply choose an account.

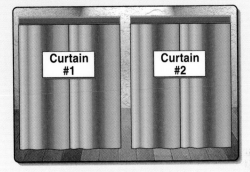

"I choose Curtain #2."

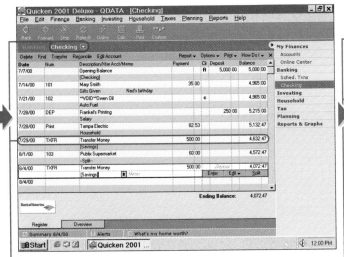

■ Quicken stores a transaction in both registers involved in the transaction.

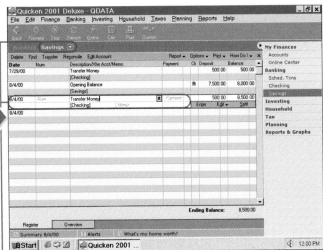

■ This example involves both the checking and savings accounts.

Note: You do not assign a category to money you are transferring between accounts.

SET UP AN ELECTRONIC FUNDS TRANSFER IN THE REGISTER

You can transfer money between Quicken accounts — and simultaneously notify your bank of the transfer. Think of online transfers as online payments. When you transfer funds between accounts using your register, start in the account that contains the money you want to move.

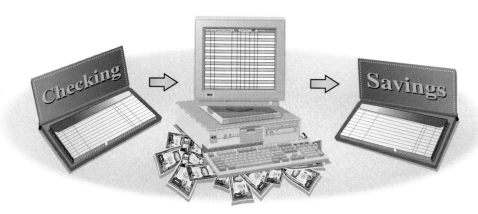

SET UP AN ELECTRONIC FUNDS TRANSFER IN THE REGISTER

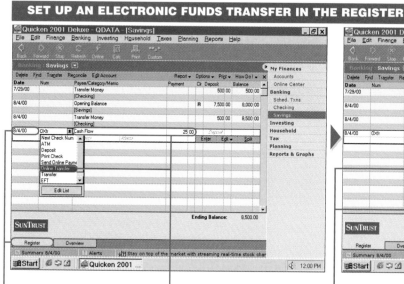

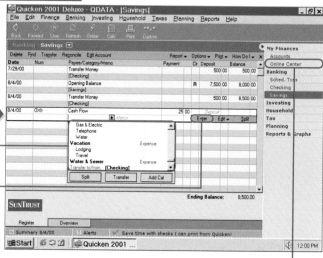

1 Display the register of the account containing the money you want to transfer.

*Note: Click a QuickTab or press **Ctrl+A** to open the Account List and double-click the account.*

2 Type a date for the transfer.

3 In the Num field, select **Online Transfer** from the pull-down menu.

4 Type information in the Payee and the Payment amount. Press Tab to move between the fields.

5 In the Category field, select the account receiving funds.

6 Press or click **Enter**.

■ Quicken stores the transaction and an online instruction for the bank.

7 To complete the transfer, click the Online Center tab and click **Update/Send**.

Note: You cannot delete a transfer after you send it. You must transfer money back to "undo" your action.

You can set up an online transfer of funds between accounts by using the Online Center.

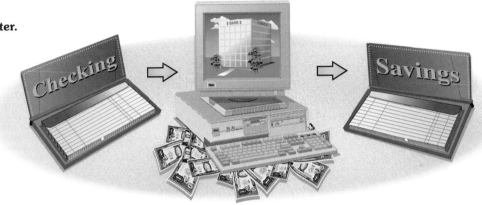

SET UP AN ELECTRONIC FUNDS TRANSFER IN THE ONLINE CENTER

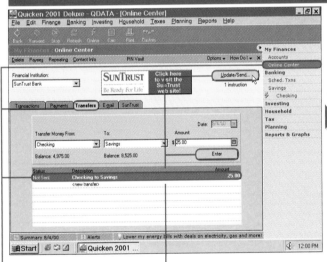

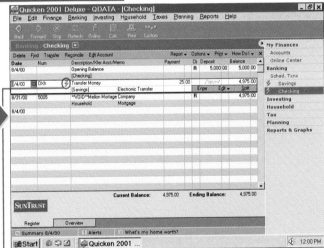

1 Click the **Online Center** QuickTab.

2 Click the **Transfers** tab.

3 Select accounts to use when transferring money and type an amount to transfer.

4 Click **Enter**.

■ Quicken stores an instruction and transactions in both affected registers.

5 Click **Update/Send**.

■ After Quicken sends the instruction, the transaction appears with a lightning bolt in the register of the account from which you withdrew money.

Note: If you delete a transfer after you send it, you affect only your register– not the bank's. Do not delete the transfer; instead, transfer money back to "undo" your action.

ORDER CHECKS

With Quicken, you can print checks instead of writing them by hand. You must order checks that work with your printer. Laser checks come with either one or three checks to a page, and dot matrix checks run continuously.

When you order computer checks, you must include a regular blank voided

ORDER CHECKS

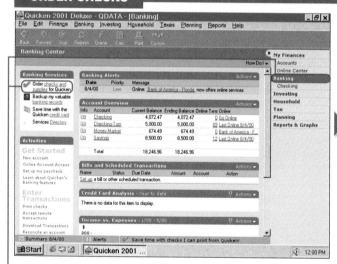

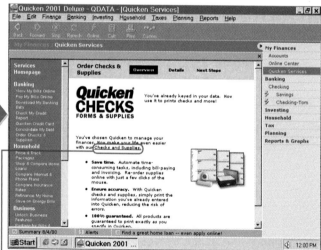

1 Click the **Banking** QuickTab.

■ Quicken displays the Banking Center.

2 Click the **Order checks and supplies for Quicken** link.

■ You see the Quicken Services window.

3 Click the **Checks and Supplies** link.

■ Quicken displays a message that you are about to connect to the Internet.

4 Click **OK** to connect to the Internet.

How do I select the correct check form for my needs?

You can print checks onto three different types of forms in Quicken:

STANDARD CHECKS **VOUCHER CHECKS** **WALLET CHECKS**

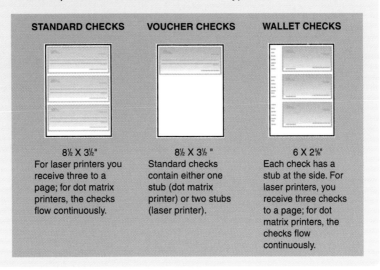

8½ X 3½"
For laser printers you receive three to a page; for dot matrix printers, the checks flow continuously.

8½ X 3½ "
Standard checks contain either one stub (dot matrix printer) or two stubs (laser printer).

6 X 2⅝"
Each check has a stub at the side. For laser printers, you receive three checks to a page; for dot matrix printers, the checks flow continuously.

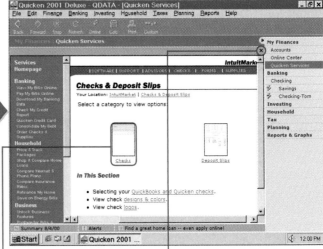

■ You see the IntuitMarket home page.

5 Click the **Checks & Deposits** link.

■ You see a page where you choose between checks and deposit slips.

6 Click the **Checks** link.

*Note: You might see a security warning. If so, click **Yes**.*

7 Click the type of check you want to order.

8 Follow the prompts on-screen to finish your order.

9 Disconnect from the Internet by clicking ⊠ on the Quicken Services page.

PRINT CHECKS

With Quicken, you can print checks for any entry in your check register to which you have assigned *Print* in the Num field.

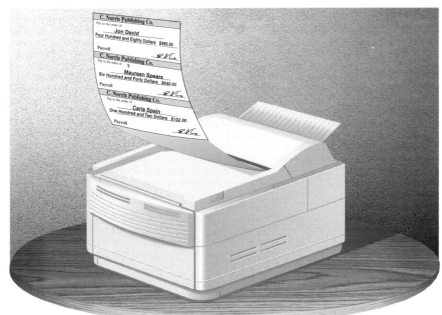

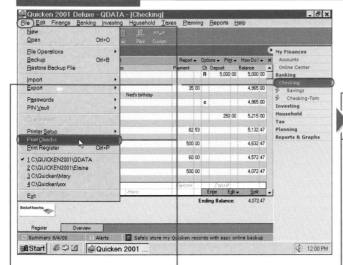

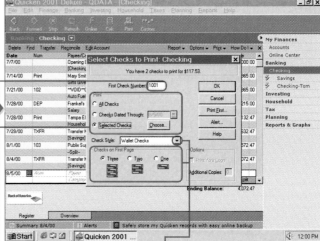

1 Click the QuickTab of the account register that contains checks to print.

*Note: If you do not see the QuickTab, press **Ctrl+A** to open the Account List and double-click the account.*

2 Click **File**.

3 Click **Print Checks**.

■ Quicken displays the Print Checks window.

4 Confirm that the First Check Number is correct.

5 Click to select the checks you want to print (○ changes to ⦿). For selected checks, click **Choose**.

6 Click ⊡, and select a check style.

7 For laser printers, click the number of checks on the first page of check forms (○ changes to ⦿).

Do I have to view my check register to print checks or can I start in the Write Checks window?

You do not need to view either your register or the Write Checks window when you decide to start these steps *unless* you have more than one checking account. Then you need to view either the register or Write Checks window for the account containing checks you want to print.

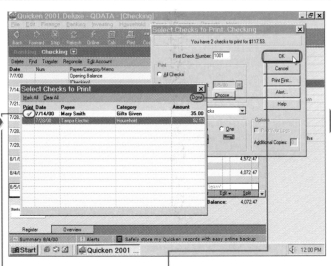

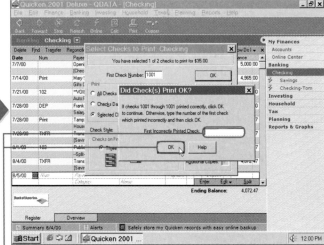

■ Quicken displays the Select Checks to Print window.

8 Click any entry to avoid printing a check for it.

Note: Click Clear All to unmark all checks.

9 Click **Done** to redisplay the preceding window in this task.

10 Click **OK** to print checks.

■ Quicken displays the Did Check(s) Print OK? window.

■ You can type the number of the first check that did not print properly.

11 If all checks printed correctly, click **OK**.

■ Quicken assigns numbers to correctly printed checks. Incorrectly printed checks retain the number "Print."

■ If you did not print all checks, click **Cancel** in the Select Checks to Print window.

DOWNLOAD TRANSACTIONS FROM YOUR BANK

You can keep your register balance completely up-to-date by downloading transactions from your bank. Whenever you make an update, an instruction appears in the Instructions to Send window that tells the bank to download the latest cleared transactions and balances since your last update.

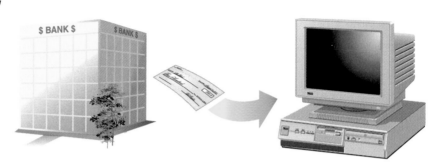

You need to match or add these transactions to your Quicken register so that you and the bank agree on the amount of money you have.

DOWNLOAD TRANSACTIONS FROM YOUR BANK

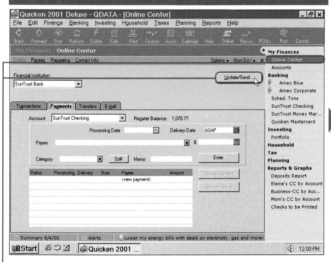

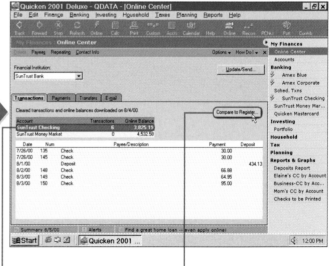

1 Click the **Online Center** QuickTab.

Note: If you do not see the Online Center QuickTab, see the Section "Create Online Payees" to display it.

2 Click **Update/Send**.

3 Type your PIN in the Instructions to Send window.

■ After you communicate with the bank, Quicken displays the Transactions tab if new transactions exist.

4 Select the first account containing new transactions.

5 Click **Compare to Register**.

Sometimes I see *New* and sometimes I see *Match* in the Status column. Why?

Quicken tries to match downloaded transactions to ones already in your register. Quicken uses the date, amount, and check number to identify matching transactions, and then highlights the matching transactions in the top portion of the window for you. If Quicken misses a match, edit the transaction in the register that *should* match to give it the same date, amount, and check number as the downloaded transaction. If Quicken matches a transaction it *should not* match, highlight the erroneously matched transaction and click **Unmatch** in the window at the bottom of the register.

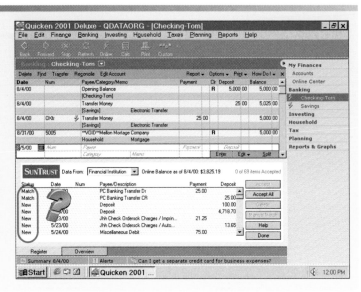

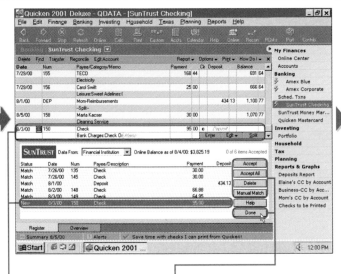

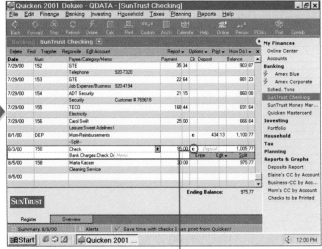

■ You see a modified register window.

6 Click a transaction; it appears in both parts of the window.

■ If necessary, type a category for the transaction.

7 Click **Accept**, **Accept All**, **Delete**, or **Manual Match**, as appropriate.

8 Repeat Steps 6 and 7 until you account for all transactions.

9 Click **Done**.

■ Quicken redisplays your register.

■ A **c** appears in the Clr field in your register, indicating that you have downloaded the transaction from the bank but not yet cleared it during an account reconciliation.

PRINT THE REGISTER

You can print the check register. Suppose, for example, that you are having trouble reconciling your account and you want to study the transactions away from your computer.

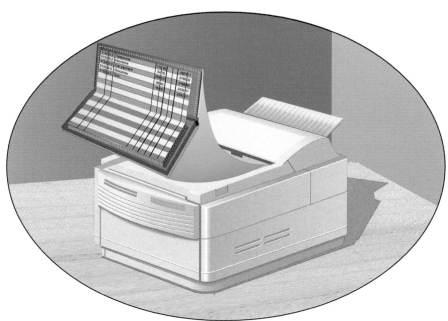

PRINT THE REGISTER

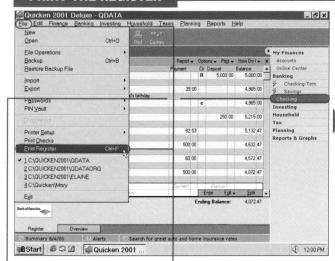

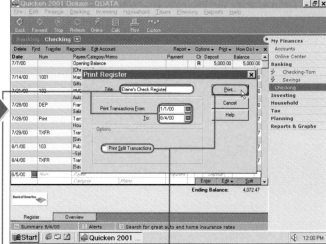

1 Click the QuickTab of the account register that you want to print.

*Note: If you do not see the QuickTab, press **Ctrl+A** to open the Account List and double-click the account.*

2 Click **File**.

3 Click **Print Register**.

■ Quicken displays the Print Register dialog box.

4 Type a title for the report.

5 Set the date range for transactions you want to include.

■ You can select whether to print the breakdown of split transactions (☐ changes to ☑).

6 Click **Print**.

Can I display the report on my monitor?

No, you cannot display this report on-screen. You can print to a printer, create an ASCII file that you can view in Notepad, create a tab-delimited file that can be read by many spreadsheet and database programs, or create a file that can be read in Lotus 1-2-3's graphics package.

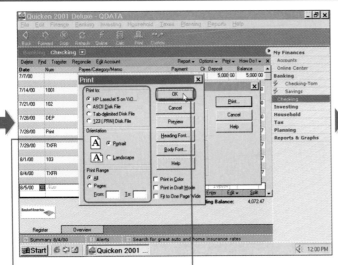

■ Quicken displays the Print dialog box.

7 Choose to print to a printer or a file, and select an orientation and a print range (○ changes to ●).

8 Click **OK**.

■ Quicken prints the report.

Healthly Living Health Club	6/30/00	$30.65
Daily News - Jan - June	7/1/00	$90.00
Phone bill	7/1/00	$60.86
City Wide Electricity	7/16/00	$56.53
Groceries	7/18/00	$86.34
Cell phone bill	7/19/00	$12.14
Insurance	7/19/00	$17.35
Mortgage	7/19/00	$865.35
Gas	7/21/00	$40.00
Birthday gifts	7/22/00	$75.90
Car payments	7/23/00	$326.89
Water	7/23/00	$54.01
Clothes	7/25/00	$101.13
Theater	7/29/00	$150.80

July 16, 2000

City Wide Electricity $56.53

Fifty-four & 53/100

Elec. - June/July   James Marlen

CHAPTER 3

Balance Your Checking Account

Do you want Quicken to help you balance your checkbook? Read this chapter.

RECONCILE AN ACCOUNT

You can easily match your Quicken entries to the bank's monthly statement by reconciling the account.

You can also reconcile other types of accounts besides bank accounts.

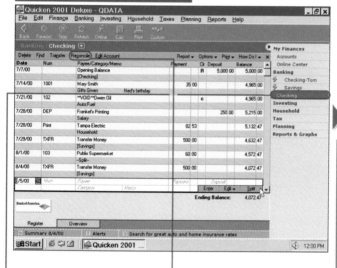

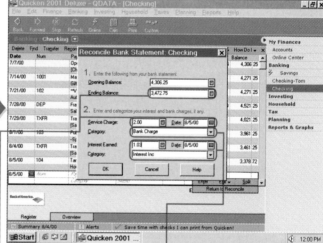

1 Click the QuickTab of the account register that you want to reconcile.

*Note: If you do not see the QuickTab, press **Ctrl+A** to open the Account List and double-click the account.*

2 Click **Reconcile**.

■ Quicken displays the Reconcile Bank Statement window.

3 Type the ending balance that appears on the bank statement.

4 Type any service charges that appear on your bank statement and type the date.

5 Click 🔽 and select a category for service charges.

6 From your bank statement, type the amount of earned interest, type the date, and select a category for interest you earned.

What will my Reconciliation Report show?

When you set up the report, you can choose the **Summary and Uncleared** option and print two pages. The first page sums cleared and uncleared transactions and matches your ending balance to the bank's statement ending balance. The second page lists uncleared checks. If you choose the **All Transactions** option, the second page lists *cleared* checks, and Quicken prints two additional pages of uncleared transactions.

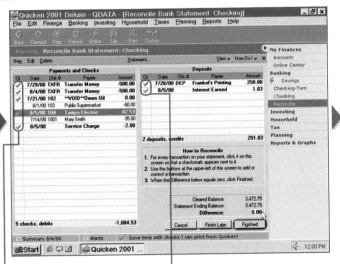

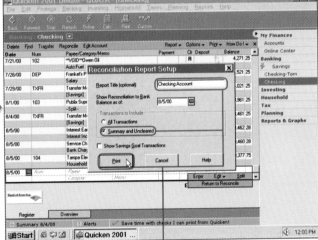

7 When you click **OK**, Quicken displays the Reconcile Bank Statement window.

8 In the left **Clr** column, click the payments and checks that appear on your bank statement.

9 In the right **Clr** column, click the deposits that appear on your bank statement.

10 When the Difference is 0.00, click **Finished**.

■ Quicken asks if you want to print a reconciliation report.

11 Click **Yes**.

■ Quicken displays the Reconciliation Report Setup window.

■ You can type a report title and date.

12 Click **Summary and Uncleared** (○ changes to ●) to print a summary and detail of cleared checks.

13 Click **Print**.

CONTINUED

RECONCILE AN ACCOUNT

You can set up your
printer to describe the
way you want your
report to look or simply
accept the defaults that
Quicken suggests.

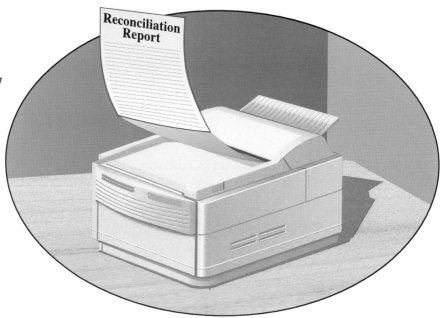

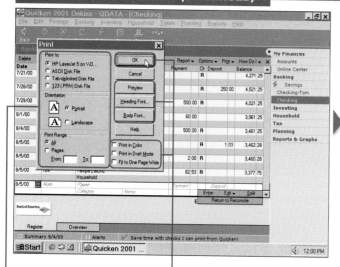

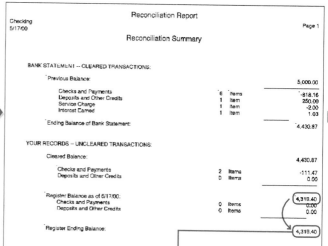

■ The Print window
displays.

14 Click print options (○
changes to ●) to select a
printer or file type, report
orientation, and the pages
you want to print.

■ You can click these
buttons to customize fonts
and preview the report.

■ You can click these boxes
(☐ changes to ☑) to select
the print quality.

15 Click **OK**.

■ The Reconciliation
Report prints.

■ The first page of the
report summarizes the
bank's statement and the
uncleared transactions in
your Quicken register.

■ The Ending Balance of
the Bank Statement should
match the Register Ending
Balance.

What are Savings Goal Transactions and should I show them on my Reconciliation Report?

Savings goal accounts, available only in Quicken Deluxe and Quicken Home and Business, are accounts you set up in Quicken (but do not have at the bank) to help you save for a special purpose — like a vacation or a new stereo system. Periodically, you transfer money from your checking account to your savings goal account. At your bank, the money never leaves your checking account, but in Quicken, you can tell, at a glance, your saving progress. If you include these transfers on your Reconciliation Report, Quicken prints the transfers on the Uncleared Transaction page. Since these are not "real" transactions, you can exclude them.

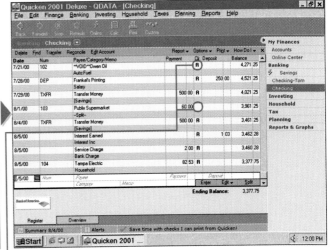

■ The second page of the Reconciliation Report groups uncleared transactions by transaction type and lists each cleared transaction.

■ The total of each section will match the same total in the Your Records section of the summary page.

■ After reconciling, you see **R** in the Clr column of the register next to cleared transactions.

■ A blank Clr column means that you have not reconciled the transaction.

■ A **c** means you started but did not complete the reconciliation – you clicked **Finish Later**.

ADD, CHANGE, AND DELETE ITEMS DURING RECONCILIATION

You can make corrections as you reconcile — you do not need to quit reconciling. If you discover missing or erroneous transactions, fix them from the Reconciliation window.

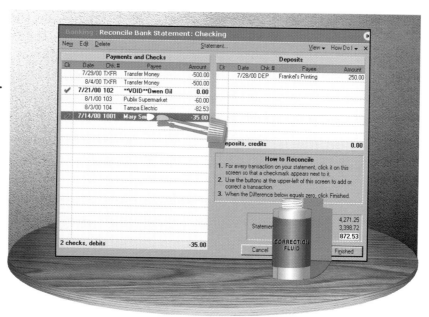

ADD, CHANGE, AND DELETE ITEMS DURING RECONCILIATION

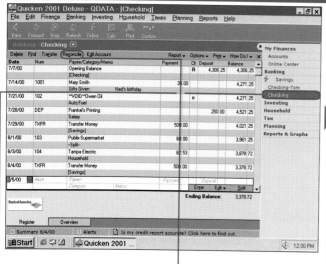

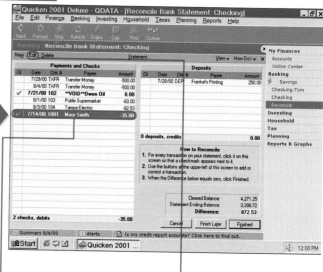

1 Click the QuickTab of the account register that you want to reconcile.

*Note: If you do not see the QuickTab, press **Ctrl+A** to open the Account List and double-click the account.*

2 Click **Reconcile**.

■ You see the Reconcile Bank Statement dialog box.

3 Complete the dialog box using Steps 3 through 6 in the Section "Reconcile an Account" and click **OK**.

■ Quicken displays the Reconcile Bank Statement window.

4 Click the transaction you want to change.

5 Click **Edit**.

I just noticed that I forgot to record an ATM withdrawal in Quicken. How do I add it?

In the Reconcile Bank Statement window, click **New**. Quicken displays your register with a blank line selected. Simply fill in the transaction and click **Return to Reconcile** to finish the reconciliation process. And, if you find a transaction in the Reconciliation window that you need to delete, click it and then click **Delete**. Quicken asks if you want to delete the current transaction. When you click **Yes**, Quicken deletes the transaction from the reconciliation window and the register.

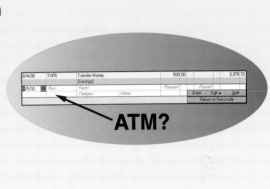

ATM?

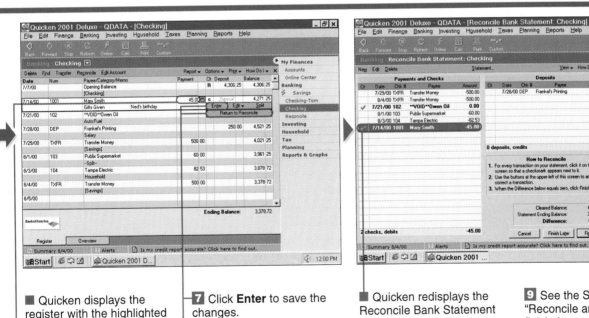

■ Quicken displays the register with the highlighted transaction selected.

■6 Type your changes.

■7 Click **Enter** to save the changes.

■8 Click **Return to Reconcile**.

■ Quicken redisplays the Reconcile Bank Statement window with the transaction change.

■9 See the Section "Reconcile an Account" to finish the reconciliation.

SEARCH FOR DIFFERENCES

Quicken can help you search for differences when the bank statement does not reconcile. What happens when you mark everything and the Difference does not equal 0.00. You can click Finish Later in the window where you clear transactions and do a little detective work.

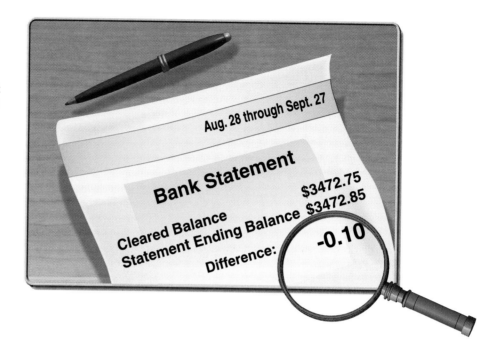

Aug. 28 through Sept. 27

Bank Statement

Cleared Balance $3472.75
Statement Ending Balance $3472.85
Difference: -0.10

CHECK FOR MISSING TRANSACTIONS

The bank may have recorded a transaction that you have not recorded in Quicken. The Missing Checks Report can help you identify checks you did not record in Quicken.

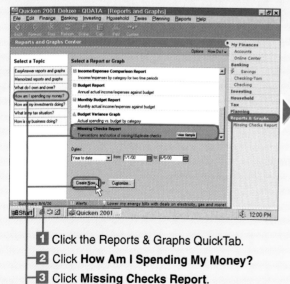

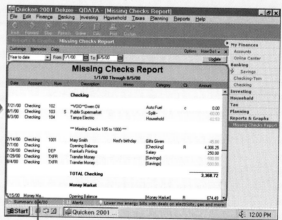

1 Click the Reports & Graphs QuickTab.

2 Click **How Am I Spending My Money?**

3 Click **Missing Checks Report**.

4 Click **Create Now**.

5 Examine your bank statement for deposits you forgot to enter. Check reorder charges, service charges, or—if your account is interest-bearing—interest payments.

CHECK THE STATEMENT ENDING BALANCE

You might have recorded the Ending Balance from the bank statement incorrectly. Make sure you typed the amount correctly.

CHECK FOR AMOUNTS THAT DO NOT MATCH

The bank might have recorded a transaction *for a different amount* than you recorded in Quicken. Compare the amounts of checks and deposits that you have recorded in your Quicken register to the amounts listed on the bank statement.

CHECK FOR TRANSPOSED FIGURES

Add the digits of the Difference and see if they equal 9 or a multiple of 9. If so, you have transposed the digits on one or more checks or deposits.

CHECK FOR ERRORS WHILE CLEARING

You might have cleared a transaction that did not clear the bank. Or, you might *not* have cleared a transaction that the bank *did* clear. Review the transactions you have cleared.

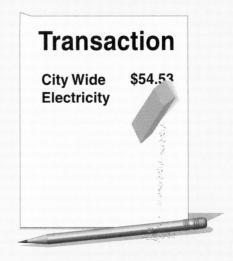

CORRECT DIFFERENCES

Quicken allows you to adjust your balance when you cannot find the difference between your register and the bank's statement. When you decide to write off the difference as a lost cause, you can record the adjustment transaction in your register balance.

Do not make a habit of this — adjustments can come back to haunt you.

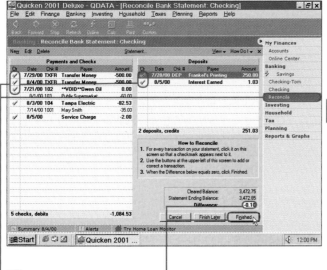

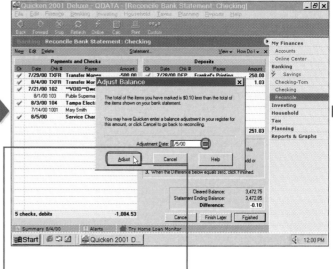

■1 Click **Reconcile** in the register window and fill in the bank statement information (see the Section "Reconcile an Account").

■2 In the Reconcile Bank Statement window, click transactions to clear them.

■ The Difference might not be 0.00.

■3 Click **Finished**.

■ Quicken displays the Adjust Balance window.

■4 Click ▦ and select a date for the adjustment transaction.

■5 Click **Adjust**.

84

Can I assign my balance adjustment to a category of my choosing?

Yes. After Quicken finishes creating the transaction, edit the transaction in the register to change the category.

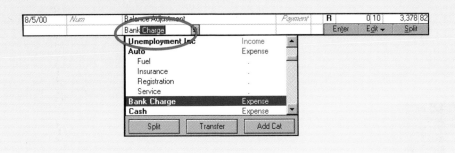

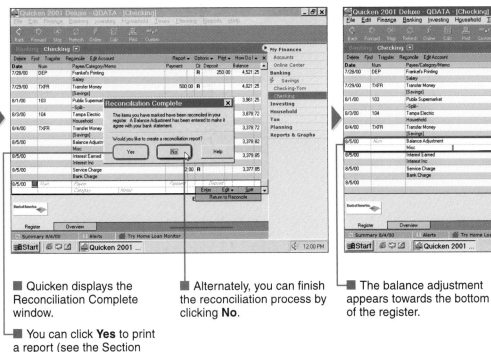

■ Quicken displays the Reconciliation Complete window.

■ You can click **Yes** to print a report (see the Section "Reconcile an Account").

■ Alternately, you can finish the reconciliation process by clicking **No**.

■ The balance adjustment appears towards the bottom of the register.

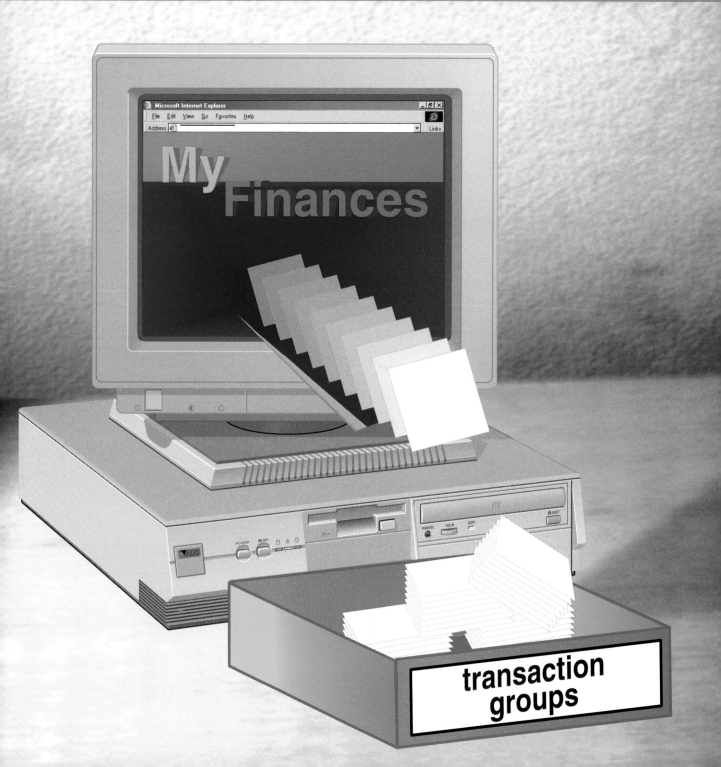

CHAPTER 4

Automate Transactions

Do you want to automate the tasks you do regularly? This chapter will help you.

2001

Alert
Robot

MEMORIZE TRANSACTIONS

You can manage the list of transactions that Quicken automatically creates.

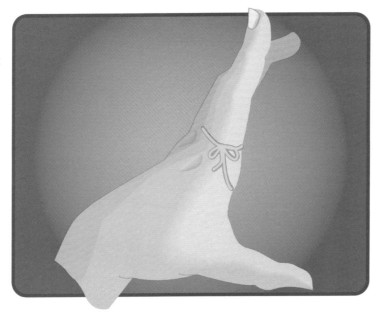

As you enter transactions, Quicken checks the payee against the Memorized Transaction List. If the payee appears in the list, Quicken fills in the rest of the transaction information.

MEMORIZE TRANSACTIONS

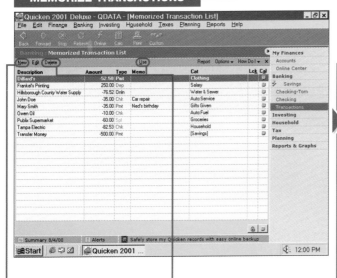

1 Press **Ctrl+T** to open the Memorized Transaction List.

■ Quicken displays up to 2,000 transactions.

■ You can click **New** to add a transaction manually.

■ You can click a transaction and then **Delete** to remove it from the list.

■ You can click a transaction and then **Use** to enter it into the register.

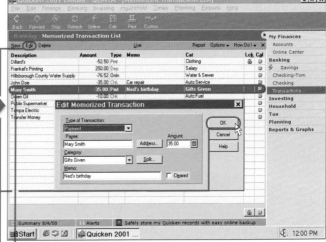

2 Click a transaction.

3 Click **Edit** to display the Edit Memorized Transaction dialog box.

4 Change any field and click **OK**.

■ Quicken changes the transaction.

*Note: You can lock the information for a transaction by clicking the **Lck** column. A 🔒 appears in the column.*

If I can memorize only 2,000 transactions, is there an easier way to keep the list clean than by manually deleting transactions?

Yes. Using the last steps in this Section, you can set Quicken's General Options to automatically remove unused transactions after a specified number of months. By doing this, you do not clutter the list with "one-time" transactions and you leave room for Quicken to continue to memorize transactions automatically.

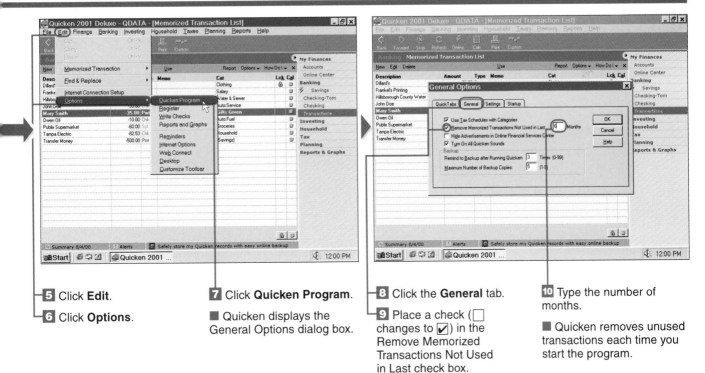

-5 Click **Edit**.

-6 Click **Options**.

7 Click **Quicken Program**.

■ Quicken displays the General Options dialog box.

8 Click the **General** tab.

-9 Place a check (☐ changes to ☑) in the Remove Memorized Transactions Not Used in Last check box.

10 Type the number of months.

■ Quicken removes unused transactions each time you start the program.

SCHEDULE TRANSACTIONS

Scheduling transactions helps you save time when you pay bills. You can set up a scheduled transaction for each bill when it arrives and let Quicken enter the transaction automatically. You can also use the list to select bills to pay.

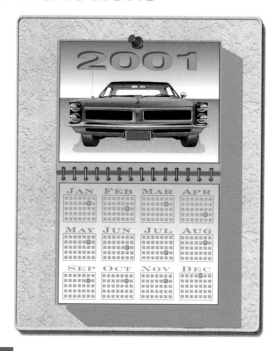

While scheduled transactions work particularly well for repeating bills of the same amount, they are equally useful for bills of different amounts.

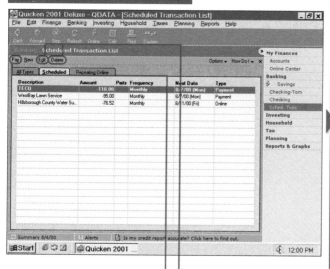

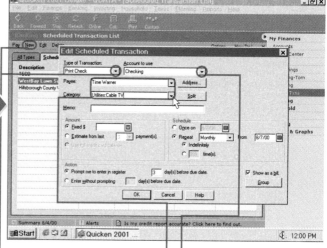

1 Press **Ctrl+J** to display the Scheduled Transaction List.

■ Quicken displays a list of scheduled transactions.

■ You can select a transaction and click **Edit** to modify it or click **Delete** to remove it from the list.

■ You can click a transaction and click **Pay** to enter the transaction into the register.

2 Click **New**.

3 Click ▼ and select a transaction type.

■ If you select **Print Check**, click **Address** to type an address that shows in a window envelope.

4 Click ▼ and select an account.

5 Type a Payee and click ▼ to select a Category.

■ You can click **Split** to assign several categories.

Suppose that I pay a bill every month, but the amount varies. How can I set up a scheduled transaction for it?

Set up the transaction for any amount. Before you pay the bill, change the amount. You can record the transaction in the register (or let Quicken record it automatically) and then change the amount.

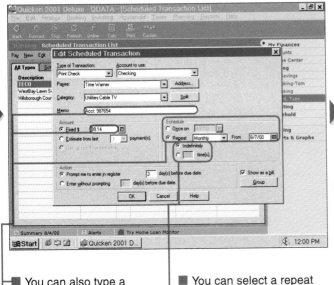

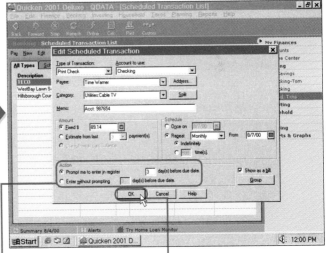

■ You can also type a Memo.

6 Type the amount.

7 Click a schedule option (○ changes to ◉) and type the next date you will pay it in the From box.

■ You can select a repeat frequency for those bills that you pay regularly.

■ You can click **Indefinitely** or type the number of times to schedule the transaction (○ changes to ◉).

8 In the Action box, select a method to enter the transaction (○ changes to ◉) and type a number of days before the due date.

■ If you opt to be prompted, Quicken reminds you to enter the transaction.

■ If you opt not to be prompted, Quicken enters the transaction when its scheduled date arrives.

9 Click **OK**.

■ The Scheduled Transaction List reappears.

CREATE A TRANSACTION GROUP

Suppose that you pay several scheduled transactions at the same time every month. You can create a scheduled transaction group that contains all these transactions and then record the group instead of recording each individual transaction. Quicken creates the group using transactions you recorded in your register.

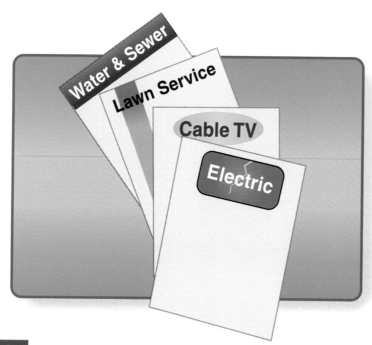

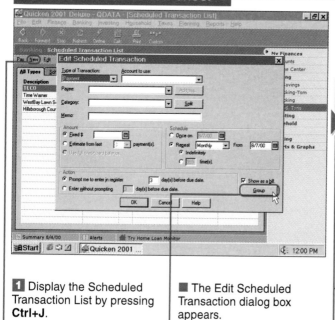

1 Display the Scheduled Transaction List by pressing **Ctrl+J**.

2 Click **New**.

■ The Edit Scheduled Transaction dialog box appears.

3 Click **Group**.

■ You can click ▼ to change the account and ▦ to change the date.

4 Type a group name.

5 Click ▼ to select a frequency and method to record the group.

6 Type the number of payments and the number of days in advance you want the transactions entered in the register.

7 Click **OK**.

Can I change the transactions that I include in a scheduled transaction group?

Yes. After you create the group, click it and click **Edit**. Quicken displays the window where you assign a name to the group. Click **OK,** and Quicken displays the list of transactions that you can assign to the group. To remove a transaction from the group, highlight it and click **Mark**.

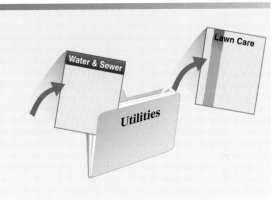

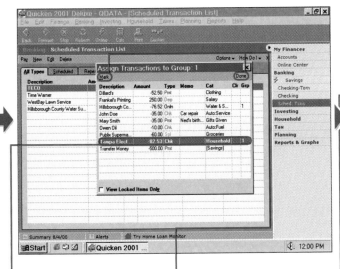

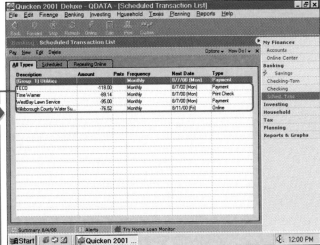

■ The Assign Transactions to Group window appears.

8 Click a transaction that you want to include in the group.

9 Click **Mark**.

10 Repeat Steps 8 and 9 for each transaction you want to include in the group.

11 Click **Done** to save the transaction.

■ Quicken places a scheduled transaction group in the window.

SET UP ALERTS

You can use alerts in Quicken to notify yourself of financial events that you might miss or forget. You can set alerts for almost anything: when to reorder checks, when an account reaches a particular balance, or when mortgage rates drop below your current mortgage rate. Once you set up an alert, you will see it on the My Finances page and in the Reminders window.

SET UP ALERTS

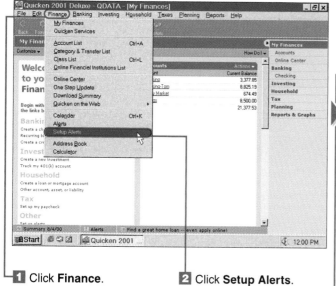

1 Click **Finance**.

2 Click **Setup Alerts**.

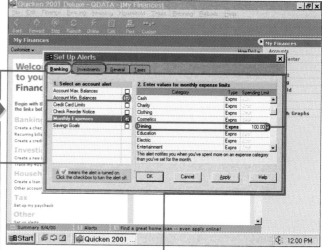

■ Quicken displays the Set Up Alerts dialog box.

3 Click the **Banking** tab and place a check next to the alert you want to use (☐ changes to ☑).

■ On the right side of the screen, you can type appropriate information.

4 Click the **Investments** tab.

Automate
Transactions **4**

What do the alerts on the General tab do?

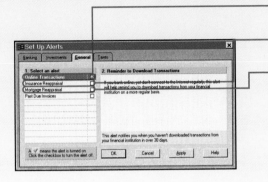

■ The Online Transactions alert reminds you to download.

■ The Insurance Reappraisal alert reminds you two months before a policy expires.

■ The Mortgage Reappraisal alert notifies you three months before a mortgage converts from variable to fixed (or vice versa).

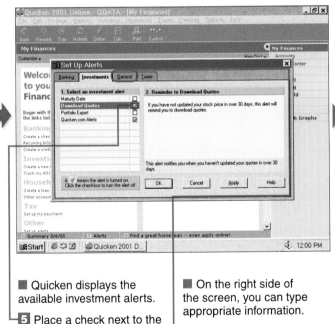

■ Quicken displays the available investment alerts.

5 Place a check next to the alert you want to use (☐ changes to ☑).

■ On the right side of the screen, you can type appropriate information.

6 Click the **General** tab.

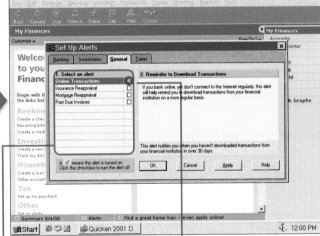

■ Quicken displays the available general alerts.

7 Place a check next to an alert to use it (☐ changes to ☑).

CONTINUED ➤

SET UP ALERTS

You can set up tax-related alerts and then view alerts in different ways.

SET UP ALERTS (CONTINUED)

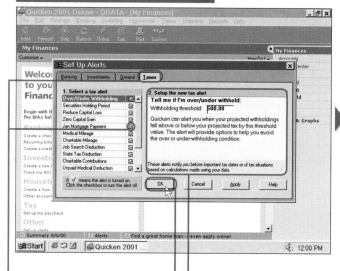

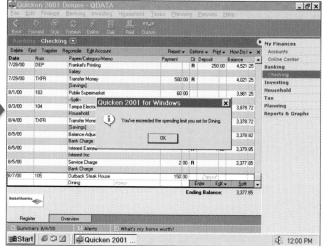

■8 Click the **Taxes** tab.

■ Quicken displays the available alerts for taxes.

■9 Place a check (☐ changes to ✓) next to the alert you want to use.

■ On the right side of the screen, you can type appropriate information.

■10 Click **OK**.

■ Nothing happens in Quicken until you perform an action that triggers an alert. Quicken's reaction depends on the alerts you have selected.

■ Some alerts pop up on-screen.

Can I make up my own alerts?

No, but you can put notes on Quicken's Financial Calendar; notes on the calendar appear in the Reminders window along with alerts and scheduled transactions. To learn more about notes, see the Section, "Add Notes to the Calendar."

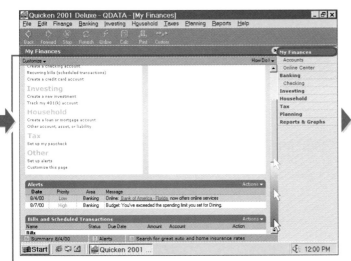

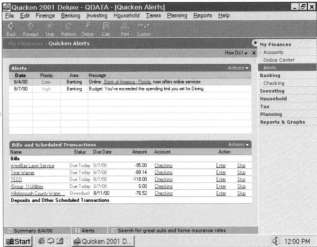

■ You can click **My Finances** and scroll down to see all alerts that have occurred.

Note: you can also view alerts in the Alerts window (see the Section "View Alerts").

VIEW ALERTS

After setting up alerts and scheduling payments, you can see everything simultaneously in the Alerts window.

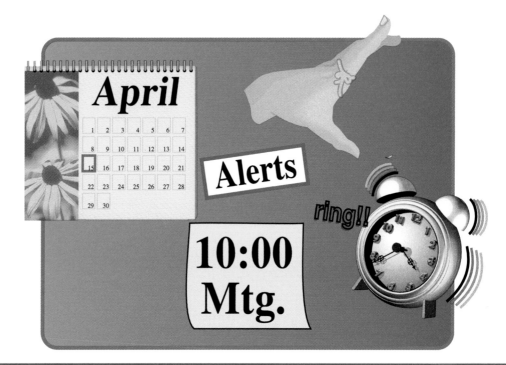

VIEW ALERTS

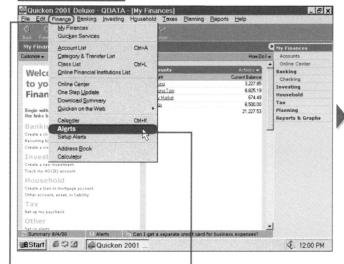

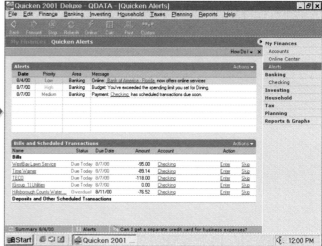

1 To view the Alerts window, click **Finance**.

2 Click **Alerts**.

■ Quicken displays the Alerts window.

■ Alerts appear in the top of the window; scheduled transactions appear in the bottom.

Note: See Chapter 11 to display the Alerts window every time you open Quicken or change the timeframe for information shown in the Alerts window.

VIEW THE FINANCIAL CALENDAR

The Financial Calendar lets you see scheduled transactions, financial events, and notes in a 30-day calendar format.

VIEW THE FINANCIAL CALENDAR

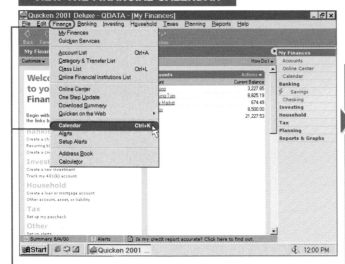

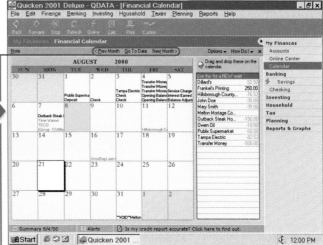

1 Click **Finance**.

2 Click **Calendar**.

■ Alternately, you can press **Ctrl+K**.

■ Quicken displays the Financial Calendar.

■ Use the navigation buttons to change calendar views.

Note: Today's date is outlined in red, transactions in the register appear in black, and scheduled transactions appear in red.

ADD NOTES TO THE CALENDAR

You can use calendar notes to include non-financial reminders — such as birthdays or appointments — on Quicken's calendar.

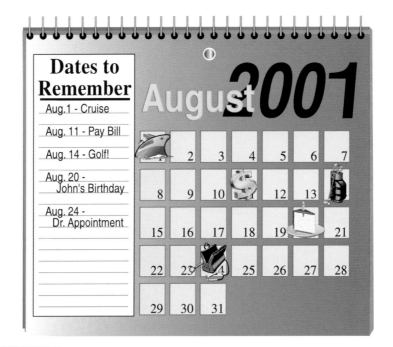

Dates to Remember

Aug.1 - Cruise

Aug. 11 - Pay Bill

Aug. 14 - Golf!

Aug. 20 - John's Birthday

Aug. 24 - Dr. Appointment

ADD NOTES TO THE CALENDAR

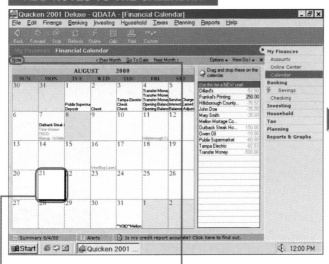

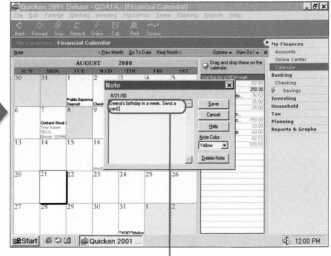

1 Press **Ctrl+K** to display the Financial Calendar.

2 Select the date on which you want to add a note.

3 Click **Note**.

■ Quicken displays the Note window.

4 Type the text of your note.

How many notes can I add to the calendar?

You can add one note per day to Quicken's financial calendar.

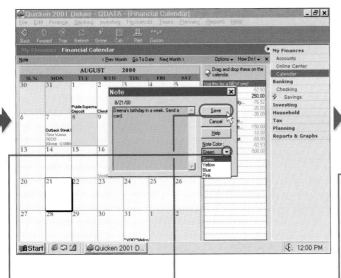

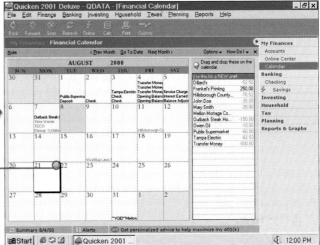

■ You can click ▼ and select a different color for the note.

■ You can color code notes to make them more identifiable.

5 Click **Save**.

■ Quicken displays ▦ on the calendar. The icon appears in the color you selected for the note.

CUSTOMIZE THE MY FINANCES PAGE

You can customize the My Finances page or create several different pages. By default, Quicken displays the My Finances page when you start the program. The My Finances page can show you more than alerts, reminders, and notes.

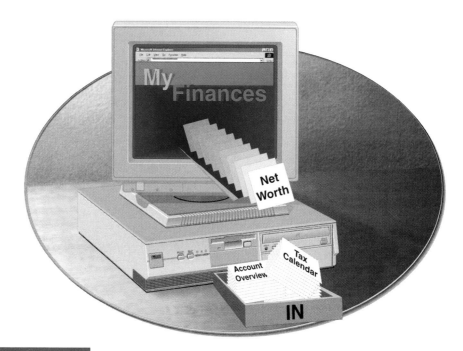

CUSTOMIZE THE MY FINANCES PAGE

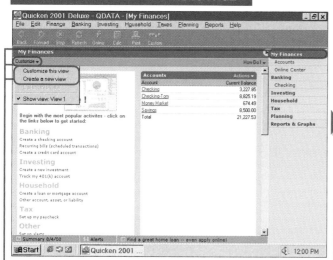

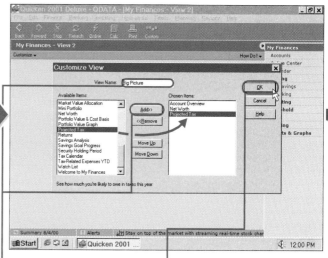

1 Click **My Finances**.

2 Click **Customize**.

3 Select a view.

■ You can create a view or customize the current view.

■ The Customize View dialog box appears.

4 Type a name for the view.

5 Click an item in the Available Items list.

6 Click **Add**.

■ The item appears in the Chosen Items list.

7 Repeat Steps 4 through 6 to add more items.

■ You can click the **Move Up** and **Move Down** buttons to reorder the list.

8 Click **OK**.

I want to avoid scrolling to see everything. How many views can I create?

You can create up to 11 views of the My Finances page. You can switch from one to another by clicking **Customize** at top of the window. You can then select the desired view from the bottom of the drop-down menu that appears.

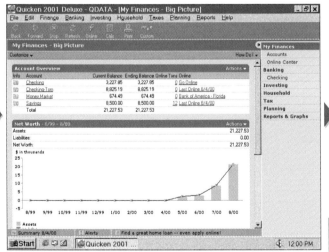

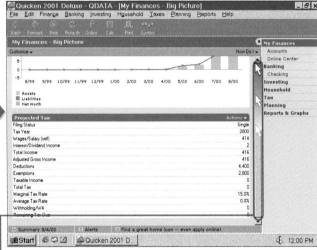

■ Quicken displays the new My Finances page.

■ Use the scroll bar on the side to view more of the page.

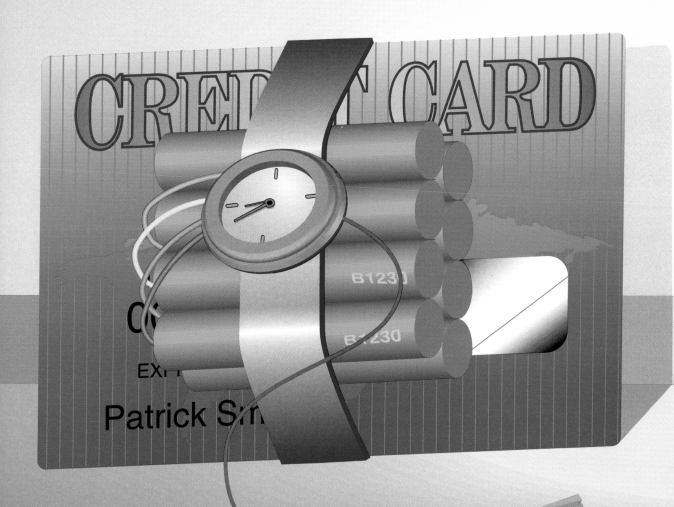

CHAPTER 5

Track Credit Card Debt

Do you feel like your credit cards are bombs waiting to explode? Read this chapter to learn how Quicken can help you track and manage your credit card spending.

SET UP A CREDIT CARD ACCOUNT

In Quicken, you can track credit card transactions and balances to more effectively manage your debt.

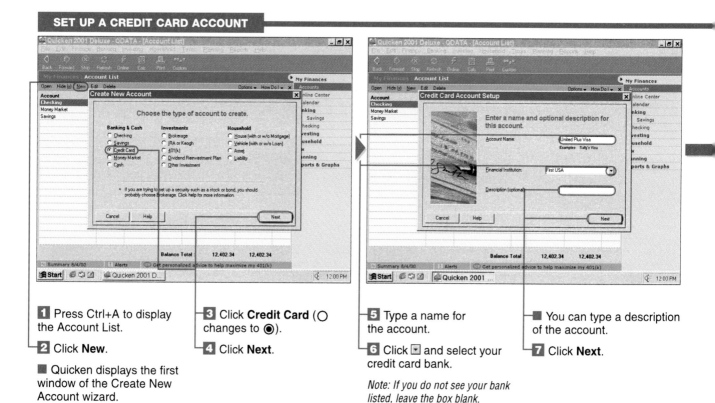

1 Press Ctrl+A to display the Account List.

2 Click **New**.

■ Quicken displays the first window of the Create New Account wizard.

3 Click **Credit Card** (○ changes to ◉).

4 Click **Next**.

5 Type a name for the account.

6 Click ▤ and select your credit card bank.

Note: If you do not see your bank listed, leave the box blank.

■ You can type a description of the account.

7 Click **Next**.

What do I do if I do not have my last credit card statement?

When you indicate that you do not have your last credit card statement, Quicken displays a window informing you that Quicken will set the account balance to zero and that you can change it later, if necessary.

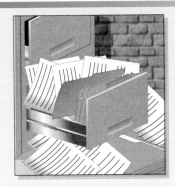

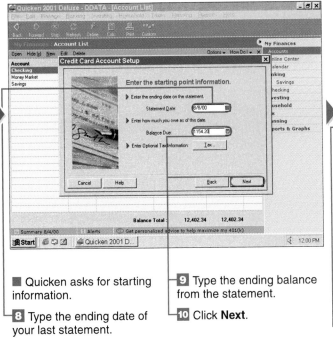

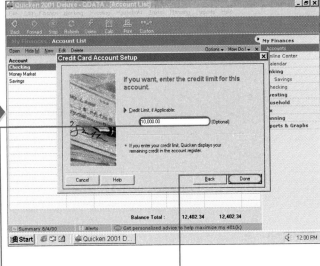

■ Quicken asks for starting information.

8 Type the ending date of your last statement.

9 Type the ending balance from the statement.

10 Click **Next**.

■ Quicken displays a window asking if you want to enter a credit limit.

■ You can type a credit limit for this card.

11 Click **Done**.

■ Quicken redisplays the Account List, which includes an entry for the new credit card account you just created.

RECORD A CREDIT CARD PURCHASE

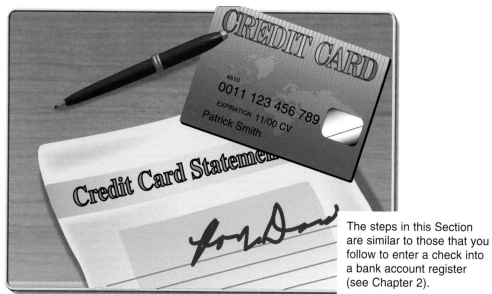

When you buy something using your credit card, you can save the receipt and record the transaction in Quicken. This enables you to track outstanding balances.

The steps in this Section are similar to those that you follow to enter a check into a bank account register (see Chapter 2).

RECORD A CREDIT CARD PURCHASE

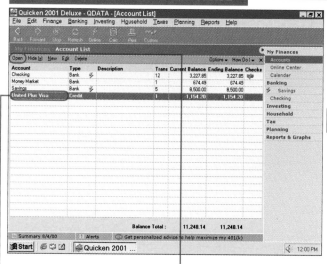

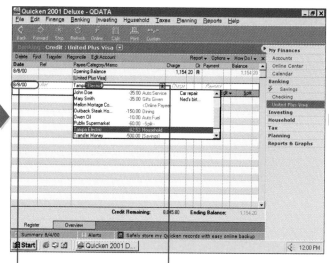

1 Press **Ctrl+A** to display the Account List.

2 Click the credit card account into which you want to record a transaction.

3 Click **Open** to display the credit card register.

■ Alternatively, you can double-click the credit card account to display its register.

4 Type the transaction date in MM/DD/YY format.

■ You can use the ➕ or ➖ keys to add or subtract days.

5 Press Tab twice.

6 In the Payee field, type the name of the business you paid with the card.

■ Quicken automatically opens a list of the last 2,000 payees.

What is the purpose of the Ref field?

If you want, you can enter the approximately 20-digit transaction number that appears on your credit card receipt — but most people have better things to do.

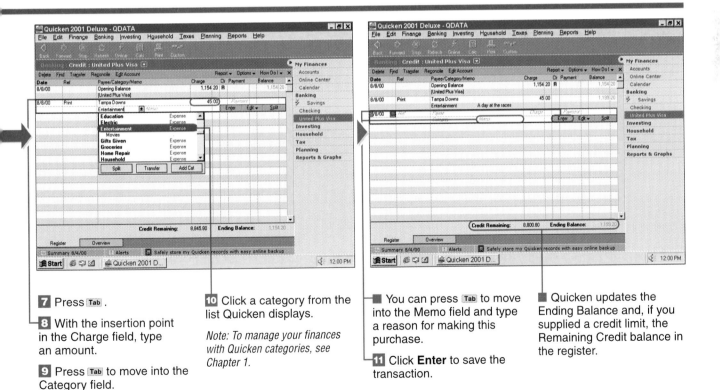

7 Press Tab.

8 With the insertion point in the Charge field, type an amount.

9 Press Tab to move into the Category field.

10 Click a category from the list Quicken displays.

Note: To manage your finances with Quicken categories, see Chapter 1.

■ You can press Tab to move into the Memo field and type a reason for making this purchase.

11 Click **Enter** to save the transaction.

■ Quicken updates the Ending Balance and, if you supplied a credit limit, the Remaining Credit balance in the register.

PAY A CREDIT CARD BILL

When you receive a bill from your credit card company, you can pay it in Quicken. The transaction you enter reduces your bank account, and, at the same time, reduces the balance in your credit card account.

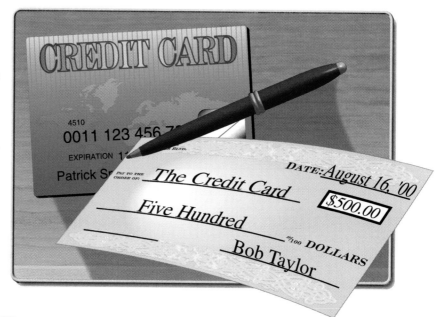

PAY A CREDIT CARD BILL

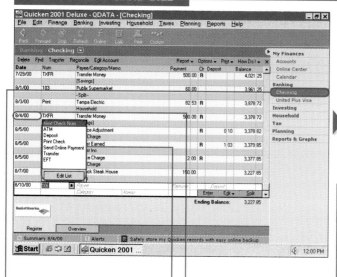

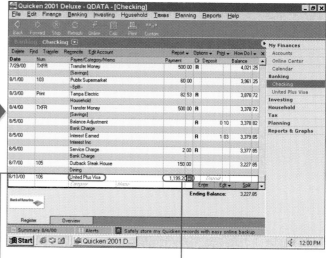

1 From the Banking QuickTab, click the account from which you want to pay the credit card bill.

*Note: If you do not see the account, press **Ctrl+A** to open the Account List and double-click the account.*

■ If necessary, change the date of the transaction.

2 In the Num field, click **Print Check**, **Next Check Num**, or **Send Online Payment**.

3 In the Payee field, type the name of the credit card company.

■ Quicken automatically opens a list of the last 2,000 payees; if you select one, Quicken fills in your last transaction to that payee.

4 In the Payment field, type the amount you want to pay.

Do I need to do anything differently if I do not want to pay the entire credit card bill?

No. When you supply the amount in the Payment field, simply enter the amount you want to pay.

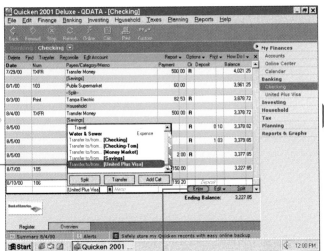

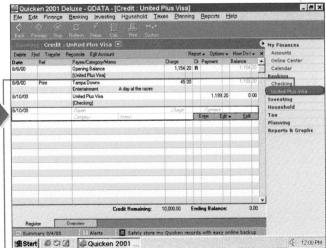

5 In the Category field, scroll to the bottom of the list Quicken displays and click the credit card account.

■ In the Memo field, you can type a reason for writing this check.

Note: If you print the check, Memo text prints in the Memo block on your check.

6 Click **Enter** to save the transaction.

■ You can click the credit card account under the Banking tab to see the Payment transaction created from your check.

Note: The Payment transaction increases the Credit Remaining and reduces the Ending Balance of the credit card account.

ENABLE ONLINE ACCESS FOR A CREDIT CARD ACCOUNT

You can download credit card transactions to save yourself the trouble of entering them. If your credit card company does not offer this option, you can apply for a free Quicken MasterCard that provides it. To download transactions, you must have information from your credit card company to enable your credit card account for online access.

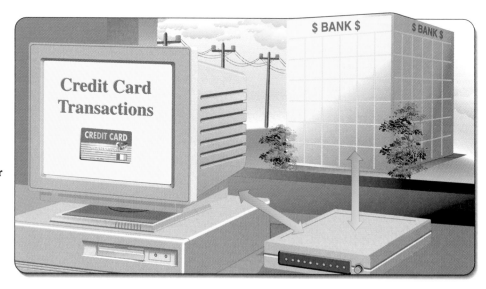

ENABLE ONLINE ACCESS FOR A CREDIT CARD ACCOUNT

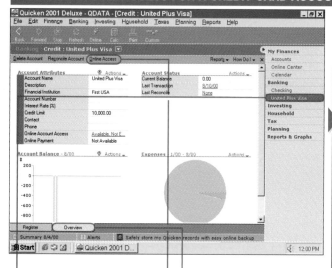

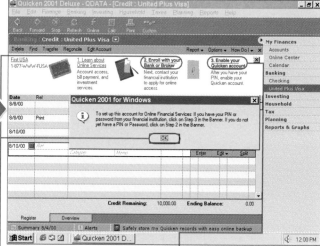

1 Click the credit card account under the **Banking** QuickTab.

*Note: If you do not see the account, press **Ctrl+A** to open the Account List and double-click the account.*

2 Click the **Overview** tab.

3 Click **Online Access**.

■ Quicken displays the register with new icons and a message that explains the icons.

4 Click **OK**.

5 If you have not received information from your bank, click **2** to contact your bank.

6 When you receive information from your bank, repeat Steps 1 through 3 in this section. Then click **3**.

What is a *routing number*?

Every transaction you make through a financial institution (and your credit card company is a financial institution) actually goes first to the Federal Reserve. Each financial institution has an account with the Federal Reserve, and the number that identifies the account is called the routing number. Why? Because the Federal Reserve uses the number to disperse (or "route") transactions to the correct financial institution.

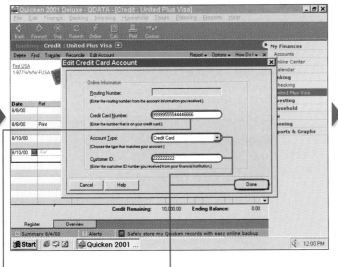

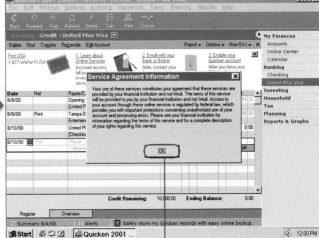

■ Quicken connects to the Internet and then displays the Edit Credit Card Account window.

7 Type your credit card number.

8 Click ▾ and select **Credit Card** or **Line of Credit**.

9 Type your customer PIN number.

10 Click **Done**.

■ Quicken displays a service agreement window.

11 Click **OK** to display the credit card account register.

DOWNLOAD CREDIT CARD TRANSACTIONS

After you have enabled a credit card account for downloading, you can download the transactions into your Quicken account.

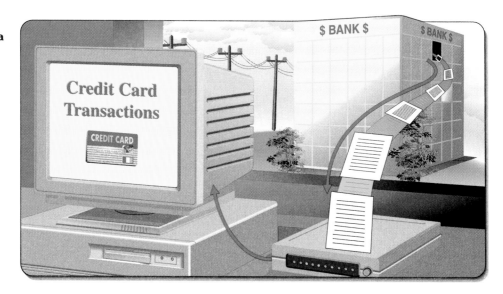

DOWNLOAD CREDIT CARD TRANSACTIONS

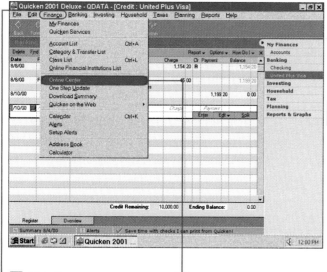

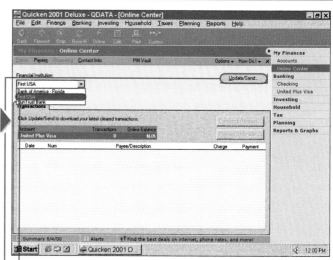

1 Click **Finance**.

2 Click **Online Center**.

Note: If you see the Online Center QuickTab, you can click it instead.

3 Click ☑ and select your credit card company.

4 Click **Update/Send**.

■ Quicken displays a window asking you to enter your PIN number.

5 Enter your PIN number and click **Send**.

■ After you connect with the bank, Quicken indicates the number of new transactions downloaded.

6 Click **OK**.

In my register, some transactions have "c" in the Clr field, and some transactions have nothing in the Clr field. Why?

c in the Clr field

Downloaded transactions display a "c" in the Clr field; the "c" simply means that you have downloaded the transaction from the bank but have not yet cleared it during an account reconciliation.

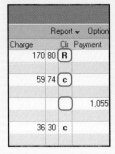

Blank Clr field

If the Clr field is blank, you entered the transaction instead of downloading it.

R in the Clr field

The "R" indicates that you have cleared the transaction during a reconciliation.

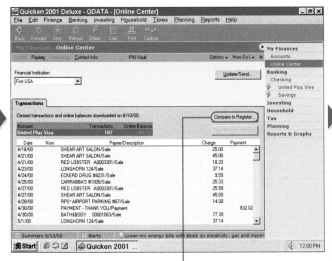

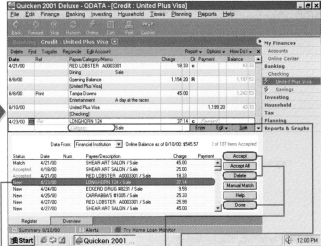

■ Quicken redisplays the Online Center and your downloaded transactions.

7 Click **Compare to Register**.

■ You see the register, modified to include credit card transactions.

8 Click a transaction.

■ It appears in both the lower and upper portions of the window.

9 Enter a category for the transaction.

10 Click **Accept** or **Delete**.

11 Repeat Steps 8 through 10 until you account for all transactions.

12 Click **Done**.

RECONCILE A CREDIT CARD ACCOUNT

You can match your Quicken entries to your credit card statement by reconciling the account against your online balance or, as you see in this Section, your paper statement. You can reconcile before or after you pay the bill.

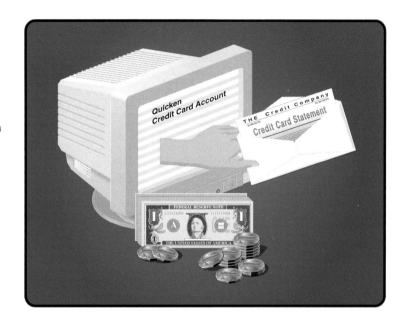

RECONCILE A CREDIT CARD ACCOUNT

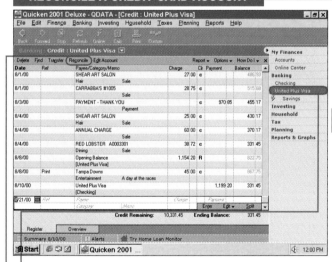

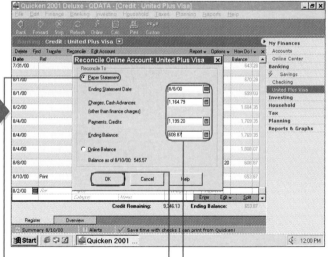

1 Click the QuickTab of the credit card account.

*Note: If you do not see the QuickTab, press **Ctrl+A** and open the register from the Accounts window.*

2 Click **Reconcile**.

■ Quicken displays the Reconcile Online Account window.

Note: A message might appear suggesting that you update your downloaded data. See the Section "Download Credit Card Transactions."

3 Click **Paper Statement** (○ changes to ◉).

*Note: Accounting professionals recommend reconciling against a paper statement in order to synchronize monthly with the credit card bank. Therefore, this example selects **Paper Statement**.*

4 Type the ending date, the new charges total, payments and credits, and the ending balance that appear on your statement.

5 Click **OK**.

What will my Reconciliation Report and register look like after I reconcile?

When you set up the report, you can select the **Summary and Uncleared** option and print two pages. The first page sums cleared and uncleared transactions and matches your ending balance to the credit card statement's ending balance. The second page lists uncleared transactions. If you select the **All Transactions** option, the second page lists *cleared* transactions, and Quicken prints two additional pages of uncleared transactions. In your register, after reconciling, you will see **R** in the Clr column next to cleared transactions. If you see a **c** or a blank Clr column in the register, see the Section "Download Credit Card Transactions" for more information.

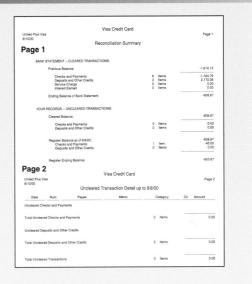

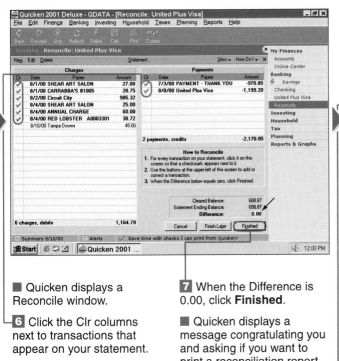

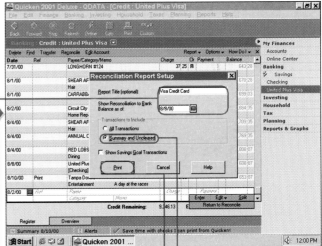

■ Quicken displays a Reconcile window.

6 Click the Clr columns next to transactions that appear on your statement.

7 When the Difference is 0.00, click **Finished**.

■ Quicken displays a message congratulating you and asking if you want to print a reconciliation report.

■ You can click **Yes** to print the report.

■ Quicken displays the Reconciliation Report Setup window.

■ You can type a report title and a new date.

■ You can click **Summary and Uncleared** (○ changes to ◉) to print a summary of cleared transactions.

■ You can print the report by clicking **Print**.

To help you monitor your
credit card spending, you
can set up a credit limit
and have Quicken "alert"
you when you exceed it.
You can use a limit other
than that established by
your credit card company.

MONITOR SPENDING

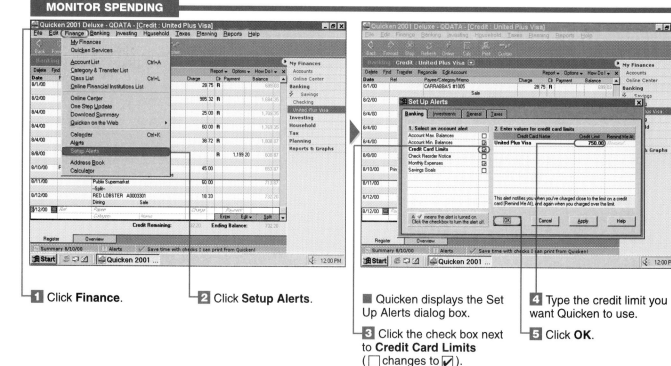

1 Click **Finance**.

2 Click **Setup Alerts**.

■ Quicken displays the Set
Up Alerts dialog box.

3 Click the check box next
to **Credit Card Limits**
(☐ changes to ☑).

4 Type the credit limit you
want Quicken to use.

5 Click **OK**.

If I set up this credit card limit alert, will it continue to "nag" me each time I enter a transaction once I have exceeded the limit?

No. Quicken only alerts you once when you exceed the credit limit. The alert appears again *after* you make a payment that gives you a "positive" Credit Remaining amount and then make another purchase that causes you to exceed the limit.

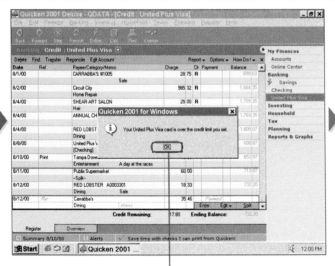

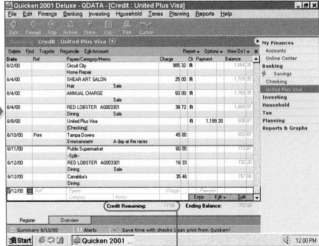

6 In the credit card account register, type a transaction.

■ If the transaction causes you to exceed the credit limit you set, you see a warning message.

7 Click **OK** to clear the message.

■ Quicken updates both the Credit Remaining and the Ending Balance.

■ The Credit Remaining continues to be a negative number until you make a payment that exceeds the Credit Remaining amount.

MONITOR CREDIT CARD BALANCES ON THE MY FINANCES PAGE

You can add credit card balances to the My Finances page, which Quicken displays when you start the program. Adding credit card balances to the My Finance page helps you keep track of them.

MONITOR CREDIT CARD BALANCES ON THE MY FINANCES PAGE

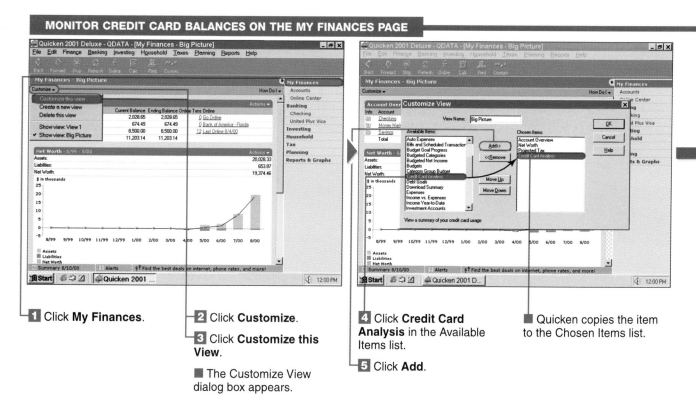

1 Click **My Finances**.

2 Click **Customize**.

3 Click **Customize this View**.

■ The Customize View dialog box appears.

4 Click **Credit Card Analysis** in the Available Items list.

5 Click **Add**.

■ Quicken copies the item to the Chosen Items list.

Besides viewing the balances, are there other benefits to adding credit cards to the My Finances page?

By clicking links on the My Finances page, you can change the credit card's credit limit and interest rate and view the credit card account's register.

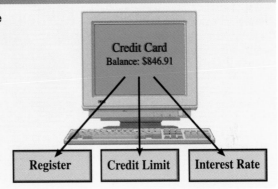

Credit Card
Balance: $846.91

Register | Credit Limit | Interest Rate

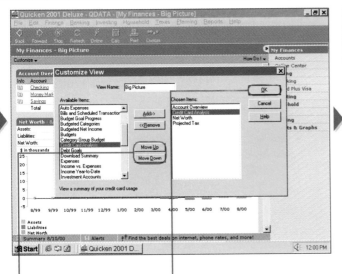

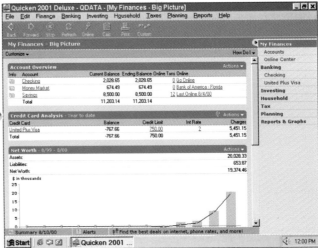

■ You can click the **Move Up** or **Move Down** buttons repeatedly to reorder Credit Card Analysis in the Chosen Items list.

⬛6 Click **OK**.

■ Quicken displays the new My Finances page that includes credit card account information and links.

STEPS TO DEBT REDUCTION

You can reduce debt using the Debt Reduction Planner. Misusing credit cards can easily lead to financial trouble, because you lose track of how much you are spending. You can find yourself with high debt on several credit cards, making minimum payments to keep the creditors satisfied.

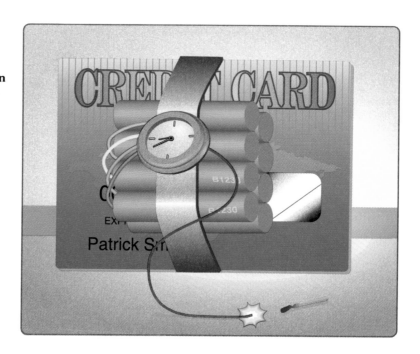

1 DEBT REDUCTION PLANNER

Quicken's Debt Reduction Planner can help you figure out the best way to get out of debt quickly. The Debt Reduction Planner helps you assess your debts, evaluate your resources, and establish cost-cutting measures to get you out of debt.

2 PAY OFF THE MOST COSTLY DEBT FIRST

The Debt Reduction Planner sorts your debts and suggests that you pay off the most expensive debt first and make minimum payments on the others. This approach saves you money in interest payments.

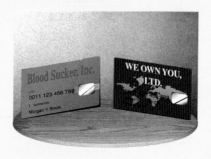

3 EVALUATE YOUR RESOURCES

The Debt Reduction Planner compares the interest you earn on your savings or investments to the interest you are paying on your debts.

MAKE THE BEST USE OF MONEY ON HAND

If you earn less interest than you pay, the Debt Reduction Planner suggests that you use some of your savings or investments to reduce your debt — again, saving you money in the long term.

 BUDGET TO REDUCE YOUR SPENDING

The Debt Reduction Planner suggests that you budget to spend less in various categories and apply the cutback amount to paying off your debt. This step helps you make more than the minimum monthly payment on your most expensive debt.

 CREATE AN ACTION PLAN

The Debt Reduction Planner sorts your debts and suggests that you pay off the most expensive debt first and make minimum payments on the others. This approach saves you money in interest payments.

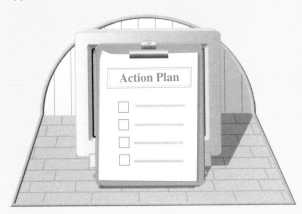

 **TRACK YOUR PROGRESS**

You also can let Quicken alert you if you fall behind your debt reduction plan and set up scheduled payments for your monthly payments.

USING THE DEBT REDUCTION PLANNER

Quicken's Debt Reduction Planner can help you get out of debt and pay the minimum amount to do it. The Debt Reduction Planner helps you identify which debts cost you the most; determines whether to use savings to reduce your debt; and calculates how to cut spending, so that you can use the extra money to pay off your debts.

USING THE DEBT REDUCTION PLANNER

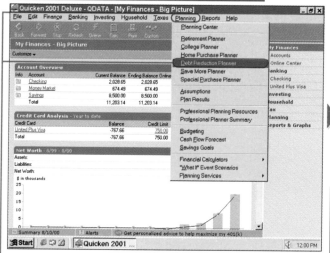

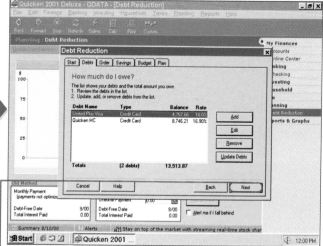

1 Click **Planning**.

2 Click **Debt Reduction Planner**.

■ Quicken starts the Debt Reduction Planner wizard.

3 Insert your Quicken CD and click **Next**.

■ A multimedia clip explains how the Debt Reduction Planner works.

4 When the clip finishes, click **Next**.

■ Quicken displays your current debt.

5 Click **Next**.

■ Quicken displays a message indicating that it needs extra information about your debts.

6 Click **OK** to close the message.

■ Quicken displays the Edit Debt Reduction dialog box.

I would like a schedule of my payments. Can I get one?

The Action Plan you produce in the Debt Reduction Planner contains a schedule (see Steps 19 through 22 in this Section). To print a schedule:

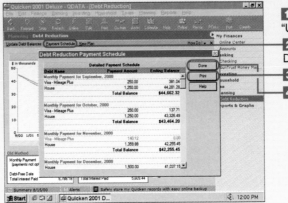

1 Perform the steps in the Section "Using the Debt Reduction Planner."

2 Click **Payment Schedule** in the Debt Reduction window.

3 Click **Print**.

4 Click **Done**.

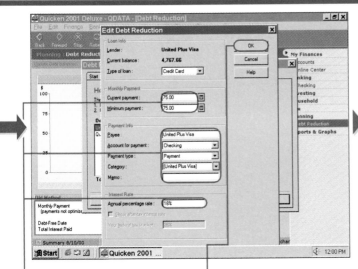

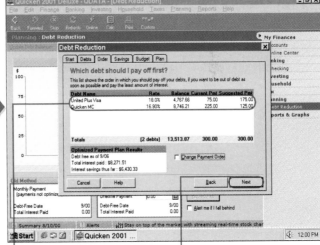

7 Type the current and minimum monthly payment amounts.

8 Type your payment information.

9 Confirm the interest rate.

10 Click **OK**.

11 Repeat Steps 7 through 10 for each debt.

■ Quicken assesses and sorts your debts.

12 Click **Next** twice.

■ Quicken sorts your debts in the order that minimizes the amount of interest you pay and the time you remain in debt.

13 Click **Next**.

■ Another multimedia clip presents the concept of using savings or investments to reduce debt.

14 When the clip finishes, click **Next**.

CONTINUED

125

In the Debt Reduction Planner, you can apply a one-time payment from your savings or investments to reduce your debt. The Debt Reduction Planner also helps you identify spending areas you can reduce.

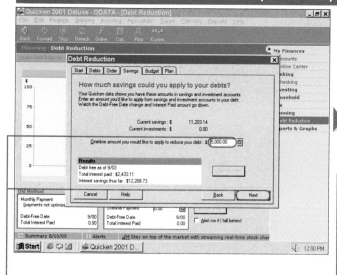

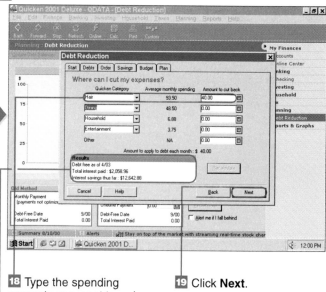

■ Quicken displays your current savings and investment balances.

15 Type a one-time amount you are willing to apply to your debt.

16 Click **Next**.

■ Another multimedia clip presents the idea of cutting spending in various categories and using the money you save to pay your debts.

17 When the clip finishes, click **Next**.

18 Type the spending amounts you want to reduce.

■ Quicken updates the Results.

19 Click **Next**.

What happens if things change and I need a new plan?

You can either discard the current plan and start a new one or edit an existing plan. Note that Quicken tracks only one debt reduction plan at a time — you cannot create and use multiple plans. To create a new plan, click **New Plan** and follow the steps in this section. To edit the current plan:

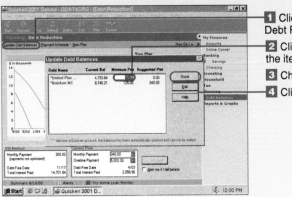

1 Click **Update Debt Balances** in the Debt Reduction window.

2 Click the **Minimum Pmt** column of the item that you want to change.

3 Change the amount you want to pay.

4 Click **Done**.

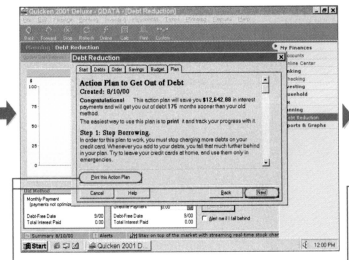

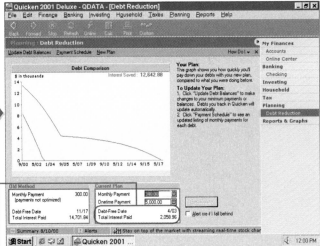

■ Quicken displays your Action Plan.

■ You can click **Print this Action Plan** for a paper copy.

20 Click **Next**.

■ Quicken displays a window in which you can set up scheduled debt payments and alerts to warn you if you fall behind your payments.

21 Click **Next**.

22 Click **Done**.

■ You see the Debt Reduction Plan graph, which compares the debt-free dates (month and year) and the total interest paid of the old method and the new plan.

*Note: You may see messages about the size of your monthly payment and about scheduled payments. If so, click **OK**.*

CREATE SPENDING REPORTS

You can create a variety of reports and graphs to monitor your spending. The steps to create each report are the same; final information depends on which report you select.

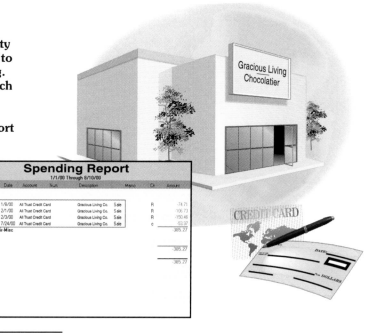

Spending Report

To determine which report or graph best meets your needs, see the Section, "View Spending Reports."

CREATE SPENDING REPORTS

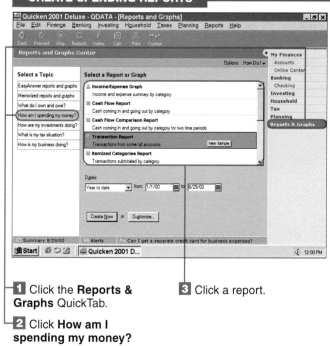

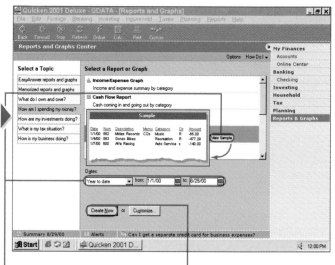

1 Click the **Reports & Graphs** QuickTab.

2 Click **How am I spending my money?**

3 Click a report.

■ You can click **View Sample** to view a thumbnail layout of any report.

■ You can change the dates or click **Customize** to exclude accounts or categories.

4 Click **Create Now**.

■ Quicken displays the report or graph you selected.

With Quicken, you can view your expenses and spending habits on different spending reports. To create a spending report, see the Section, "Create Spending Reports."

INCOME/EXPENSE GRAPH

When you are trying to cut costs, Quicken's Income/Expense Graph allows you to identify areas of spending and lets you compare monthly income with monthly expenses. You can place the mouse pointer over a bar or pie slice to see details about that bar or pie slice.

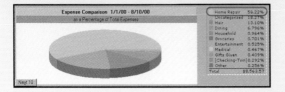

ITEMIZED CATEGORIES REPORT

You can use Quicken's Itemized Categories Report to list transactions, sorted by category. This allows you to see all transactions that relate to a particular category and the total expenditures in that category. You see income categories, followed by expense categories with a subtotal for each category.

Note: See Chapter 1 for a full explanation of categories and what they can do for you.

TRANSACTION REPORT

You can print Quicken's Transaction Report to list, in chronological order, all transactions for all categories in selected accounts. You can customize the report to include all accounts or a set of accounts or change the categories included on the report.

INCOME / EXPENSE COMPARISON REPORT

You can look at the amount you spent last year for a certain category and compare it to the amount you spent this year. A large increase or decrease can signal an area of concern.

BANKING SUMMARY REPORT

You can print the Banking Summary Report to see totals for each category. The other reports in this section provide transaction details. This report lists income categories, followed by expense categories. The report prints totals for the categories. You can double-click a dollar amount to see the transactions that comprise that amount.

CHAPTER 6

Manage Your Property

Did you know that Quicken can help you manage and value personal property, such as your house, car, and belongings? This chapter explains how.

VIEW THE HOUSEHOLD CENTER

The Household Center QuickTab provides an overview of your personal property situation.

Household Services

Click any of these links to perform common functions related to household spending.

Asset & Liability Accounts

You can review the balances in your asset and liability accounts, click a link to open the register, create a new account, or create an inventory of your personal possessions.

Household and Car Alerts

This section displays alerts you have set about your car and household information.

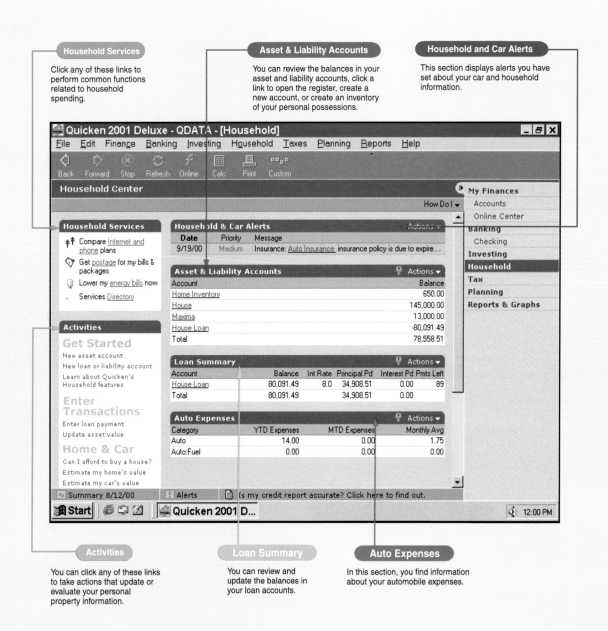

Activities

You can click any of these links to take actions that update or evaluate your personal property information.

Loan Summary

You can review and update the balances in your loan accounts.

Auto Expenses

In this section, you find information about your automobile expenses.

USING AN ASSET ACCOUNT

Let Quicken help you assess your financial picture. Quicken can do much more than just write checks and manage credit cards.

YOUR NET WORTH

Possessions: $250,000   Debts: $200,000

Net Worth: $50,000

Set up asset accounts in Quicken that represent things you own, such as your home and your car. If you do not own these things outright, also set up loan accounts to offset them. Then, Quicken can calculate how much your assets are really worth to you.

ASSET ACCOUNTS AND PROPERTY

Use asset accounts to track the value of securities but not their performance. For example, you can set up asset accounts for Treasury Bills, CDs, precious metals, or fixed annuities.

FIND MORTGAGE RATES

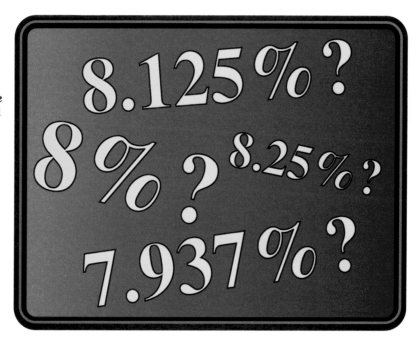

Quicken can help you research current interest rates. Suppose that you are researching mortgage rates on a new home and wonder what to expect from lenders. Quicken can help you find them.

FIND MORTGAGE RATES

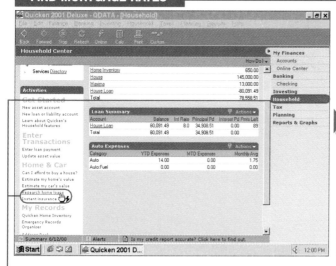

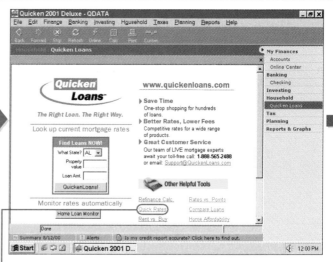

1 Click the **Household** QuickTab.

2 Click **Research home loans**.

■ Quicken connects to the Internet. You see the Quicken Loans Web page.

Note: When you point at a link and see a lightning bolt attached to the mouse pointer, clicking the link connects you to the Internet.

3 Click the **Quick Rates** link under **Other Helpful Tools**.

■ Quicken displays the Mortgage Tools Quick Rates page at Quicken.com.

What do the other calculators on the Quicken Loans page do?

Rent vs. Buy link

You can receive guidance on which option is more sound financially.

Refinance Calc link

This link helps you decide if you need to refinance your current mortgage.

Compare Loans link

You can compare the loans that are available to you based on information you provide about yourself and your proposed purchase.

Rates vs. Points link

This helps you determine which rate/point combination yields the lower long-term cost of your loan.

Home Affordability link

You can obtain a basic idea of the home sales price and the loan amount that you can afford.

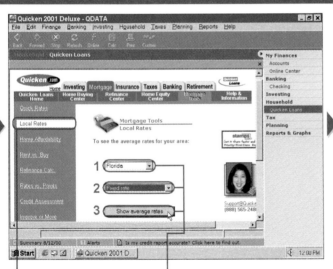

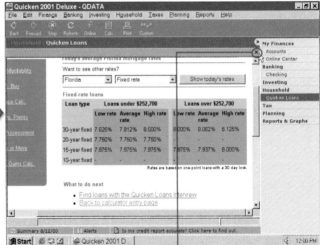

4 Click the **Local Rates** link on the left side of the page.

■ Quicken displays the Mortgage Tools Local Rates page.

5 Click ▾ and select your state from the menu.

6 Click ▾ and select a mortgage type.

7 Click **Show average rates**.

■ Quicken displays the rates for your area.

■ You can close the Mortgage tab and disconnect from the Internet by clicking ✕.

FIND AN AFFORDABLE HOUSE

Quicken can help you determine if you can afford the house of your dreams. Or, if you know you can afford a house, Quicken can help you decide how much you can afford to spend.

FIND AN AFFORDABLE HOUSE

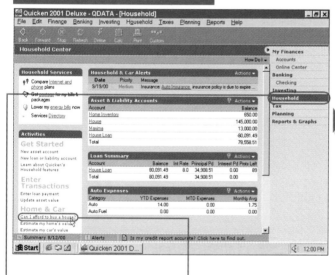

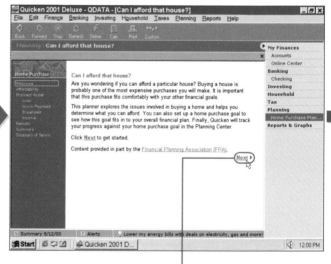

1 Click the **Household** QuickTab.

2 Click **Can I afford to buy a house?**

■ Quicken starts the Home Purchase Planner with a window that explains the process.

3 Click **Next**.

What amounts should I include when I list monthly loan and debt payments?

Include loan amounts such as car loans and college loans. Include minimum monthly credit card payments. Do not include living expenses or rent. Include mortgage payments for your current home only if you do not intend to sell it.

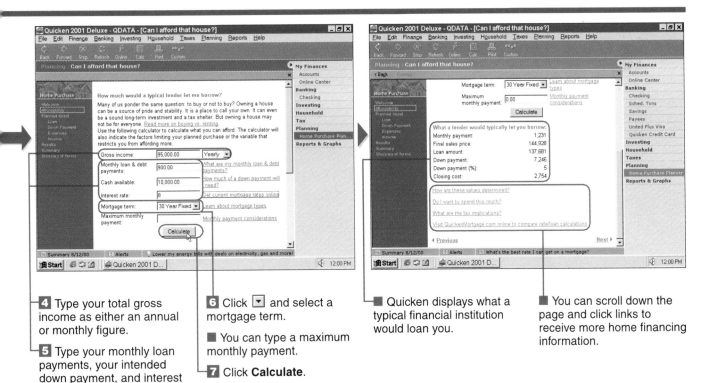

4 Type your total gross income as either an annual or monthly figure.

5 Type your monthly loan payments, your intended down payment, and interest rate.

6 Click ▾ and select a mortgage term.

■ You can type a maximum monthly payment.

7 Click **Calculate**.

■ Quicken displays what a typical financial institution would loan you.

■ You can scroll down the page and click links to receive more home financing information.

SET UP HOUSE ACCOUNTS

With Quicken, you can calculate the *equity* in your house. The difference between your home's value — an asset — and the remaining balance on your mortgage — a liability — represents your home's equity. For an accurate financial picture, you must include your home's value and its associated mortgage in Quicken.

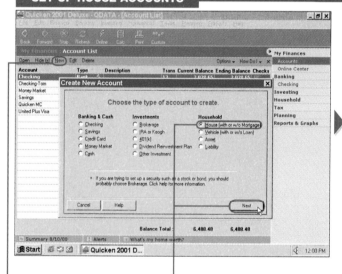

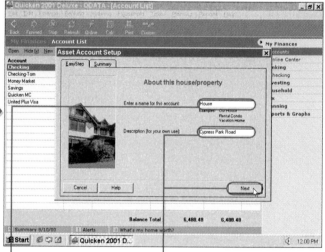

1 Press **Ctrl+A** to display the Account List.

2 Click **New**.

■ Quicken starts the Create New Account wizard.

3 Click **House (with or w/o Mortgage)** (O changes to ◉).

4 Click **Next**.

5 Type a name for the account.

■ You can type a description of the account.

6 Click **Next**.

What do I enter if I do not know my purchase price and current property value?

Take guesses. You will be able to change these amounts later, and Quicken includes some tools to help you estimate the current value of the property.

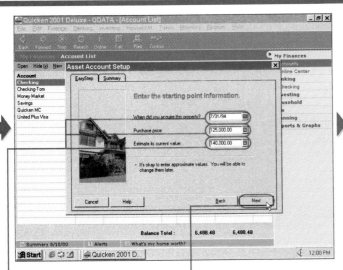

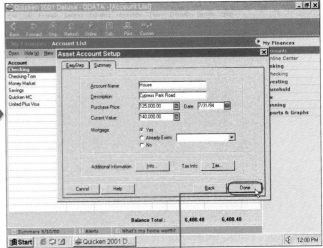

- 7 Type the date you bought the property.

- 8 Type the purchase price of your house.

- 9 Type the estimated current property value.

- 10 Click **Next**.

■ Quicken asks if you need to set up a mortgage.

- 11 Click **Yes, create a liability account**.

- 12 Click **Next**.

■ Quicken displays a summary of your entries.

- 13 Click **Done**.

CONTINUED

SET UP HOUSE ACCOUNTS

To complete the setup of the house account, you can set up the mortgage loan associated with the house.

SET UP HOUSE ACCOUNTS (CONTINUED)

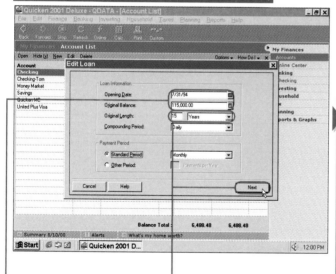

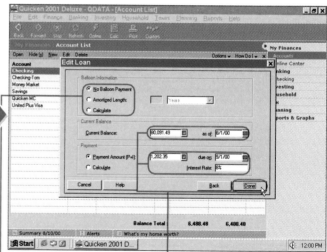

■ The Edit Loan dialog box appears.

14 Type the starting date of the loan and the original loan balance.

15 Type the original loan term.

■ If necessary, you can change the payment period (○ changes to ◉).

16 Click **Next**.

17 Select a Balloon Information option (○ changes to ◉).

Note: Balloon notes typically require one large payment at the end of the note.

18 Type the outstanding balance and date on your mortgage.

19 Type the payment amount, next date due, and the loan interest rate.

20 Click **Done**.

What do I do if I already set up an account for my mortgage?

To attach your house asset to an existing Quicken account:

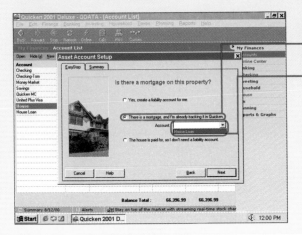

1 Follow Steps 1 through 10 in this section.

2 Click **There is a mortgage and I'm already tracking it in Quicken** (○ changes to ⊙).

3 Click ▾ and select your mortgage account from the list Quicken provides.

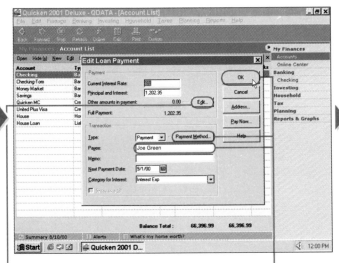

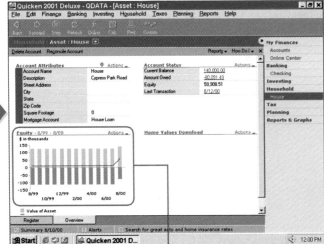

■ In the Edit Loan Payment box, you can click **Edit** to add homeowners insurance, escrow amounts for property taxes, and so on.

Note: By default, Quicken sets up the payment as a memorized transaction.

■ You can click **Payment Method** to set up the payment as a scheduled transaction.

21 Type the name of the mortgage company.

22 Click **OK**.

■ Quicken offers to download recent home sales in your area to estimate the value of your home.

23 Click **Cancel**.

■ Quicken redisplays the account list with both your house accounts in it.

■ You can view your home's equity on the Overview tab of your House asset account.

ESTIMATE THE VALUE OF A HOUSE

Thinking of selling your house? Wonder how much it is worth? You can estimate the value of your home at any time.

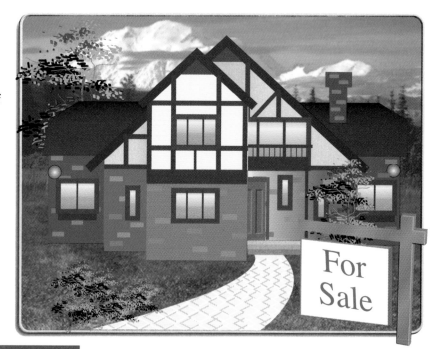

ESTIMATE THE VALUE OF A HOUSE

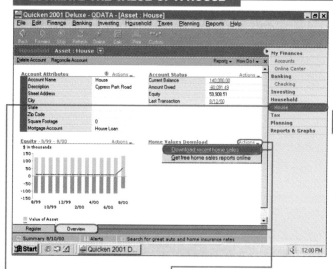

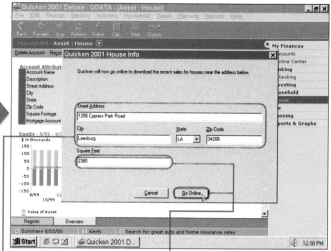

1 Click the **House** asset account QuickTab.

*Note: If you do not see the account, press **Ctrl+A** to open the Account List, and double-click the account.*

2 Click the **Overview** tab of the house asset account.

3 Click **Actions**.

4 Select **Download recent home sales** from the drop-down menu.

■ Quicken displays the House Info window.

5 Type your address, city, state, and zip code in the appropriate boxes.

6 Type the square footage of your home.

7 Click **Go Online**.

**I am considering buying a new
house. Can Quicken tell me the
value of homes in a new
neighborhood?**

Yes. When you estimate the value
of "your" home, type an address
in the neighborhood you are
considering.

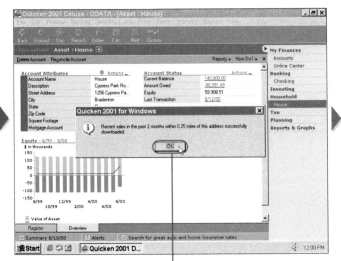

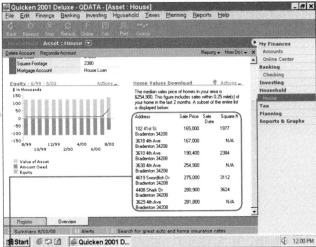

■ Quicken connects to the
Internet and displays a
message saying that the
requested information has
downloaded.

■8 Click **OK**.

■ Quicken redisplays the
Overview tab, updated with
home values in your
neighborhood.

ESTIMATE THE VALUE OF A CAR

You can estimate the
value of your car by
setting up an asset
account in Quicken.

ESTIMATE THE VALUE OF A CAR

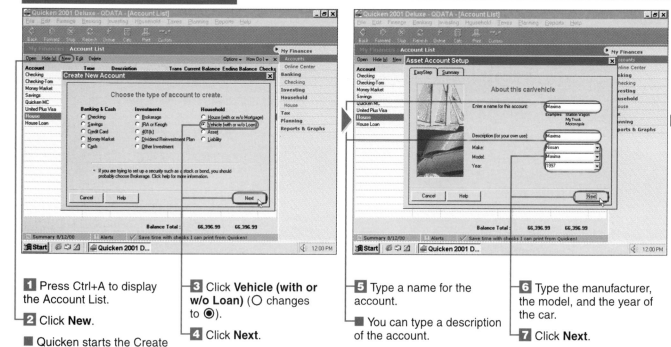

1 Press Ctrl+A to display
the Account List.

2 Click **New**.

■ Quicken starts the Create
New Account wizard.

3 Click **Vehicle (with or
w/o Loan)** (○ changes
to ◉).

4 Click **Next**.

5 Type a name for the
account.

■ You can type a description
of the account.

6 Type the manufacturer,
the model, and the year of
the car.

7 Click **Next**.

I am considering buying a new car. Can I receive an estimate of the price of the new car?

Yes. After connecting to www.edmunds.com, use the steps described in this task, but supply the manufacturer, model, and year of the car you want to buy.

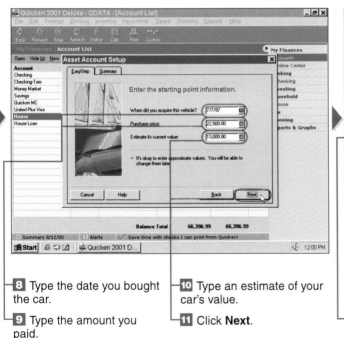

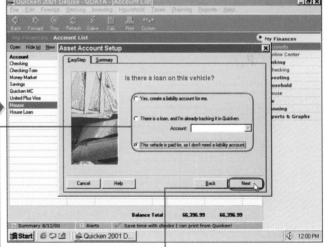

■8■ Type the date you bought the car.

■9■ Type the amount you paid.

■10■ Type an estimate of your car's value.

■11■ Click **Next**.

■ Quicken asks for loan information.

■12■ Click a loan option (○ changes to ●) to create a car loan account, indicate that you have a car loan account, or indicate that you own the car.

■ This example assumes that the car is paid in full.

Note: See the Section "Set Up House Accounts" to set up assets you do not own.

■13■ Click **Next**.

CONTINUED

ESTIMATE THE VALUE OF A CAR

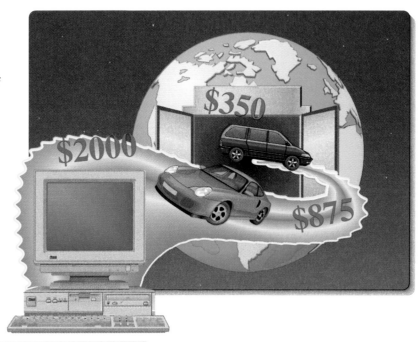

You can connect to the
Internet and download
estimates of the value of
your car.

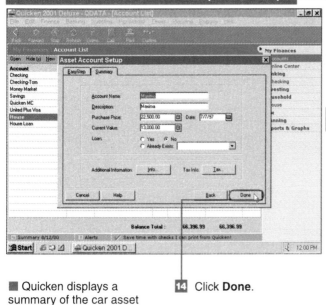

■ Quicken displays a
summary of the car asset
account.

14 Click **Done**.

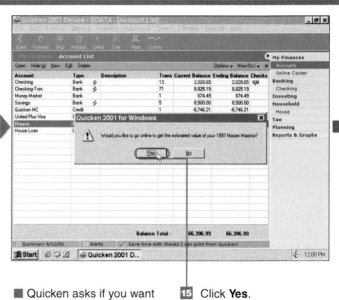

■ Quicken asks if you want
to go online to receive an
estimated value for your car.

15 Click **Yes**.

Who is Edmunds?

Edmunds is a privately held
California company that has
specialized, since 1966, in
providing pricing information and
reviews for new and used
vehicles — both cars and trucks.

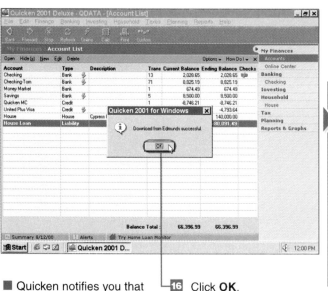

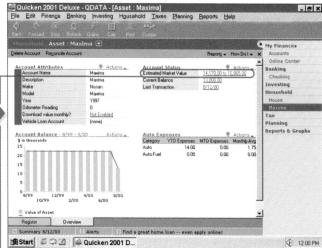

■ Quicken notifies you that
the download is complete.

16 Click **OK**.

■ Quicken displays the
estimated market value of
your car.

UPDATE THE ESTIMATED VALUE OF A CAR

You can update the
estimated value of your
car. You can even can
tell Quicken to update
the estimate once a
month.

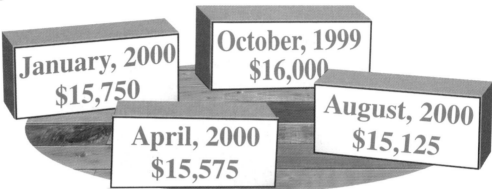

UPDATE THE ESTIMATED VALUE OF A CAR

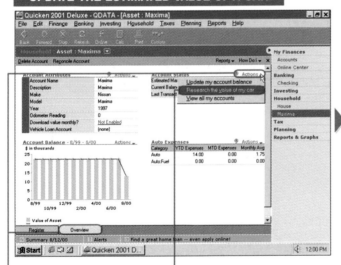

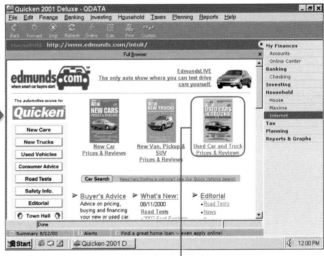

1 Click the **Overview** tab of
the car asset account.

*Note: If you do not see the
account, press **Ctrl+A** to open the
Account List and double-click the
account.*

2 Click **Actions**.

3 Select **Research the
value of my car** from the
drop-down menu.

4 When Quicken prompts
you to connect to the
Internet, click **OK**.

■ Quicken connects to
edmunds.com.

5 Click **Used Car and
Truck Prices and Reviews**.

What kind of reviews can I expect from edmunds.com?

Edmunds.com provides a wide variety of reviews that include short term and long term road tests, comparisons between popular models, and a list of the "most wanted" vehicles for a particular year. You also can attend "EdmundsLIVE" auto shows, held on a variety of dates in several cities, and road test vehicles without dealers present. All this information is available at edmunds.com.

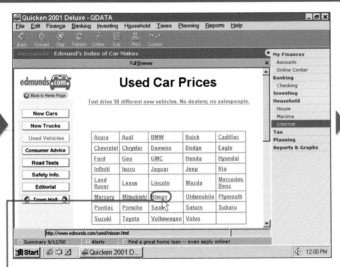

■ edmunds.com displays the Used Car Prices Web page.

6 Click your vehicle manufacturer.

■ Edmunds.com displays a Web page of years for your car manufacturer.

7 Click the year of your car.

■ edmunds.com displays a Web page of models for the year you selected.

8 Click the model of your car.

CONTINUED

UPDATE THE ESTIMATED VALUE OF A CAR

You can receive an estimate of the value of your car if you provide information at edmunds.com.

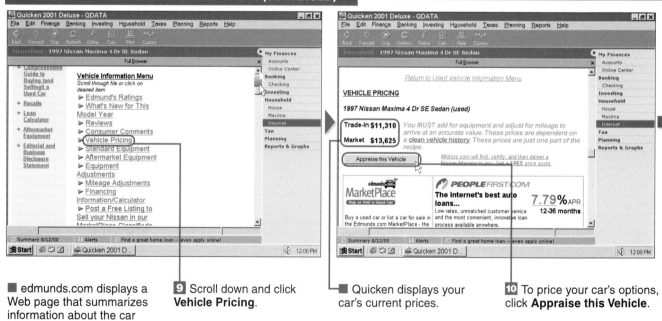

■ edmunds.com displays a Web page that summarizes information about the car make, model, and year you chose.

9 Scroll down and click **Vehicle Pricing**.

■ Quicken displays your car's current prices.

10 To price your car's options, click **Appraise this Vehicle**.

How can I find out more information about the auto shows sponsored by edmunds.com?

Complete Steps 1 through 4 of this section. Click the link to EdmundsLIVE at the top of the page.

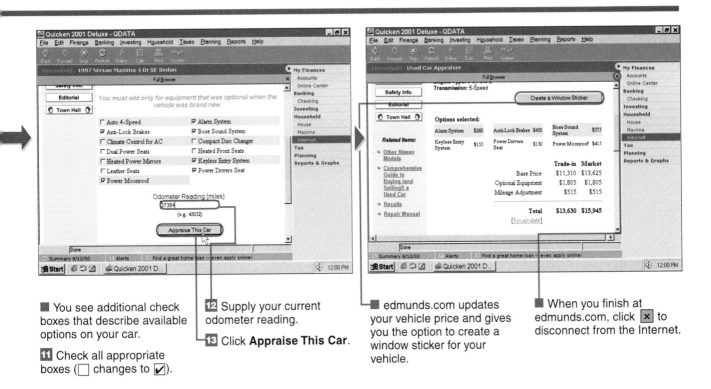

■ You see additional check boxes that describe available options on your car.

11 Check all appropriate boxes (☐ changes to ☑).

12 Supply your current odometer reading.

13 Click **Appraise This Car**.

■ edmunds.com updates your vehicle price and gives you the option to create a window sticker for your vehicle.

■ When you finish at edmunds.com, click ☒ to disconnect from the Internet.

FIND INSURANCE QUOTES

Need insurance? Let Quicken help you find the best rates for any type of insurance: home, car, life, and medical.

FIND INSURANCE QUOTES

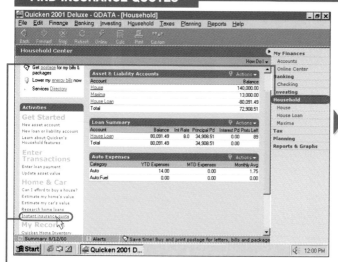

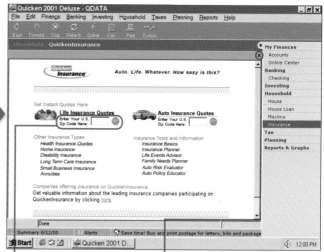

1 Click the **Household** QuickTab.

2 Click **Instant insurance quote**.

■ Quicken connects to the Internet.

3 Next to the appropriate kind of insurance, type your zip code and then click **Go**.

■ You can click the links under "Other Insurance Types" for medical insurance.

■ You can click the links under "Insurance Tools and Information" for planners and auto insurance.

4 When you finish, click ☒ to disconnect from the Internet.

UPDATE THE VALUE OF AN ASSET OR LIABILITY

You can update the value of assets and liabilities to reflect fluxuations in their value. To maintain an accurate picture of your financial situation, consider updating the value of the asset or liability periodically.

UPDATE THE VALUE OF AN ASSET OR LIABILITY

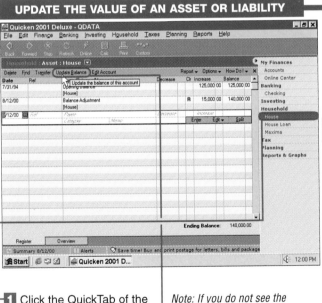

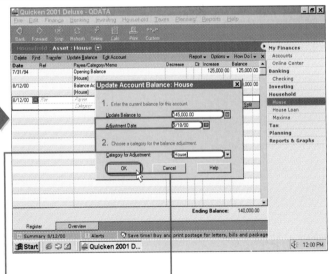

1 Click the QuickTab of the asset or liability and display the register.

Note: If you do not see the account's QuickTab, press Ctrl+A to display the Account List. Then, double-click the account.

2 Click **Update Balance**.

3 Type the new balance for the account.

4 Type a date for the adjustment.

5 Type a category for the adjustment.

Note: You can assign the adjustment to the House account.

6 Click **OK**.

■ Quicken updates the balance of the account.

TRACK HOME INVENTORY

You can use Quicken's Home Inventory to help create an accurate assessment of the value of the possessions in your home. You can use this value in the event of an insurance claim, to help determine your net worth, or to simply map the location of possessions in your home.

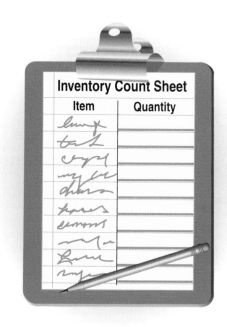

TRACK HOME INVENTORY

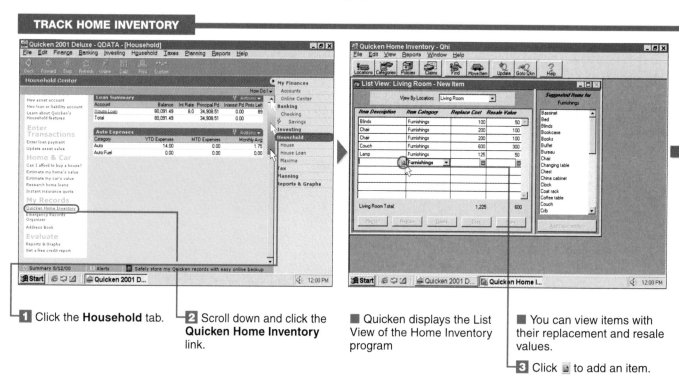

1 Click the **Household** tab.

2 Scroll down and click the **Quicken Home Inventory** link.

■ Quicken displays the List View of the Home Inventory program

■ You can view items with their replacement and resale values.

3 Click ▣ to add an item.

Can I view my inventory by room in my house?

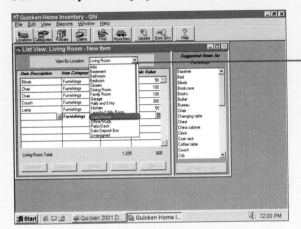

1 Follow Steps 1 through 2 in this section.

■ The List View dialog box appears.

2 Click ▼ and select a room from the View By Location list box.

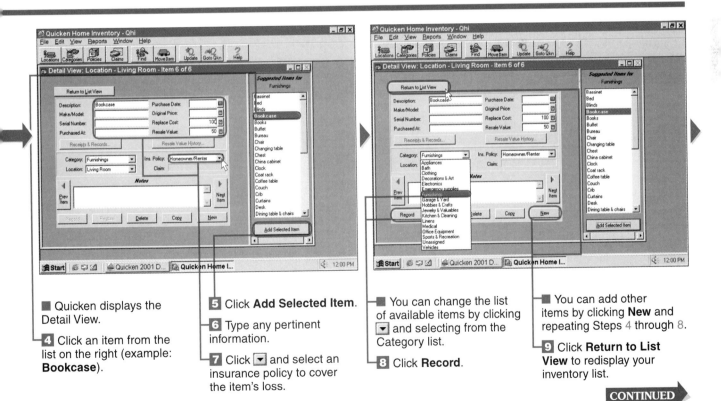

■ Quicken displays the Detail View.

4 Click an item from the list on the right (example: **Bookcase**).

5 Click **Add Selected Item**.

6 Type any pertinent information.

7 Click ▼ and select an insurance policy to cover the item's loss.

■ You can change the list of available items by clicking ▼ and selecting from the Category list.

8 Click **Record**.

■ You can add other items by clicking **New** and repeating Steps 4 through 8.

9 Click **Return to List View** to redisplay your inventory list.

CONTINUED ▶

TRACK HOME INVENTORY

You can report on your inventory from within Quicken Home Inventory. And, when you exit from Quicken Home Inventory, you can update the value of inventory that you see in Quicken on the Household page.

TRACK HOME INVENTORY (CONTINUED)

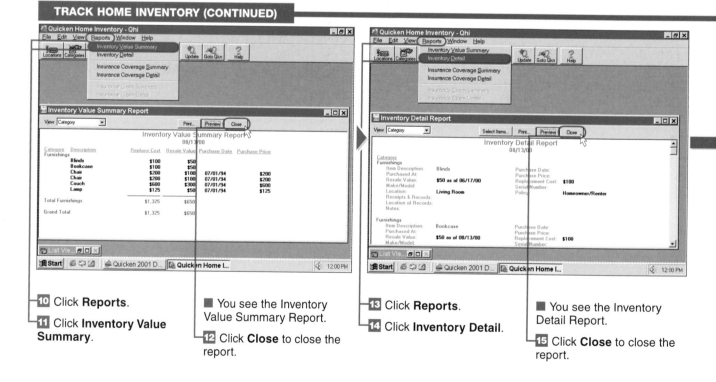

10 Click **Reports**.

11 Click **Inventory Value Summary**.

■ You see the Inventory Value Summary Report.

12 Click **Close** to close the report.

13 Click **Reports**.

14 Click **Inventory Detail**.

■ You see the Inventory Detail Report.

15 Click **Close** to close the report.

Is there some way to describe where I keep records about an inventoried item?

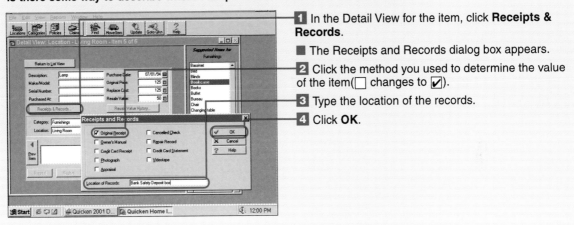

1 In the Detail View for the item, click **Receipts & Records**.

■ The Receipts and Records dialog box appears.

2 Click the method you used to determine the value of the item(☐ changes to ☑).

3 Type the location of the records.

4 Click **OK**.

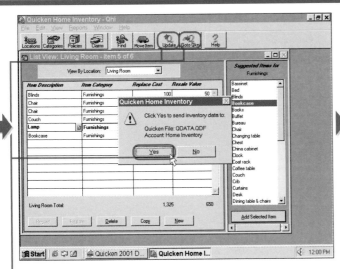

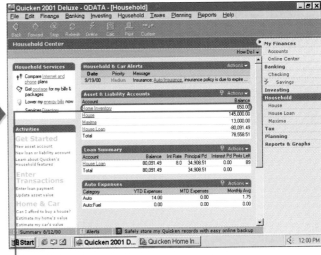

16 Click **Update**.

■ You see a box asking if you want to send data to Quicken.

17 Click **Yes**.

18 Click **Goto Qkn**.

■ Quicken Home Inventory automatically saves your entries.

■ You can close Quicken Home Inventory by clicking its icon in the Task Bar and then clicking ☒.

■ When you view the Household Center in Quicken, you see a Home Inventory.

Note: Clicking the account reopens the Quicken Home Inventory.

SET UP EMERGENCY RECORDS

You can use the
Emergency Records
Organizer to provide
important information
when you are away or in
the event of an
emergency.

You can supply as much or
as little information as you
want. Based on your needs,
you can print reports
appropriate for various

SET UP EMERGENCY RECORDS

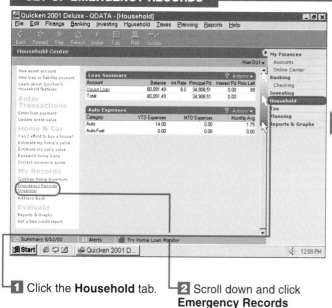

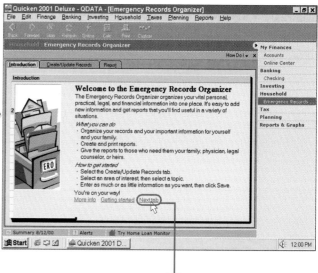

■1 Click the **Household** tab.

■2 Scroll down and click
**Emergency Records
Organizer**.

■ Quicken displays an
information screen.

■3 Click the **Next Tab** link.

What kinds of emergency information can I record?

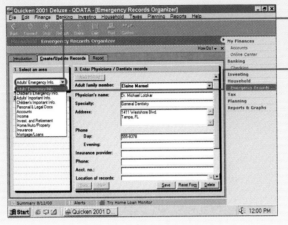

1 Click ▼ in **Select an Area**.

■ Quicken displays a list of all the types of emergency information you can record.

2 Select the emergency information type that you want.

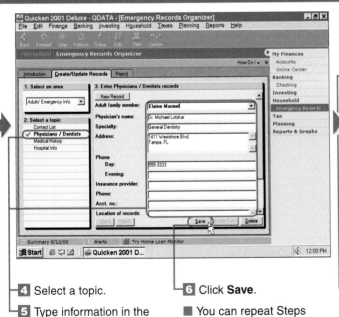

4 Select a topic.

5 Type information in the fields.

6 Click **Save**.

■ You can repeat Steps 4 through 6 to add more emergency information.

7 Click the **Report** tab.

■ Quicken automatically displays the Emergency Report.

■ You can view other reports by clicking ▼ and selecting them from the Report Type list.

■ To print a report, you can click **File** and then click **Print**.

SET UP ADDRESSES

You can use Quicken's address book to store and organize contact information (particularly useful when you are paying bills). Any payee for whom you have set up an address in the Memorized Transaction List, the Scheduled Transaction List, or the Write Checks window will appear in the Address Book window.

SET UP ADDRESSES

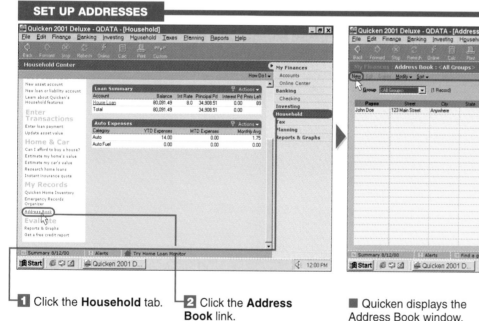

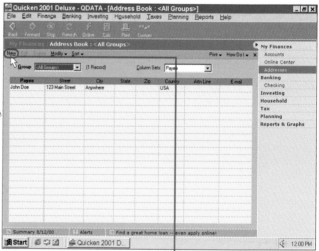

1 Click the **Household** tab.

2 Click the **Address Book** link.

■ Quicken displays the Address Book window.

3 Click **New** to display the Edit Address Book Record dialog box.

Is it possible to print labels for my Christmas card list — and include my brother on my Family list?

Yes, you can print labels from Address Book entries and you can limit the list to a particular group, such as the Christmas Card group. You can print a separate label for your brother, but it would be more efficient to simply include him in both groups.

To print labels, follow these steps:

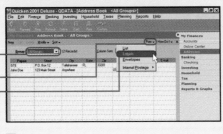

1 Click the group in the Address Book window.

2 Click **Print**.

3 Select **Labels** from the drop-down menu.

To include an addressee in more than one group, follow these steps:

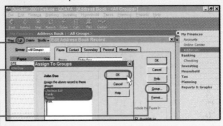

1 Click on the person you want to include in both groups.

2 Click **Edit** to open the record.

3 Click **Group** to open the Assign to Groups dialog box.

4 Click each group to which you want to assign your person.

5 Click **OK**.

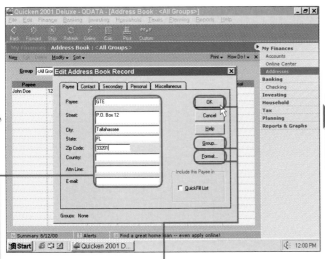

4 Type the contact information.

■ You can type detailed information in each tab in the dialog box.

■ You can click **Group** to assign addresses to groups (Work, Family, and so on).

■ To format the address for printing, you can click **Format**.

5 To save the address, click **OK**.

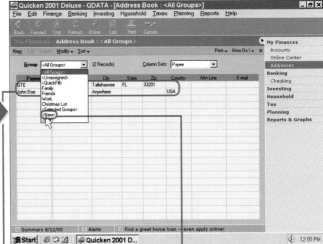

■ Quicken redisplays the address list with the new contact showing.

■ You can create a new group by clicking ▾ next to the Group box and then clicking **<New>**.

CREATE NET WORTH REPORTS

You can create a variety of reports and graphs to determine your net worth. The steps to create each report are the same; final information depends on which report you select.

You must record all your assets and liabilities in Quicken to obtain accurate reports. To determine what to record and which Net Worth Report best fits your needs, see the Section "View Net Worth Reports."

CREATE NET WORTH REPORTS

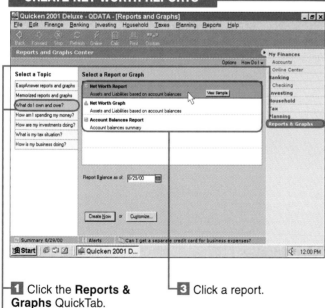

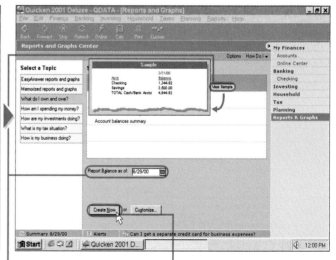

1 Click the **Reports & Graphs** QuickTab.

2 Click **What do I own and owe?**

3 Click a report.

■ You can click **View Sample** to view a thumbnail layout of any report.

■ You can change the dates or click **Customize** to exclude accounts or categories.

4 Click **Create Now.**

■ Quicken displays the report or graph you selected.

Quicken allows you to view your net worth. Net Worth equals assets minus liabilities; if you sold all your assets and paid off all your liabilities, you would be left with your net worth.

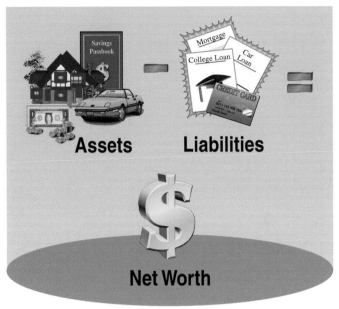

Assets **Liabilities**

Net Worth

You must record all your assets and liabilities in Quicken to obtain accurate reports. Assets include your bank accounts (Chapters 1 and 2), the value of your car, your home and its contents (Chapter 6), and your investments (Chapter 7). Liabilities include your credit card debts and loans (Chapter 5).

NET WORTH REPORT

Net Worth Report
As of 8/13/00

Account	8/13/00 Balance
TOTAL Other Assets	153,650.00
TOTAL ASSETS	**173,760.86**
LIABILITIES	
Checks Payable	82.53
Credit Cards	
Quicken MC	8,746.21
United Plus Visa	4,793.64
TOTAL Credit Cards	13,539.85
Other Liabilities	
House Loan	80,091.49
TOTAL Other Liabilities	80,091.49
TOTAL LIABILITIES	**93,713.87**
OVERALL TOTAL	**80,046.99**

In a Net Worth Report, you see the breakdown of liabilities, the total of assets and liabilities, and the net worth (Overall Total on the report).

NET WORTH GRAPH

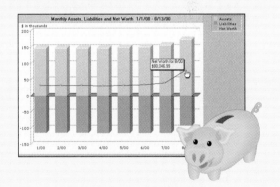

A net worth graph shows you the breakdown of your assets, liabilities, and net worth. When you point your mouse at any aspect of the graph, the pointer changes shape and reveals additional information. When you point at an orange square, you see the net worth for that period. Placing your pointer on any bar, reveals the dollar amount associated with the bar. You can double-click a bar, after the pointer changes, to see a pie chart breakdown of the bar.

CHAPTER 7

Track Investments

Do you want to use Quicken to research and track investments into financial instruments like stocks and bonds? Read this chapter.

ts

VIEW THE INVESTING CENTER

The Investing QuickTab provides an overview of the securities that you own.

Investing Services

Click any of these links to perform common functions related to investing.

Activities

Click any of these links to learn about Quicken and investing or to perform actions that update information about securities.

Personal Folders

This section displays alerts that you have set about investments. For example, you can set alerts to remind you to download quotes.

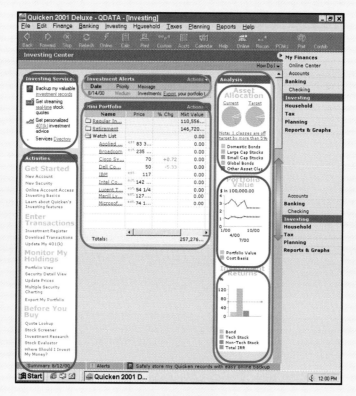

Mini Portfolio

Review the balances in your investment accounts, or click a link to open a register, create a new account or a new investment, download quotes for your securities, or view your entire portfolio. You can also set up and monitor prices and price changes for securities, even if you do not own them.

Analysis

In this section you see the Asset Allocation, Portfolio Value, and Investment Returns graphs:

Asset Allocation Graph

If you choose to classify your assets (that is, "Domestic Bonds," "Global Bonds," or "Large Cap Stocks"), you can view the allocation of your securities and compare it to a target allocation.

Portfolio Value Graph

This graph compares portfolio value to cost.

Investment Returns Graph

If you scroll down the page, you can view returns based on security type, such as Bond, Stock, and CD. (You also can establish your own security types in Quicken).

QUICKEN AND INVESTING

**You can use Quicken
to help you with your
investing activities.**

TRACK INVESTMENT ACTIVITY

In Quicken, you set up investment accounts and
record "buys" and "sells" in them. You also enter other
investment transactions, such as dividends and splits,
to keep the account values up-to-date. You can track
stocks, bonds, mutual funds, commodities,
Krugerrands — whatever you want.

DOWNLOAD STOCK PRICES

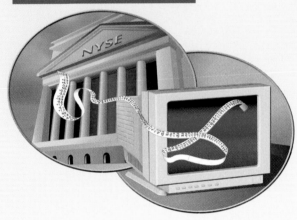

Use the Internet to download the latest prices of
securities. You can download prices of securities that
you own, or you download the prices of stocks that you
might consider buying so that you can watch their
performance before you decide.

RESEARCH

Considering the purchase of a stock or mutual fund?
Let Quicken retrieve the stock's P/E (Price/Earnings)
ratio, the annual dividend, and last year's highs and
lows. Through Quicken, you can obtain information
about mutual funds and profiles by Morningstar, one of
the leading mutual fund rating services.

MONITOR PERFORMANCE AND TAX IMPLICATIONS

Compare the performance of various securities and
asset classes. Set an asset allocation target and let
Quicken help you rebalance your portfolio. And,
estimate capital gains that you will need to report on
your tax return.

RESEARCH A STOCK OR MUTUAL FUND

Let Quicken help you find information about stocks, bonds, and mutual funds. The Investment Research window enables you to connect to Quicken.com and get all kinds of information.

RESEARCH A STOCK OR MUTUAL FUND

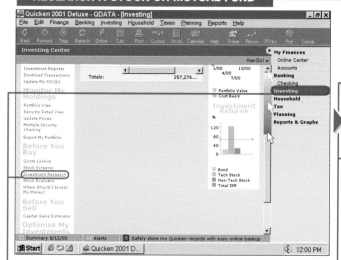

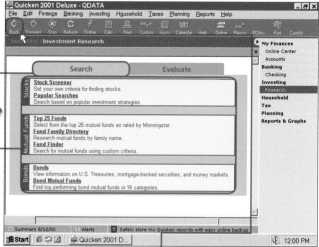

1 Click the **Investing** QuickTab.

2 Scroll down to click the **Investment Research** link.

■ Quicken connects to the Internet and displays the Investment Research window.

3 Click the **Search** tab.

4 Click a link to research stocks, mutual funds, or bonds.

■ Quicken displays Web pages that you can use to find investments.

5 Click ◀ to return to the Investment Research window.

How do I use the Investment Research window if I do not know the ticker symbol?

The Investment Research window contains a link that you can click to find a ticker symbol on the Internet. Click the link, supply the name of the company or mutual fund, and click **Search**; in response, you receive the symbol.

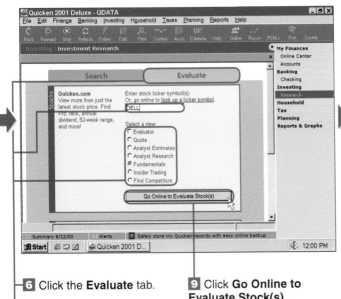

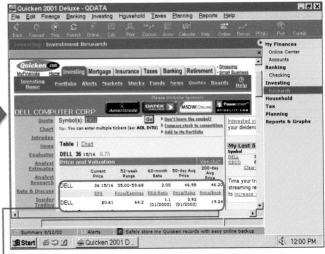

■ **6** Click the **Evaluate** tab.

■ **7** Type a stock symbol.

■ **8** Click an option to describe the information you want (○ becomes ◉).

■ **9** Click **Go Online to Evaluate Stock(s)**.

■ For mutual funds, scroll down, supply a mutual fund symbol, and click **Go Online to Evaluate Fund(s)**.

■ Quicken displays the information you requested.

QUICKEN AND INVESTMENT ACCOUNT TYPES

Quicken contains a variety of
different investment account
types to help you manage a
variety of investments.

TAX-DEFERRED INVESTMENTS

Tax-deferred investments have no effect on your
personal income taxes until you liquidate them. You
record the information you need via checking account
transactions: You write checks to make contributions
and you make deposits that represent withdrawals. Set
up accounts for tax-deferred investments only under
two circumstances:

You want or need to track tax-deferred
income or capital gains or losses.

You want a complete picture
of your net worth.

BROKERAGE ACCOUNTS

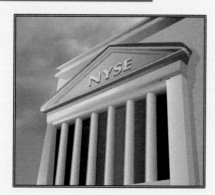

Quicken's brokerage account helps you monitor single or
multiple investments for which you want to calculate
performance. Use brokerage accounts for mutual funds,
stocks, bonds, CDs, treasury bills, collectibles, precious
metals, and fixed annuities.

401(K) AND 403B ACCOUNTS

401(k) accounts enable you to track employer retirement plans. If your plan statements include share amounts and purchase price details for every purchase, you might want to use a tax-deferred brokerage account to track performance.

IRAS

In these retirement savings accounts, earnings grow tax-deferred until withdrawal. Contributions may or may not be tax-deductible, depending on the type of plan. Quicken supports the traditional IRA, Roth IRA, Education IRA, Keogh Plan, and SEP-IRA.

DIVIDEND REINVESTMENT PLAN

You can use this account type when the dividends you receive automatically purchase additional shares of the security paying the dividend.

OTHER INVESTMENT

Use this account type for real estate investment partnerships or trusts, unit trusts, or variable annuities.

SET UP A BROKERAGE INVESTMENT ACCOUNT

You can easily set up a brokerage account to handle multiple securities.

SET UP A BROKERAGE INVESTMENT ACCOUNT

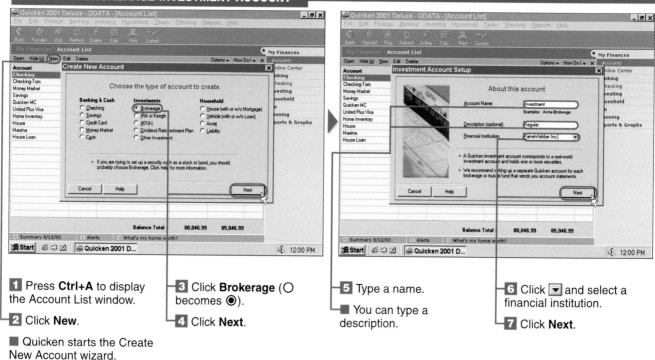

1 Press **Ctrl+A** to display the Account List window.

2 Click **New**.

■ Quicken starts the Create New Account wizard.

3 Click **Brokerage** (○ becomes ◉).

4 Click **Next**.

5 Type a name.

■ You can type a description.

6 Click ▼ and select a financial institution.

7 Click **Next**.

Should I still choose Brokerage as the account type if I track stocks, bonds, and mutual funds in the same account?

Yes. If you want to track a single mutual fund (and no other investments), you can click the **One mutual fund** option when Quicken asks for the kind of securities the account will contain.

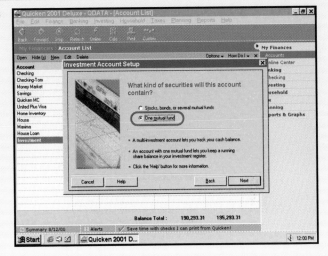

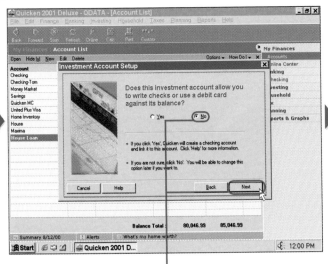

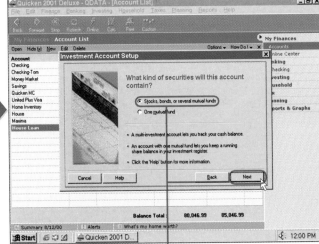

■ The wizard asks if you can write checks or use a debit card with the account.

8 Click **No** (you can change this setting later if you wish).

9 Click **Next**.

■ Quicken asks if you want to track a single security or multiple securities.

10 Click **Stocks, bonds, or several mutual funds** (○ changes to ◉).

11 Click **Next**.

CONTINUED

SET UP A BROKERAGE INVESTMENT ACCOUNT

Quicken allows you to select the tax status of your account and to use online services with the account.

SET UP A BROKERAGE INVESTMENT ACCOUNT (CONTINUED)

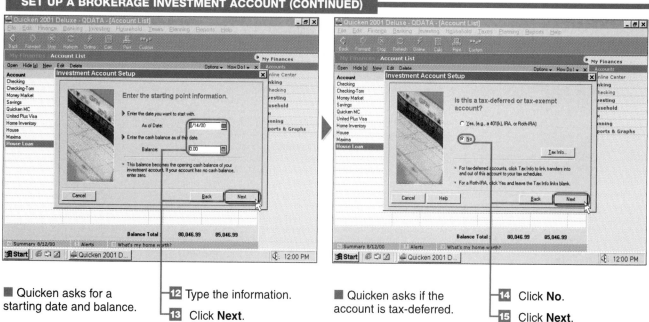

■ Quicken asks for a starting date and balance.

⏸12 Type the information.

⏸13 Click **Next**.

■ Quicken asks if the account is tax-deferred.

⏸14 Click **No**.

⏸15 Click **Next**.

What kind of online services can I use with an Investment account?

If your brokerage firm supports Quicken, you can download transactions from your brokerage firm directly into Quicken. That way, you do not need to type the transactions that occur.

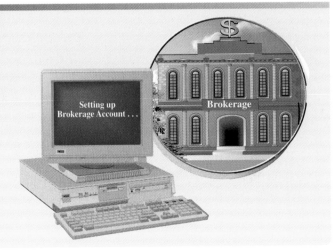

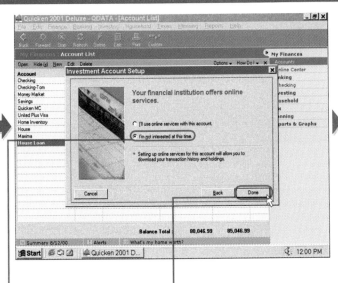

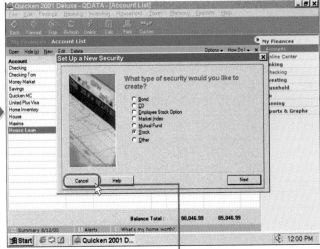

■ Quicken asks if you are interested in online services.

16 Click **I'm not interested at this time**.

Note: You must contact your brokerage firm to set up online services.

17 Click **Done**.

■ Quicken prompts you to create a security by starting the new security setup wizard.

18 Click **Cancel**.

■ To set up a new security, see the Section, "Set Up a Security."

SET UP A SECURITY

After you establish investment accounts (see the Section "Set up a Brokerage Investment Account"), you must enter the securities you already own into the accounts. Setting up a security you already own is a different process from recording a transaction to buy a new security (see the Section "Buy a Security"). In this example, you see how to set up a stock.

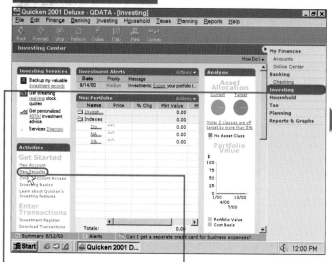

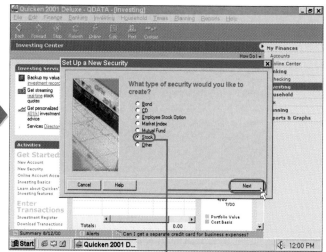

1 Click the **Investing** QuickTab.

2 Click the **New Security** link.

■ The Set Up a New Security wizard appears, asking you to choose a type of security.

3 Click **Stock** (O changes to ⦿).

4 Click **Next**.

What are investnment goals?

"Goals" is actually a misnomer. "Goals" provide a way to group securities for reporting purposes. For example, you can set up goals that correspond to industry groups so that you can view your securities by industy group. Or, you can set up goals that represent the people who recommend a particular stock. Then you can print reports by "advisor" to see who is giving you the "best advice."

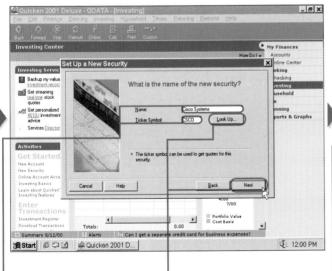

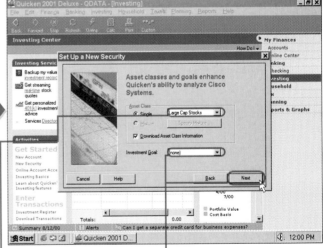

5 Type the security's name.

■ Optionally, type the security's symbol. If you do not know it, leave it blank.

■ You can click **Look Up** to use the Internet to find the symbol.

6 Click **Next**.

■ Quicken asks you to select an asset class and an investment goal.

7 Click ▾ and select an asset class.

Note: Asset classes help you categorize assets and balance your portfolio.

■ You can click ▾ and select an investment goal.

8 Click **Next**.

CONTINUED

You can create your own
investment goals; you are
not limited to using the
ones supplied by Quicken.

Investment Goals

1
2
3
4

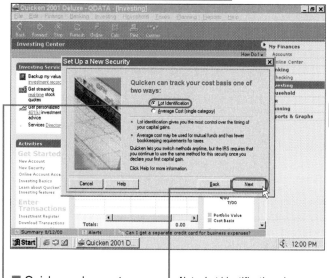

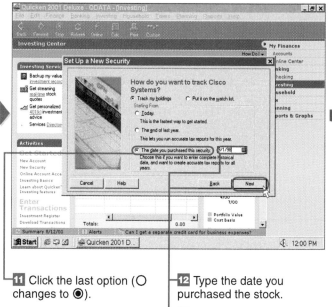

■ Quicken asks you to
select a method to track the
cost basis of the security.

9 Click **Lot Identification**.

*Note: Lot identification gives you
the most control over timing
capital gains, an important tax
consideration.*

10 Click **Next**.

11 Click the last option (O
changes to ●).

12 Type the date you
purchased the stock.

13 Click **Next**.

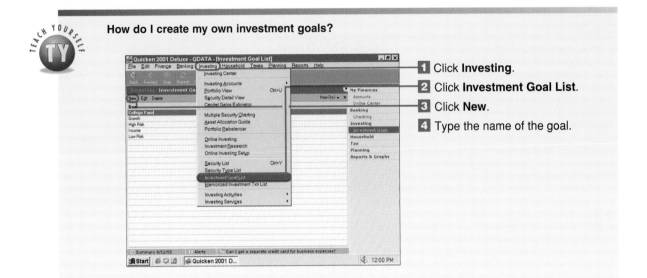

How do I create my own investment goals?

TEACH YOURSELF TY

1 Click **Investing**.

2 Click **Investment Goal List**.

3 Click **New**.

4 Type the name of the goal.

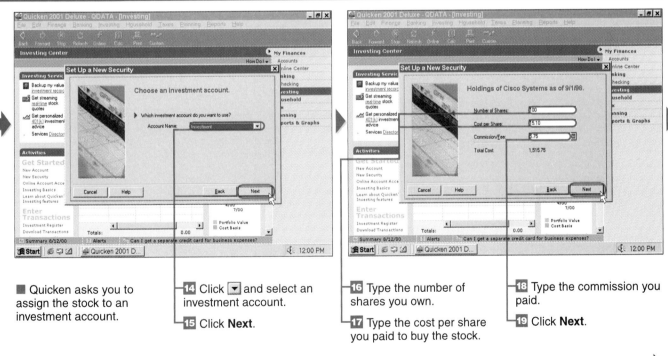

■ Quicken asks you to assign the stock to an investment account.

14 Click ▼ and select an investment account.

15 Click **Next**.

16 Type the number of shares you own.

17 Type the cost per share you paid to buy the stock.

18 Type the commission you paid.

19 Click **Next**.

CONTINUED

SET UP A SECURITY

As you complete setting up a security, the Set Up Security wizard displays a summary of the information you provided and offers you the opportunity to set up additional securities.

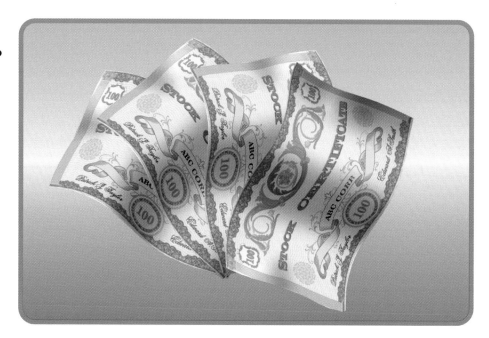

SET UP A SECURITY (CONTINUED)

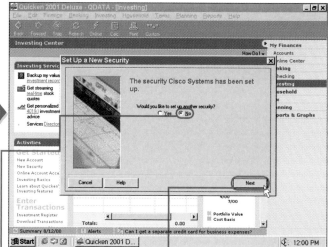

■ Quicken displays summary information for the security.

■ **20** Click **Next** if all the information is accurate.

■ The wizard asks if you want to set up additional securities.

■ **21** Click **Yes** or **No**.

■ You can click **Yes** and then **Next** to set up additional securities using the steps in this section.

■ You can click **No** if you do not want to set up another security.

■ **22** Click **Next**.

■ You can click **Yes** and then **Next** to continue to set up additional securities.

If I set up my own investment goals after I create the security, how do I assign the new goal to an existing security?

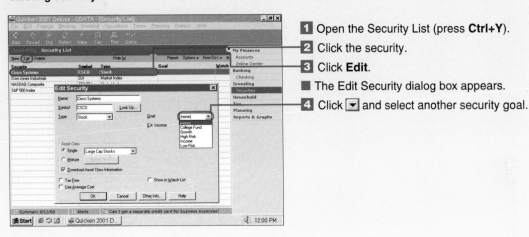

1 Open the Security List (press **Ctrl+Y**).

2 Click the security.

3 Click **Edit**.

■ The Edit Security dialog box appears.

4 Click ▼ and select another security goal.

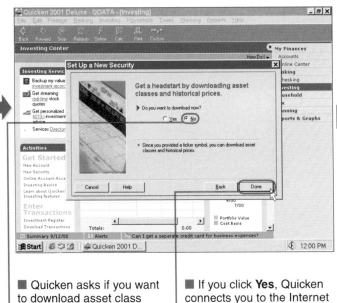

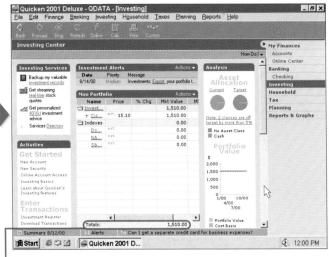

■ Quicken asks if you want to download asset class information for the security.

23 Click **Yes** or **No**.

■ If you click **No**, you avoid downloading asset classes.

■ If you click **Yes**, Quicken connects you to the Internet (see the Section "Assign Asset Classes").

24 Click **Done**.

■ Quicken redisplays the Investing Center QuickTab. The value of your investment account reflects the securities you added.

UNDERSTAND SECURITY TRANSACTIONS

You can choose from more than 30 types of transactions in the Actions menu of an investment register. Several transactions are offered in two versions; the version you select determines whether you transfer money from another Quicken account to cover any cash involved in the transaction. In addition, you can record corporate name changes, securities spin-offs, acquisitions, and reminder transactions.

Buy	Buy Security
BuyX	Buy & Transfer
CGLong	Long-term Cap Gain Dist
CGLongX	Long-term Cap Gain Dist & Transfer
CGMid	Mid-term Cap Gain Dist
CGMidX	Mid-term Cap Gain Dist & Transfer
CGShort	Short-term Cap Gain Dist
CGShortX	Short-term Cap Gain Dist & Trans...
Div	Dividend
DivX	Dividend & Transfer

Exercise	Exercise an Employee Stock Opt...
ExercisX	Exercise an Emp. Stock Opt. & Xfr
Expire	Expire an Employee Stock Option
Grant	Employee Stock Option Grant
IntInc	Interest Income
IntIncX	Interest Income & Transfer
MargInt	Margin Interest Expense
MargIntX	Margin Interest Expense & Transfer
MiscExp	Miscellaneous Expense
MiscExpX	Miscellaneous Expense & Transfer

Recording Income Events

To record income events for capital gains (long-term, mid-term, or short-term), dividends, interest, and miscellaneous income, choose CGLong, CGMid, CHShort, Div, IntInc, MiscInc or their "X" counterparts.

Buying and Selling

To purchase a new security or additional shares of an existing security using cash in the investment account, choose Buy.

To purchase a new security or additional shares of an existing security using cash in another Quicken account, choose BuyX.

To remove shares of a security from the account and store the cash in the investment account, choose Sell.

To remove shares of a security from the investment account and store the cash in a different Quicken account, choose SellX.

MiscInc	Miscellaneous Income
MiscIncX	Miscellaneous Income & Transfer
ReinvDiv	Reinvest Dividend
ReinvInt	Reinvest Interest
ReinvLg	Reinvest Long-term Cap Gain Dist
ReinvMd	Reinvest Mid-term Cap Gain Dist
ReinvSh	Reinvest Short-term Cap Gain Dist
Reminder	Reminder Transaction
RtrnCap	Return of Capital
RtrnCapX	Return of Capital & Transfer

RtrnCapX	Return of Capital & Transfer
Sell	Sell Security
SellX	Sell & Transfer
ShrsIn	Add Shares to Account
ShrsOut	Remove Shares from Account
StkSplit	Stock Split
XIn	Transfer Cash in
XOut	Transfer Cash out
Vest	Vest in an Employee Stock Option

Reinvesting

To record reinvestment transactions for capital gains, dividends, or interest, choose ReinvDiv, ReinvInt, ReinvLg, ReinvMd, ReinvSh.

Stock Splits and Return of Capital

To record a stock split, choose StkSplit.

To record any return of capital transactions, choose RtrnCap or RtrnCCapX.

Transfers Between Accounts

To add shares without affecting the cash balance of any Quicken account, choose the ShrsIn transaction. To remove shares without affecting the cash balance of any Quicken account, choose ShrsOut transaction. Use these transactions to transfer shares between investment accounts.

To transfer cash into an investment account, choose Xin.
To transfer cash out of an account, choose XOut.

Handling Employee Stock Options

To record employee stock option transactions, choose Exercise, ExercisX, Expire, Grant, and Vest.

Recording Miscellaneous Expenses

To record margin interest expenses, MargInt or MargIntX.
To record other miscellaneous expenses, choose MiscExp or MiscExpX.

BUY A SECURITY

You can record the trades you make on accounts you have set up (see the Section "Set Up a Brokerage Account"). You can also record transactions like dividends or stock splits.

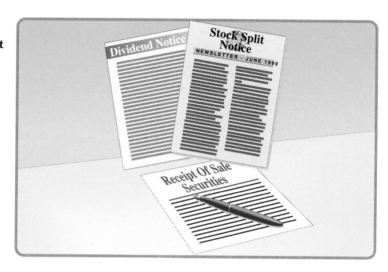

You enter various transactions in the account register in basically the same way. The type of transaction you choose may change the fields slightly. This section shows you how to buy a security. Also, buying a security is another way to set up a security.

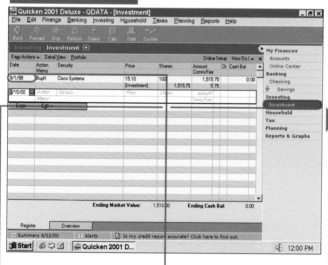

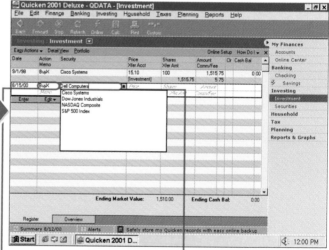

1 Click on your investment account to open it.

*Note: If you do not see the account under the Investing QuickTab, press **Ctrl+A** to open the Account List and double-click the account.*

■ Quicken displays the register.

■ You can change the date of the transaction by using the + or − keys to repeatedly increment or decrement by one day.

2 Press Tab.

3 Click **BuyX** from the list of transaction types.

4 Press Tab.

5 Type the security's name.

■ Quicken displays the last 2,000 securities; choose one, and Quicken fills in your last transaction for that security.

Can I use wizards to help me enter transactions?

Yes. You can click the **EasyActions** button in the investment account register to view its menu. You can click **Advanced** to view further options. You can select any option from either the EasyActions or the Advanced menus. Your selection starts a wizard or displays a dialog box that helps you enter the transaction.

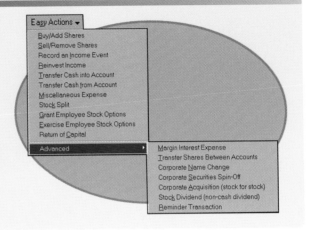

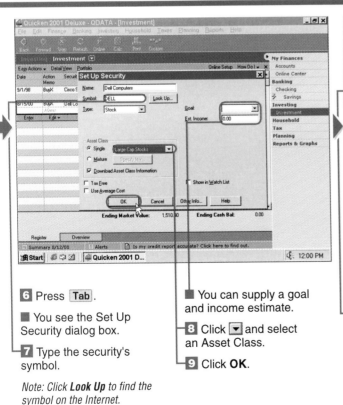

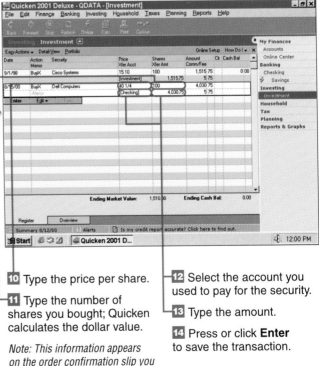

6 Press **Tab**.

■ You see the Set Up Security dialog box.

7 Type the security's symbol.

*Note: Click **Look Up** to find the symbol on the Internet.*

■ You can supply a goal and income estimate.

8 Click ▼ and select an Asset Class.

9 Click **OK**.

10 Type the price per share.

11 Type the number of shares you bought; Quicken calculates the dollar value.

Note: This information appears on the order confirmation slip you receive from your brokerage firm.

12 Select the account you used to pay for the security.

13 Type the amount.

14 Press or click **Enter** to save the transaction.

ASSIGN ASSET CLASSES

Quicken's asset classes match standards used in the industry. You can download asset class information for your securities and let Quicken assign asset classes for you. If you prefer, you can manually assign asset classes by opening the security list and editing the security.

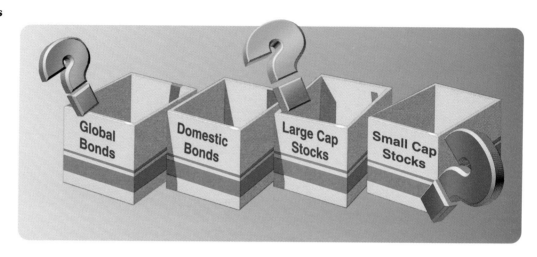

ASSIGN ASSET CLASSES

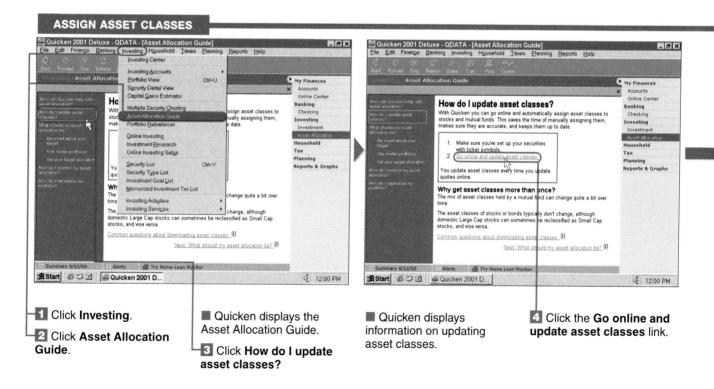

1 Click **Investing**.

2 Click **Asset Allocation Guide**.

■ Quicken displays the Asset Allocation Guide.

3 Click **How do I update asset classes?**

■ Quicken displays information on updating asset classes.

4 Click the **Go online and update asset classes** link.

How do I assign asset classes manually?

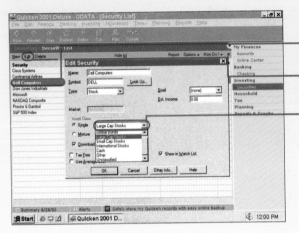

1 Press **Ctrl+Y** to open the Security List.

2 Click the security for which you want to set an asset class.

3 Click **Edit**.

■ Quicken displays the Edit Security dialog box.

4 Click ▼ and select an asset class.

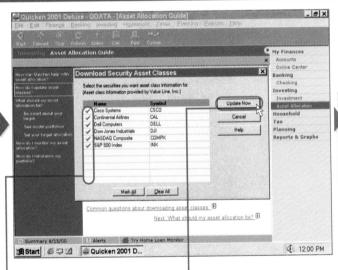

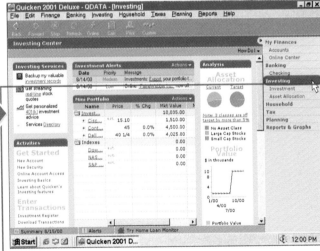

■ Quicken displays a list of securities for which you can download asset classes.

■ To avoid downloading asset classes, remove the checks in the left column.

5 Click **Update Now** to connect to the Internet to download.

6 Click **Done** when the download finishes.

7 Click the **Investing** QuickTab.

■ Quicken updates the Asset Allocation chart.

SET UP A "WATCH" LIST

Quicken enables you to track a stock that you do not own on a "watch" list. If you are considering buying shares of this stock, you can monitor its price before you decide to buy.

You can add the stock to your "watch" list in two different ways — the method you choose depends on whether you have already set up the security.

SET UP A "WATCH" LIST

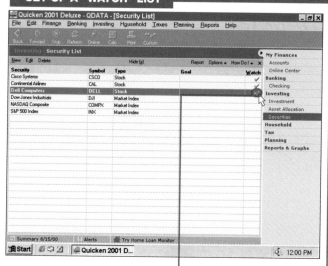

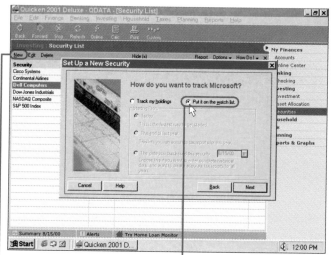

WATCH EXISTING SECURITIES

1 Press **Ctrl+Y** to display the Security List.

2 Click the Watch column for the stock you want to add to your list.

WATCH A NEW SECURITY

1 Press **Ctrl+Y** to display the Security List.

2 Click **New**.

3 Follow Steps 1 through 10 in the Section "Set Up a Security."

4 When prompted, click **Put it on the watch list**.

5 Follow Steps 13 through 19 in the Section "Set Up a Security."

You can view the "big picture" in portfolio view, which includes all investment accounts and securities. You can only view your portfolio after you have set up an investment account (or more than one investment account) and added your securities (see the Sections "Set Up a Brokerage Account" and "Set Up a Security").

VIEW YOUR PORTFOLIO

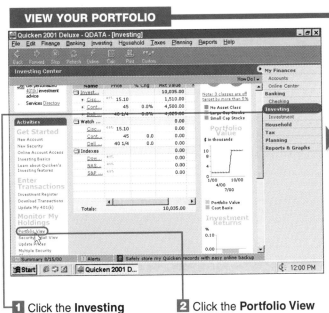

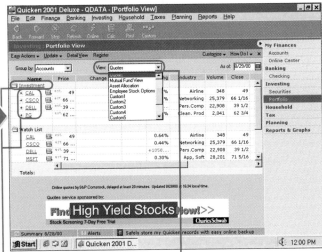

1 Click the **Investing** QuickTab.

2 Click the **Portfolio View** link.

■ Quicken displays the account as a folder.

■ Each security appears as a subfolder under the folder of the appropriate account.

■ In the Portfolio View, you can look at your investments in several ways. Use the **View** list to see views like the Quotes view, the Holdings view, and the Portfolio Performance View.

SELECT QUOTES TO DOWNLOAD

You can download quotes for any security that appears in the Security List (see the Section "Set Up A Security"). By default, Quicken assumes that you want to download quotes for all securities in the list, but you can be selective.

SELECT QUOTES TO DOWNLOAD

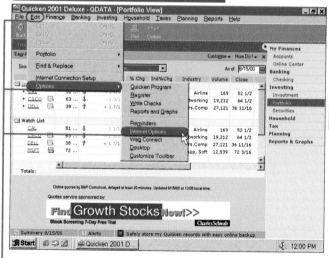

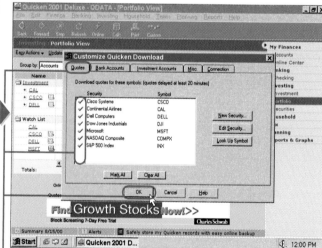

1 Click **Edit**.

2 Click **Options**.

3 Click **Internet Options**.

■ The Customize Quicken 2000 Download dialog box appears.

4 Click the **Quotes** tab.

5 Click any security to remove or add a check mark (☐ changes to ☑).

6 Click **OK** to close the dialog box.

■ When you download, Quicken downloads quotes for all securities you checked.

DOWNLOAD QUOTES

You can download
security quotes at any
time. Quicken updates
the value of your
portfolio based on the
quotes you download.

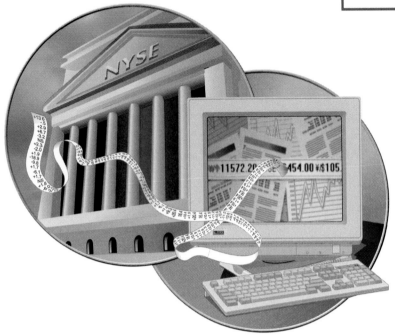

You connect to the
Internet to download
quotes.

DOWNLOAD QUOTES

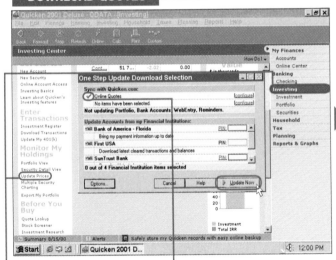

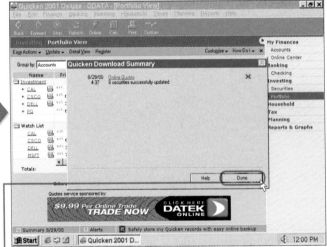

1 Click the **Investing**
QuickTab.

2 Scroll down and click
Update Prices.

■ The One Step Update
Download Selection dialog
box appears.

3 Place check marks
beside any items you
want to download. (☐
changes to ☑).

■ You can click any check
to remove it.

4 Click **Update Now**.

■ Quicken connects to the
Internet and displays the
Download Status window.
When the process finishes,
Quicken displays the
Download Summary dialog
box.

5 Click **Done**.

■ Quotes in both your Watch
List and your portfolio are
updated.

*Note: You also can click **Update** in
the Portfolio window to download
quotes.*

ESTIMATE CAPITAL GAINS

Let Quicken help you estimate your capital gains.

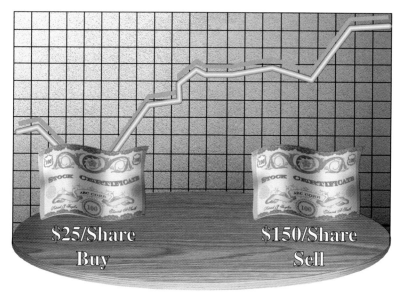

$25/Share
Buy

$150/Share
Sell

Using the Capital Gains Estimator, you create up to three scenarios where you identify sales you might make, and Quicken shows you the taxes you would pay and the net proceeds you would make from the sale.

ESTIMATE CAPITAL GAINS

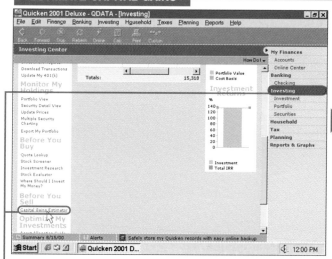

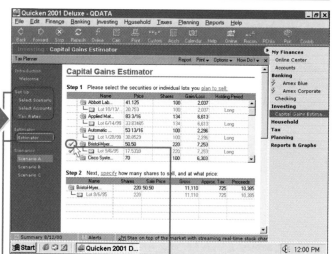

1 Click the **Investing** QuickTab.

2 Scroll down to click **Capital Gains Estimator**.

■ Quicken displays the first of several Capital Gains Estimator windows.

■ You can click links to select a scenario or investment account to estimate; or to use tax rates other than the standard rates for short and long term gains.

3 Click **Estimator**.

■ Quicken displays the Capital Gains Estimator

4 Click a security to sell (☐ changes to ☑).

■ Quicken displays the gross sale price, approximate taxes, and net proceeds of your proposed sale.

You can let Quicken calculate the adjustments you need to make to rebalance your portfolio so that it matches your target allocation (see the Section "Set Target Allocation").

Remember that adjustments (trades) can have tax implications. Revisit your allocations periodically to make sure you still want to achieve your target allocation.

REBALANCE YOUR PORTFOLIO

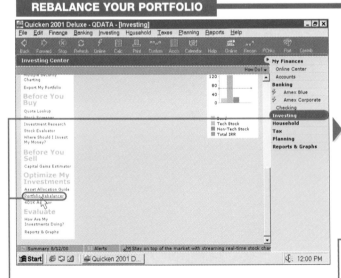

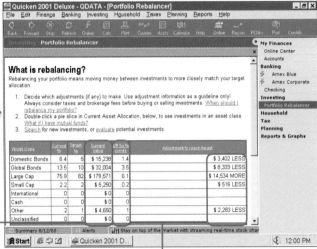

■1 Click the **Investing** QuickTab.

■2 Click the **Portfolio Rebalancer** link.

■ Quicken displays the Portfolio Rebalancer window; the pie charts for Current Asset Allocation and Target Asset Allocation appear at the bottom of the window.

■ You view your current holdings in dollars and percentages and your target holdings in percentages.

■ The Off by % Points column shows the percentage by which target holdings differ from actual holdings.

■ You view the dollar value of the adjustment you need to make.

SET ASSET ALLOCATION TARGET

You might have noticed the Target Asset Allocation graph next to the Current Asset Allocation graph. You can set a target allocation and then (in "Rebalance Your Porfolio" in this Chapter) let Quicken help you rebalance the porfolio to meet the target.

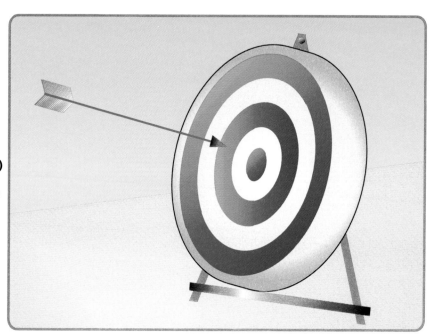

SET ASSET ALLOCATION TARGET

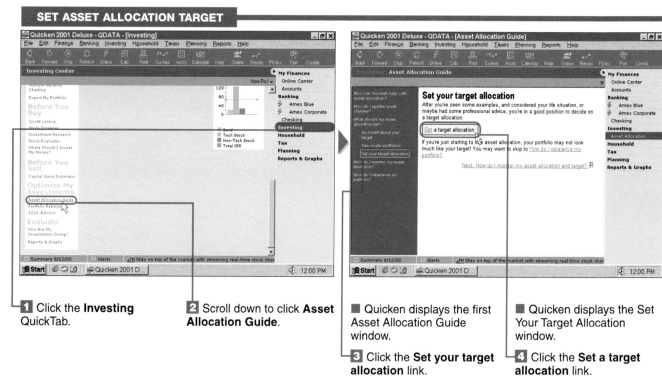

1 Click the **Investing** QuickTab.

2 Scroll down to click **Asset Allocation Guide**.

■ Quicken displays the first Asset Allocation Guide window.

3 Click the **Set your target allocation** link.

■ Quicken displays the Set Your Target Allocation window.

4 Click the **Set a target allocation** link.

How do I decide what my target allocation should be?

Use the **Be Smart about Your Target** and **See Model Portfolios** links in the Asset Allocation Guide. They provide examples and links to valuable information that will help you decide.

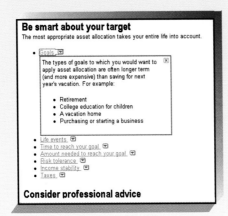

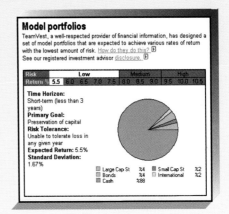

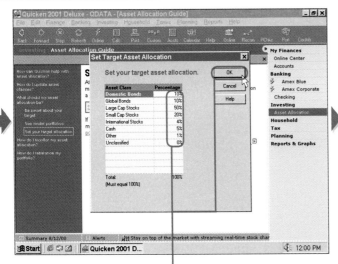

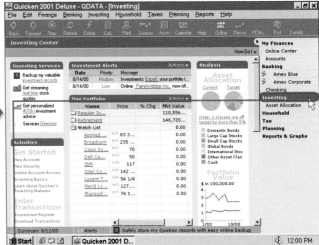

■ Quicken displays the Set Target Asset Allocation dialog box.

5 Type percentage goals for each asset classification.

6 Click **OK** to close the dialog box.

7 Click the **Investing** QuickTab.

■ Quicken updates the Target Asset Allocation graph to match your settings.

COMPARE SECURITY PERFORMANCE

The Quicken Web site at www.quicken.com enables you to chart one or more securities against standard indexes (the Dow Jones Industrial Average, the S&P 500, and the NASDAQ Composite).

COMPARE SECURITY PERFORMANCE

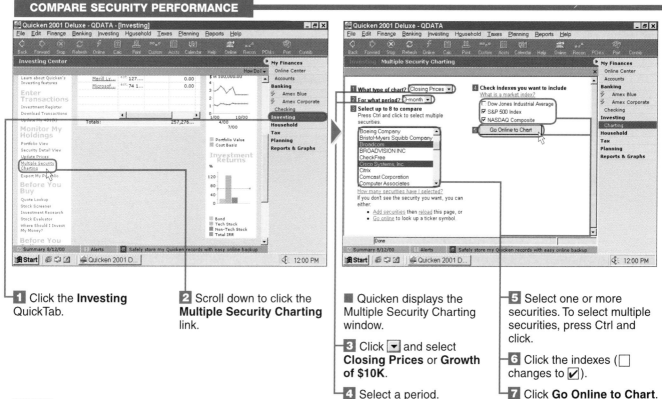

1 Click the **Investing** QuickTab.

2 Scroll down to click the **Multiple Security Charting** link.

■ Quicken displays the Multiple Security Charting window.

3 Click ▼ and select **Closing Prices** or **Growth of $10K**.

4 Select a period.

5 Select one or more securities. To select multiple securities, press Ctrl and click.

6 Click the indexes (☐ changes to ☑).

7 Click **Go Online to Chart**.

What do I do if I want to compare a security I have not set up to ones I have set up? The one I want to compare does not appear in the list.

After you connect to the Internet, you can supply the symbol of the security you want to include in the comparison.

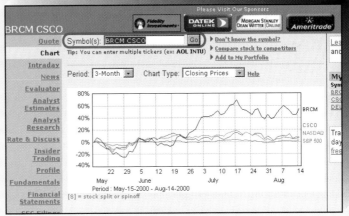

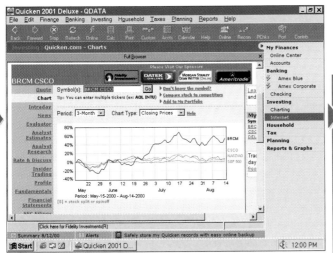

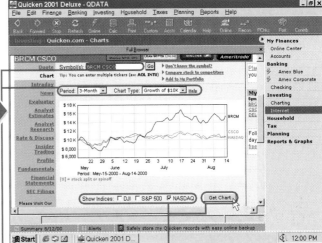

■ Quicken connects to the Internet.

■ After you are connected, you see the Charts window at Quicken.com.

■ Type new symbols to compare different stocks.

■ You can click these drop-down lists boxes to change the period and chart type.

■ You can click these check boxes to change the indices.

8 Click **Get Chart** to update the chart and include the changes.

EXPORT YOUR PORTFOLIO TO THE WEB

You can store your portfolio online in a secured section of the Quicken.com Web site. That way, you can access your portfolio anywhere in the world using a Web browser. And, Quicken.com provides a variety of services to you. For example, you can have Quicken.com notify you when a security hits a price you specify.

Before you try to export, identify the information you want to send to the Web.

EXPORT YOUR PORTFOLIO TO THE WEB

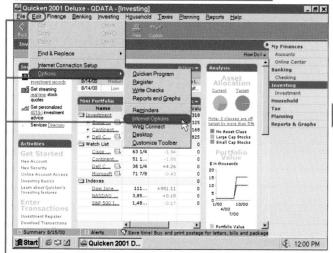

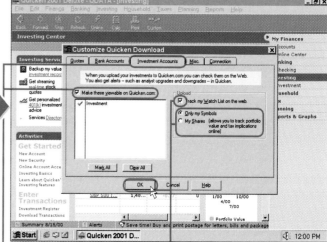

1 Click **Edit**.

2 Click **Options**.

3 Click **Internet Options**.

■ The Customize Quicken Download dialog box appears.

4 Click the **Investment Accounts** tab.

5 Click **Make these viewable on Quicken.com** (☐ changes to ☑).

■ You can click next to each account you want to export (☐ changes to ☑).

■ You can click **Track my Watch List on the web** (☐ changes to ☑).

■ You can click to send shares or only symbols (○ changes to ◉).

6 Click **OK**.

What information actually gets exported to the Web?

If you select **My Shares** in the Customize Quicken Download dialog box, Quicken sends the name of each investment account you choose, the security ticker symbols, the number of shares of each security that you currently hold, and the average price you paid per share. If you select **Symbols Only**, Quicken sends only your symbols. You can choose to send only your watch account without sending your investment account.

◉ Only my Symbols

○ My Shares (allows you to track portfolio
value and tax implications
online)

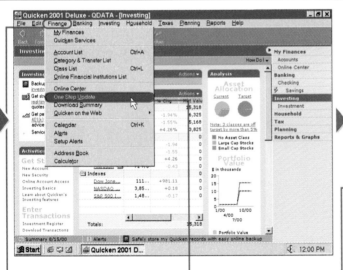

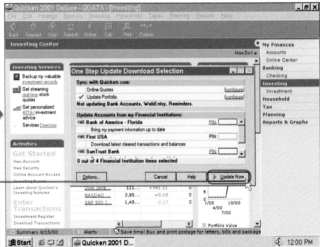

7 Click **Finance**.

8 Click **One Step Update**.

■ You see the One Step Update Download Selection window.

9 Click **Update Portfolio** (☐ changes to ☑).

10 Click **Update Now**.

■ Quicken asks if you want to enter your Quicken.com user name and password now.

11 Click **Yes**.

CONTINUED

EXPORT YOUR PORTFOLIO TO THE WEB

To place your portfolio on the Web, you must register at the Quicken.com Web site to establish a user name and password.

EXPORT YOUR PORTFOLIO TO THE WEB (CONTINUED)

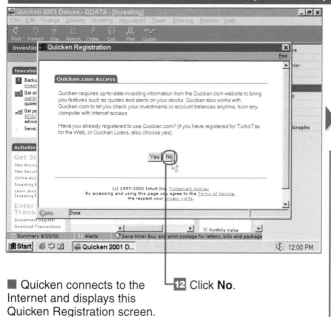

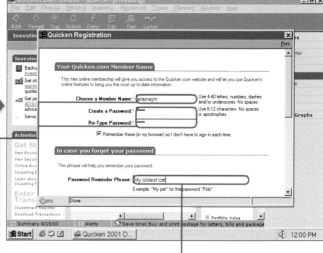

■ Quicken connects to the Internet and displays this Quicken Registration screen.

12 Click **No**.

■ You see the next registration screen.

13 Type a name you want to use for your user name.

14 Type the same password in both boxes.

15 Type a hint to remind you of your password.

Note: If you forget your password, Quicken.com displays this reminder.

What do I do if the user name I want is already taken?

If your user name is already in use, Quicken displays a window, which helps you select a different user name.

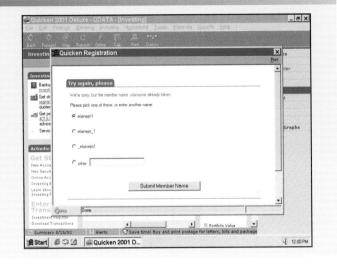

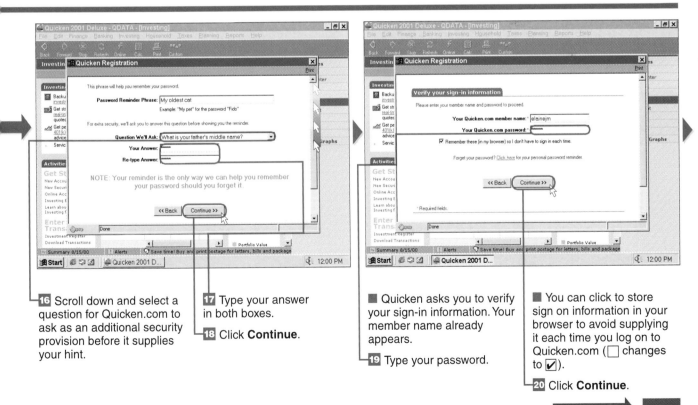

16 Scroll down and select a question for Quicken.com to ask as an additional security provision before it supplies your hint.

17 Type your answer in both boxes.

18 Click **Continue**.

■ Quicken asks you to verify your sign-in information. Your member name already appears.

19 Type your password.

■ You can click to store sign on information in your browser to avoid supplying it each time you log on to Quicken.com (□ changes to ☑).

20 Click **Continue**.

CONTINUED ▶

EXPORT YOUR PORTFOLIO TO THE WEB

Once you establish an account at Quicken.com, you can export your portfolio. If your portfolio changes after you export it to Quicken.com, simply export your portfolio again. After the first time, the export process is much shorter.

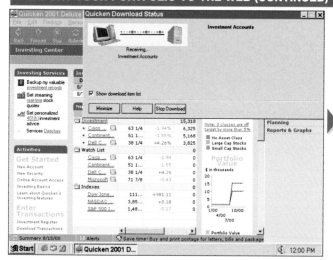

■ Quicken exports your investment account(s).

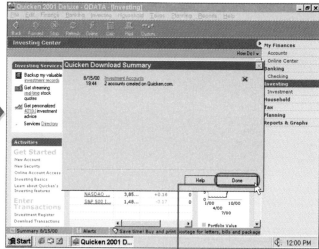

■ When the export completes, Quicken displays the Quicken Download Summary.

21 Click **Done**.

How can I set up a price alert so that Quicken.com notifies me when a stock hits a certain price?

At the Quicken.com Web site, view your portfolio. Then click **Alerts**, the link next to **Portfolio**. Quicken.com displays a page showing announcements for your stocks by investment account. Next to each account title, you see a **Setup** button. Click the **Setup** button, and Quicken.com displays the Alerts page for that account. Scroll down to the bottom of the page. You can specify target prices for stocks in that account. If the stock hits your target price, an alert will appear when you visit Quicken.com.

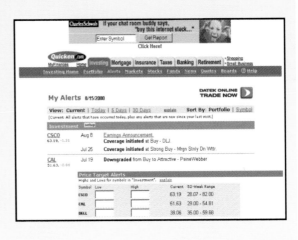

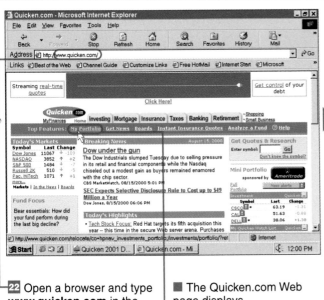

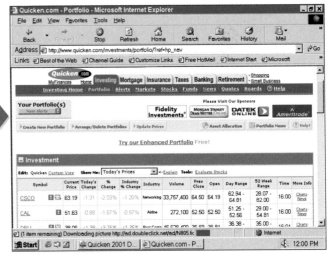

▨22 Open a browser and type **www.quicken.com** in the Address bar.

■ The Quicken.com Web page displays.

▨23 Click the **My Portfolio** link.

■ Your portfolio appears on Quicken.com.

CREATE INVESTMENT REPORTS

You can create a variety of investment reports from the Reports & Graphs Center. The steps you use to create each report are the same; the report you see when you finish depends on the report you select when you start.

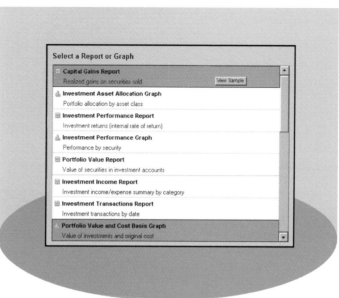

To determine which investment report or graph best meets your needs, see the Section, "View Investment Reports."

CREATE INVESTMENT REPORTS

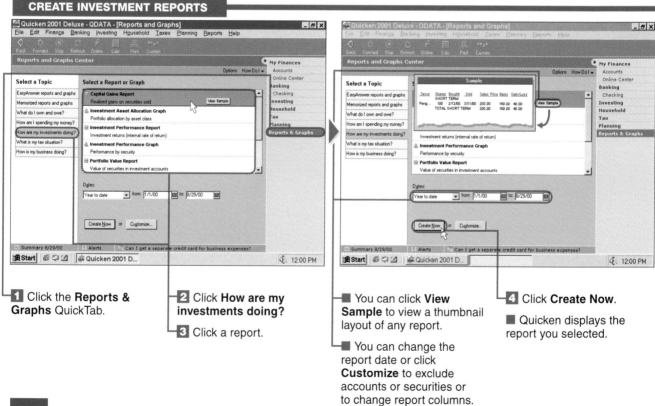

1 Click the **Reports & Graphs** QuickTab.

2 Click **How are my investments doing?**

3 Click a report.

■ You can click **View Sample** to view a thumbnail layout of any report.

■ You can change the report date or click **Customize** to exclude accounts or securities or to change report columns.

4 Click **Create Now**.

■ Quicken displays the report you selected.

VIEW INVESTMENT REPORTS

Quicken allows you to view different Investment graphs.
To generate a report, see the Section "Create Investment Reports."

TYPES OF INVESTMENT GRAPHS

INVESTMENT ASSET ALLOCATION GRAPH

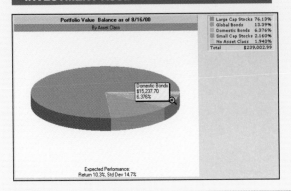

View the allocation of your assets at any time by printing the Investment Asset Allocation Graph. Pointing the mouse at any pie slice changes the pointer to a magnifying glass and you see the dollar amount related to the slice. You can also double-click any slice to view a graph of its details.

INVESTMENT PERFORMANCE GRAPH

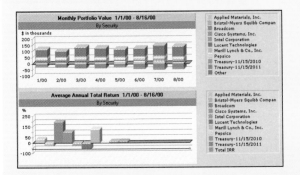

The Investment Performance Graph provides a graphic presentation of how well your stocks and bonds are performing. The graphs also show you the *internal rate of return* (IRR) of your portfolio. You compare the IRR, a percentage, to the interest rate you would receive from a bank account that compounds annually. The IRR takes into account money earned by the investment as well as changes in share price.

The upper graph shows the value of your portfolio over time. The lower graph shows the performance of individual securities. You can point at the small square on either side of the bottom graph to see the IRR for the portfolio.

PORTFOLIO VALUE AND COST BASIS GRAPH

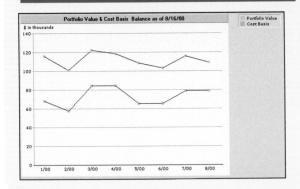

Do you want a visual representation of how well your portfolio is doing? If so, use the Portfolio Value and Cost Basis Graph, which compares the cost basis of your portfolio to its current market value.

VIEW INVESTMENT REPORTS

Quicken allows you to view different Investment reports. To generate a report, see the Section "Create Investment Reports."

TYPES OF INVESTMENT REPORTS

CAPITAL GAINS REPORT

Capital Gains Report
1/1/00 Through 8/16/00

Account	Security	Shares	Bought	Sold	Sales Price	Cost Basis	G
SHORT TERM							
Investment	WalMart	110.000	8/30/99	2/15/00	6,171.04	5,208.52	
Investment	America Online, Inc. Delaware	50.000	11/9/99	5/19/00	2,643.45	3,801.14	
Investment	Microsoft Corporation	50.000	11/9/99	5/19/00	3,173.67	4,564.38	
TOTAL SHORT TERM					**11,988.16**	**13,574.04**	
LONG TERM							
Investment	Cisco Systems, Inc.	28.000	5/1/97	5/19/00	1,458.88	195.21	
TOTAL LONG TERM					**1,458.88**	**195.21**	
OVERALL TOTAL					**13,447.04**	**13,769.25**	

Use the Capital Gains report to review the gains or losses you have made through trades. Quicken groups your capital gains by short term, mid-term, and long term.

INVESTMENT PERFORMANCE REPORT

Investment Performance Report
1/1/00 Through 4/30/00

Date	Account	Action	Description	Investments	Returns	Avg Re
			1/1/00 - 4/30/00			
1/1/00			Beg Mkt Val	127,121.29		
1/3/00	Investment	DivX	Automatic Data Processing, Inc		8.75	
1/10/00	Investment	DivX	WalMart		5.50	
2/1/00	Investment	DivX	Bristol-Myers Squibb Company		53.90	
2/15/00	Investment	SellX	110.000 WalMart		6,171.04	
2/15/00	Investment	DivX	Abbott Laboratories		17.00	
2/25/00	Investment	DivX	Fannie Mae		16.80	
3/1/00	Investment	DivX	Intel Corporation		1.50	
3/10/00	Investment	DivX	IBM		14.40	
3/10/00	Investment	DivX	EXXON MOBIL CORP		17.60	
4/3/00	Investment	DivX	Automatic Data Processing, Inc		8.75	
1/3/00	Retirement	BuyX	5.000 QUALCOMM INC	967.19		
1/4/00	Retirement	DivX	Mattel, Inc.		9.00	
2/15/00	Retirement	SellX	30.000 QUALCOMM INC		3,672.79	
2/24/00	Retirement	DivX	Merill Lynch & Co., Inc.		27.00	
3/1/00	Retirement	DivX	Lucent Technologies		4.40	
3/2/00	Retirement	BuyX	70.000 Certificate of Accrual-...	3,816.19		

You can create an Investment Performance Report to show the internal rate of return (IRR) on your investments. You compare this rate to what you might receive, with compounded annual interest, from a bank account. Comparing rates helps you determine if your investments are earning more than money placed in a bank account. The report shows your average annual total return and accounts for dividends, interest, other payments, plus increases and decreases in the market value of securities.

PORTFOLIO VALUE REPORT

Portfolio Value Report
As of 8/16/00

Security	Shares	Price	est	Cost Basis	Gain/Loss	Balance
Abbott Laboratories	100.000	40.188	*	2,075.30	1,943.45	4,018.75
Applied Materials, Inc.	134.000	77 13/16	*	4,533.87	5,893.01	10,426.88
Automatic Data Processing, Inc	100.000	58 1/8	*	3,085.29	2,727.21	5,812.50
Bristol-Myers Squibb Company	220.000	52.875	*	3,857.46	7,775.04	11,632.50
Dallas-02/15/2013	100.000	48.741	*	4,775.03	99.07	4,874.10
EXXON MOBIL CORP	40.000	81.313	*	0.00	3,252.50	3,252.50
Fannie Mae	60.000	57.563	*	3,466.02	-12.27	3,453.75
IBM	20.000	130.000		897.58	1,702.42	2,600.00
Metropolitan Pier	100.000	54.714	*	5,028.14	443.26	5,471.40
Montgomery Cnty Bond	100.000	48.922	*	4,837.35	54.85	4,892.20
TOTAL Investments				**32,556.04**	**23,878.54**	**56,434.58**

The Portfolio Value Report shows you exactly that — the value of your portfolio on a specific date. The report also shows your cost for each security and your unrealized gains or losses. The report shows how your portfolio is doing on a specific date, including your unrealized gains.

INVESTMENT INCOME REPORT

Investment Income Report
1/1/00 Through 8/16/00

Category Description	1/1/00-8/16/00
INCOME	
_DivInc	665.80
_RlzdGain	-322.21
TOTAL INCOME	**343.59**
EXPENSES	
Uncategorized	0.00
TOTAL EXPENSES	**0.00**
TRANSFERS	
FROM Reg. Invest-Cash	15,438.55
TO Reg. Invest-Cash	-24,533.38
TOTAL TRANSFERS	9,094.83

You can use the Investment Income Report to prepare Schedule B of your tax return. The report shows investment income and expenses. You can subtotal the report by security. The report shows income from dividends, interest, capital gains, and employee stock options. It also shows expenses from margin interest or other investment expenses.

INVESTMENT TRANSACTIONS REPORT

Investment Transactions Report
1/1/00 Through 8/16/00

Date	Account	Action	Security	Category	Price	Shares	Com
1/3/00	Investment	DivX	Automatic Data Processing, Inc	_DivInc			
				[Reg. Invest-Cash]			
1/10/00	Investment	DivX	WalMart	_DivInc			
				[Reg. Invest-Cash]			
2/1/00	Investment	DivX	Bristol-Myers Squibb Company	_DivInc			
				[Reg. Invest-Cash]			
2/15/00	Investment	SellX	WalMart		57 1/4	-110.000	
				_RlzdGain			
				[Reg. Invest-Cash]			
2/15/00	Investment	DivX	Abbott Laboratories	_DivInc			
				[Reg. Invest-Cash]			
2/25/00	Investment	DivX	Fannie Mae	_DivInc			
				[Reg. Invest-Cash]			
3/1/00	Investment	DivX	Intel Corporation				

This report lists investment transactions, and you can choose to include or exclude unrealized gains on this report. Your choice determines the use of the report.

If you include unrealized gains, this report shows the change in market value of your investments over the report's time period. If you exclude unrealized gains, the report shows the change in the cost basis of your securities over the report's time period.

Form **W-4**

Employee's Witholding Allowance Certificate

Department of the Treasury
Internal Revenue Service

For Privacy Act and Paperwork Reduction Act Notice, see page 2.

2000

| 1 | Type or print your first name and middle initial | Last name | 2 | Your Social Security number |

Home address (number and street or rural code)

3 ☐ Single ☐ Married ☐ Married, but witholding at the higher Single rate.

City or Town, state and ___ ___ de

__r last name differs from that on your Social Security Card, check here___ __must call **1-800-772-1213** for a new card.

Deductions

CHAPTER 8

Quicken and Taxes

Did you know that Quicken can help you estimate your income tax liability and prepare your income tax return? This chapter explains how.

REVIEW THE TAXES CENTER

Quicken contains many features that can help you with your taxes.

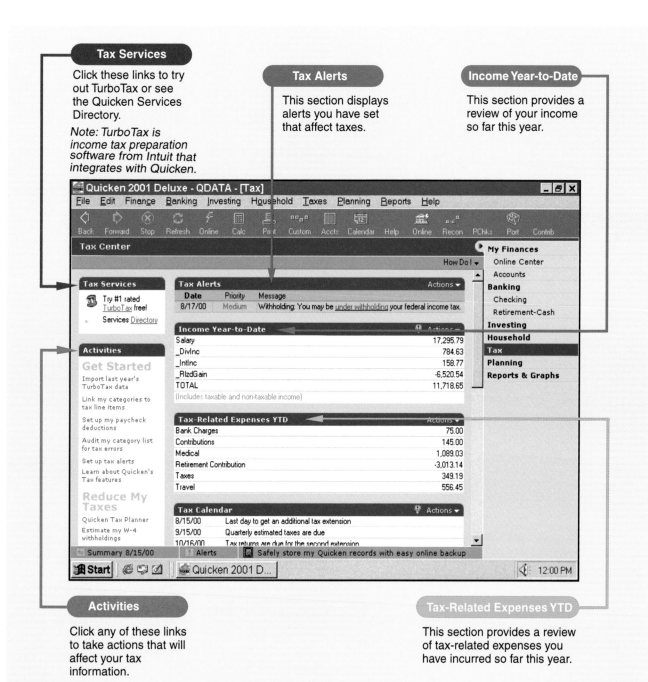

Tax Services

Click these links to try out TurboTax or see the Quicken Services Directory.

Note: TurboTax is income tax preparation software from Intuit that integrates with Quicken.

Tax Alerts

This section displays alerts you have set that affect taxes.

Income Year-to-Date

This section provides a review of your income so far this year.

Activities

Click any of these links to take actions that will affect your tax information.

Tax-Related Expenses YTD

This section provides a review of tax-related expenses you have incurred so far this year.

Tax Calendar

Scroll down to see
important "tax-related"
dates, such as
deadlines for estimated
tax payments.

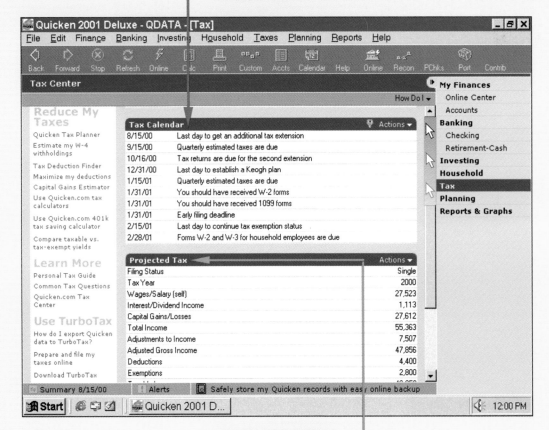

Projected Tax

This section, possibly
the most interesting,
forecasts your taxes
for the year.

You can store paycheck information for tax purposes by describing your last paycheck. Quicken enters all the information into the register and, optionally, creates a scheduled transaction. By default, Quicken tracks Federal and State income taxes, Social Security, Medicare, and disability insurance deductions.

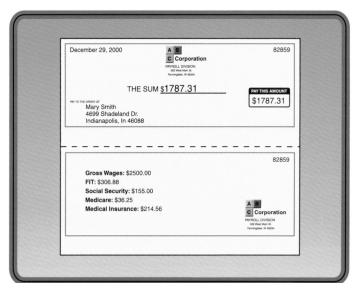

In addition, Quicken tracks other deductions you specify, such as retirement plans or flexible spending accounts. You complete an extra wizard screen for each additional deduction you track.

SET UP YOUR PAYCHECK

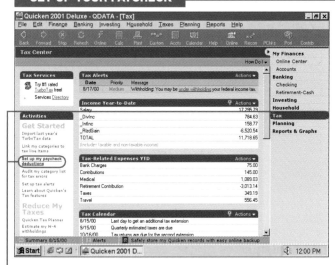

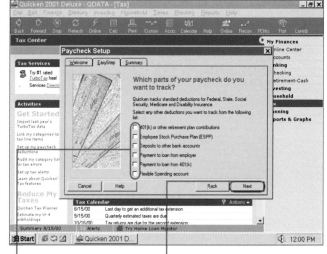

1 Click the **Tax** QuickTab.

2 Click the **Set up my paycheck deductions** link.

■ Quicken displays the Manage Paychecks window.

3 Click **New**.

■ Quicken displays the Welcome screen of the Paycheck Setup wizard.

4 Click **Next**.

5 Remove checks from deductions that do not appear on your paycheck (☑ changes to ☐).

■ After you enter standard deduction information, the wizard displays one window for each deduction that remains checked.

■ If appropriate, answer the questions that are specific to the deduction.

6 Click **Next**.

What is the purpose of the Manage Paychecks window?

It helps you track more than one paycheck. To set up additional paychecks, repeat the steps in this section. Each time, Quicken asks you to specify a name for additional paychecks; you can track your paychecks by their names, and you can view them all in the Manage Paychecks window.

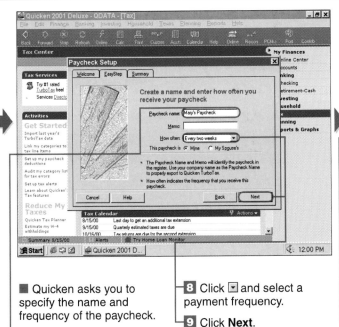

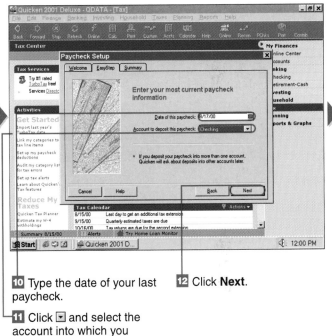

■ Quicken asks you to specify the name and frequency of the paycheck.

7 Type a name for the paycheck.

8 Click ▾ and select a payment frequency.

9 Click **Next**.

10 Type the date of your last paycheck.

11 Click ▾ and select the account into which you deposited the paycheck.

Note: If you split the paycheck between accounts, you describe the split later.

12 Click **Next**.

CONTINUED

SET UP YOUR PAYCHECK

When you set up
your paycheck, you can
describe gross and
net pay, standard payroll
taxes, and other payroll
taxes, such as local taxes.

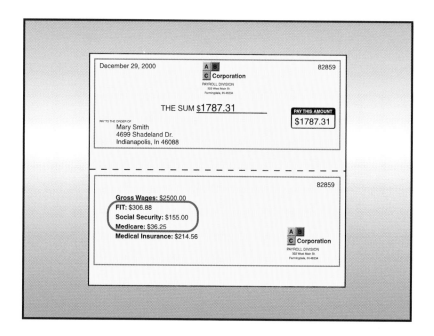

SET UP YOUR PAYCHECK (CONTINUED)

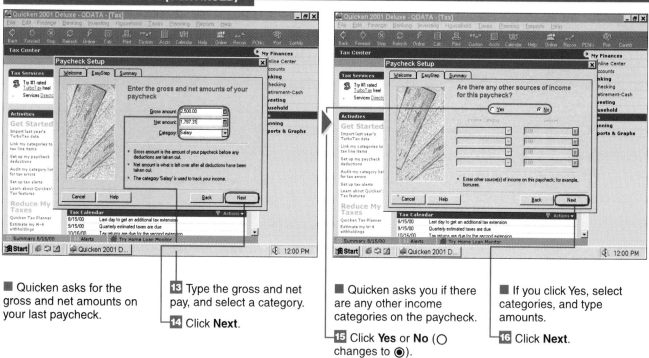

■ Quicken asks for the
gross and net amounts on
your last paycheck.

13 Type the gross and net
pay, and select a category.

14 Click **Next**.

■ Quicken asks you if there
are any other income
categories on the paycheck.

15 Click **Yes** or **No** (○
changes to ●).

■ If you click Yes, select
categories, and type
amounts.

16 Click **Next**.

Do I HAVE to track the payroll taxes?

No. You can set up a "net only" paycheck. Type the net amount of your paycheck in both Gross and Net boxes of wizard and set the Standard deductions values on the other screens to $0.00. Quicken records a paycheck that posts the net amount to the Salary category.

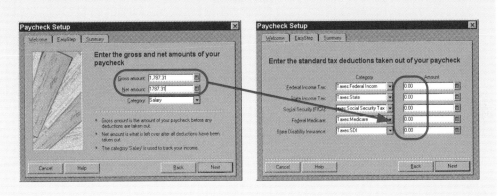

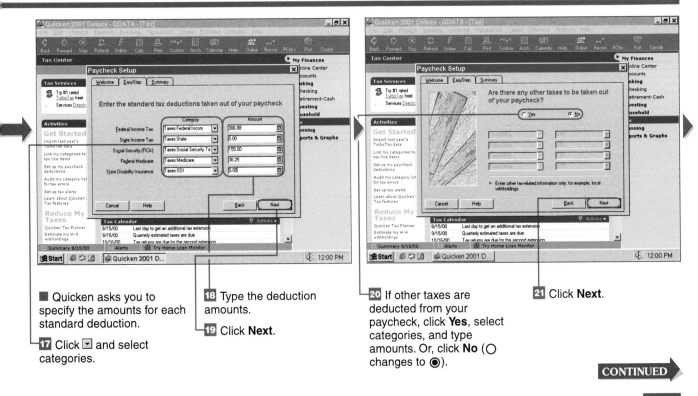

■ Quicken asks you to specify the amounts for each standard deduction.

17 Click 🔽 and select categories.

18 Type the deduction amounts.

19 Click **Next**.

20 If other taxes are deducted from your paycheck, click **Yes**, select categories, and type amounts. Or, click **No** (○ changes to ◉).

21 Click **Next**.

CONTINUED

SET UP YOUR PAYCHECK

You can also set up other deductions, such as medical insurance.

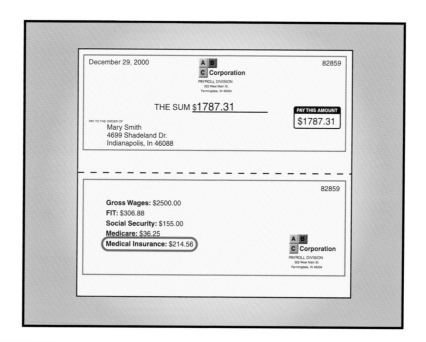

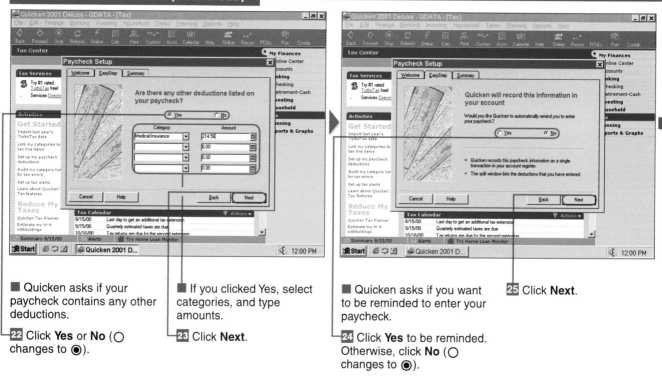

■ Quicken asks if your paycheck contains any other deductions.

22 Click **Yes** or **No** (○ changes to ◉).

■ If you clicked Yes, select categories, and type amounts.

23 Click **Next**.

■ Quicken asks if you want to be reminded to enter your paycheck.

24 Click **Yes** to be reminded. Otherwise, click **No** (○ changes to ◉).

25 Click **Next**.

Can I set up a paycheck if my gross and net amounts vary each payday?

Yes. To set up your paycheck:

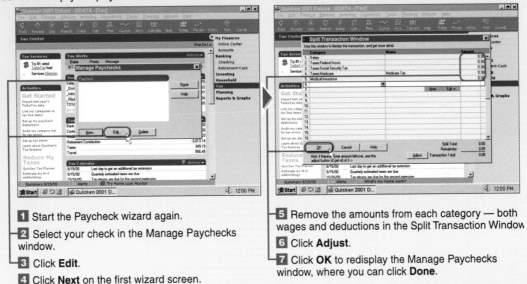

1 Start the Paycheck wizard again.

2 Select your check in the Manage Paychecks window.

3 Click **Edit**.

4 Click **Next** on the first wizard screen.

5 Remove the amounts from each category — both wages and deductions in the Split Transaction Window.

6 Click **Adjust**.

7 Click **OK** to redisplay the Manage Paychecks window, where you can click **Done**.

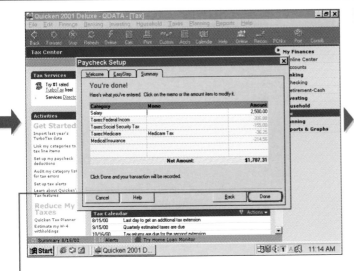

■ Quicken displays a summary of your paycheck. It should match your check stub.

26 Click **Done**.

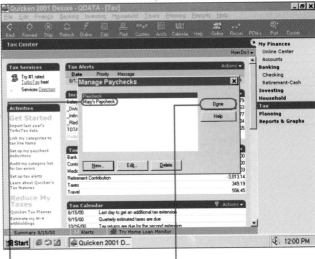

■ Quicken redisplays the Manage Paychecks window, and your paycheck appears.

27 Click **Done**.

■ Quicken records your last paycheck in the register and creates a scheduled transaction.

CONTINUED

CONFIRM WITHHOLDING AMOUNTS

Quicken can help you determine if you are withholding enough money to cover your tax liability. Use the Am I under or over withholding? window, a "what-if" tool, to see what happens when you change withholdings. When you finish, you can submit an adjusted W-4 form to your employer.

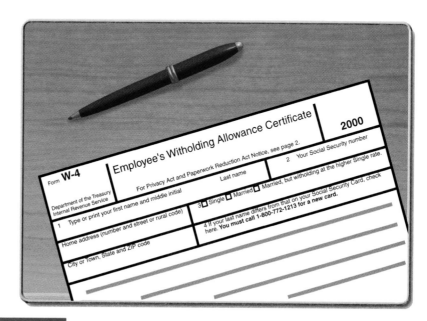

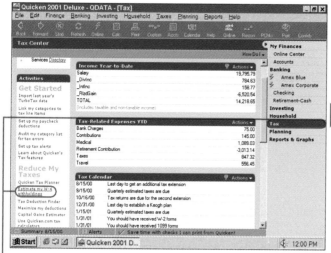

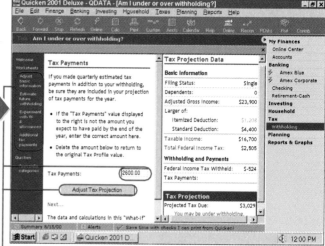

1 Click the **Tax** QuickTab.

2 Click **Estimate my W-4 withholdings**.

■ Quicken displays the Am I under or over withholding? window.

3 Click a link to provide estimates in the left window.

4 Type estimates as required.

5 Click **Adjust Tax Projection**.

■ Quicken adjusts the numbers on the right side of the screen.

Note: Your guesses do not affect your Quicken data.

6 Repeat steps 3 through 5 for all estimates that apply to you.

Quicken enables you to assign tax-related categories to tax forms. In your daily routine, you already assign transactions to categories (See "Enter a Transaction in the Register" in Chapter 1). Your hard work pays off when you produce reports in seconds that help you prepare your income tax return.

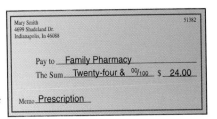

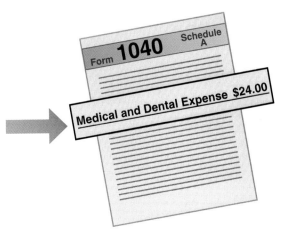

Assigning categories to tax forms also helps if you use TurboTax to prepare your income tax return.

ASSIGN CATEGORIES TO TAX FORMS

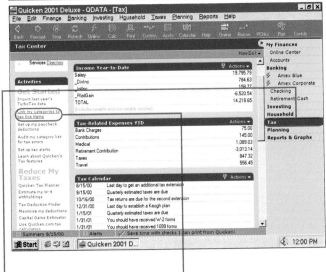

1 Click the **Tax** QuickTab.

2 Click the **Link my categories to tax line items** link.

■ Quicken displays the Tax Link Assistant.

3 Click a category to which you want to assign a tax form.

4 Click the tax form line to which you want to assign the category.

5 Click **Assign Line Item to Category**.

6 Repeat Steps 3 through 5 until you assign all tax-related categories to tax forms.

7 Click **OK**.

USING THE TAX PLANNER

Using information from your Tax Profile, the Tax Planner helps you plan several tax-related areas. For example, you can project the effect that receiving that wage increase, increasing your deductions, or changing your exemptions will have on your tax liability.

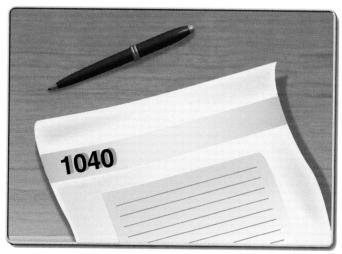

The Tax Planner is a "what-if" tool. You can make changes in it to see the effect of the changes on your tax liability for 2000 and 2001. You can store up to four sets of numbers in four different scenarios. Changes that you make in the Tax Planner do not affect your Quicken data.

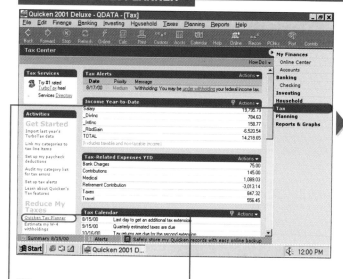

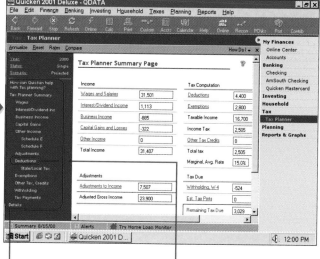

1 Click the **Tax** QuickTab.

2 Click the **Quicken Tax Planner** link.

■ Quicken displays the Tax Planner Summary Page, prefilled with information from your Quicken data file.

■ You can click any of these links to see the source of its corresponding number on the Tax Planner Summary Page.

3 Click **Deductions**.

How do I switch to a different scenario?

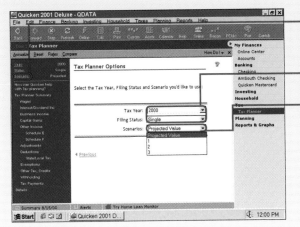

■ **1** Click **Scenario** on the left side of the page.

■ The Tax Planner Options page appears on the right side of the page.

■ You can click ▼ and select a different tax year or filing status.

2 Click ▼ and select a different scenario.

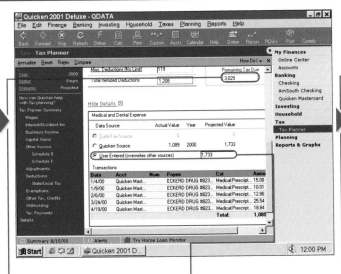

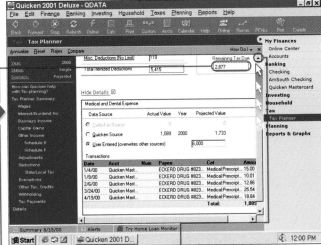

■ You see details for the medical and dental deductions on Schedule A.

4 Take note of the amount in the Remaining Tax Due box, which is the amount your changes may affect.

5 Click **User Entered** (○ changes to ◉) and type an amount.

6 Press Tab on your keyboard.

■ If your "what-if" amount affects your tax liability, you see the change in the Remaining Tax Due box.

■ To change other deductions that appear on Schedule A, scroll up and click a link for a particular deduction to see details and supply a "what-if" amount.

SEARCH FOR DEDUCTIONS

The Deduction Finder
helps you identify tax
deductions for which you
are eligible.

SEARCH FOR DEDUCTIONS

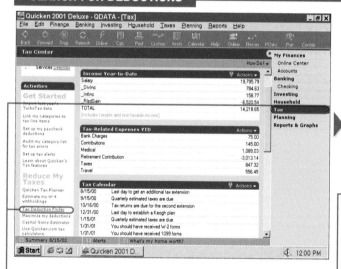

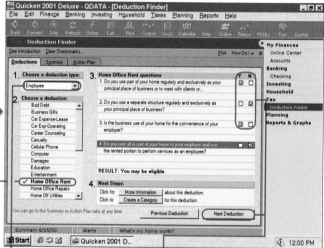

1 Click the **Tax** QuickTab.

2 Click the **Tax Deduction Finder** link.

■ Quicken displays a window that explains how to use the Deduction Finder.

3 Click **OK**.

Note: To avoid seeing this box again, check the box in the lower left corner.

■ Quicken displays the Deduction Finder window.

4 Click ▾ and select a deduction type.

■ You see deductions based on your choice.

5 Select a deduction.

6 Answer the questions (☐ changes to ☑).

■ Quicken evaluates your eligibility.

7 Select another deduction or click Next Deduction.

8 Repeat Steps 4 through 7 until you finish.

What do I see if I click More Information while answering questions about a deduction?

You see the same information you see on the Action Plan tab with one addition: the Quicken Steps section.

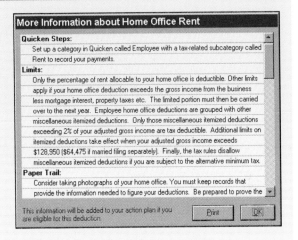

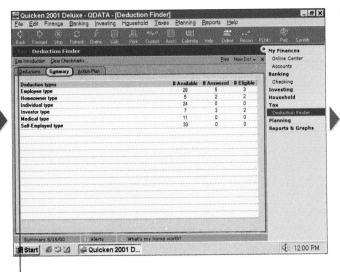

9 Click the **Summary** tab.

■ Quicken displays a summary of the deductions you evaluated.

10 Click the **Action Plan** tab.

■ Quicken displays information about each eligible deduction.

■ You see eligibility criteria, limits for the deduction, documents you need to keep, and tax forms to use (and not use). Additional information appears under a category called "More Info," which you must scroll down to see.

MAXIMIZE DEDUCTIONS

Quicken can help you find tax deductions that are often missed.

MAXIMIZE DEDUCTIONS

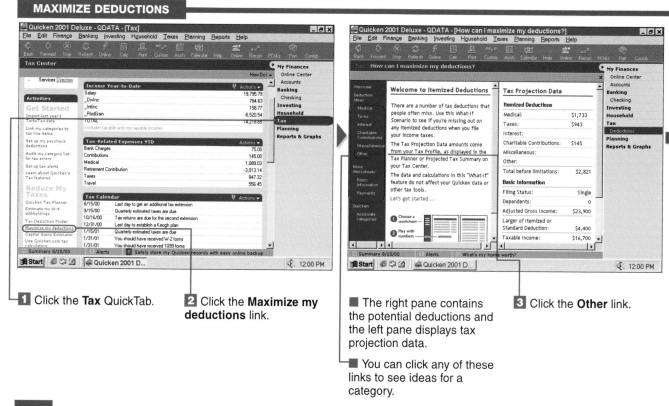

1 Click the **Tax** QuickTab.

2 Click the **Maximize my deductions** link.

■ The right pane contains the potential deductions and the left pane displays tax projection data.

■ You can click any of these links to see ideas for a category.

3 Click the **Other** link.

What will I see if I click the links under "More Worksheets"?

Under Basic Information, you can change filing status, number of dependents, and gross income. Under Tax Payments, you can change the tax payment information displayed at the bottom of the Tax Projection Data pane.

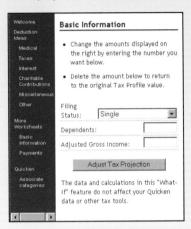

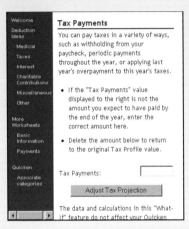

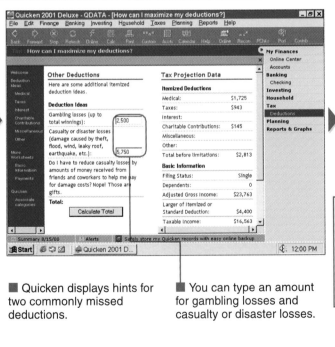

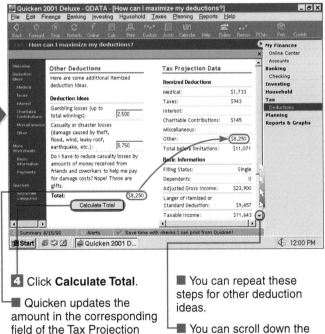

■ Quicken displays hints for two commonly missed deductions.

■ You can type an amount for gambling losses and casualty or disaster losses.

4 Click **Calculate Total**.

■ Quicken updates the amount in the corresponding field of the Tax Projection Data pane.

■ You can repeat these steps for other deduction ideas.

■ You can scroll down the Tax Projection Data pane to see your updated Tax Projection.

CREATE TAX REPORTS

You can create a variety of reports and graphs to calculate your tax liability. The steps to create each report are the same; the final information depends on which report you select.

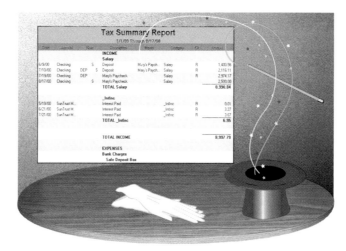

See the Section, "View Tax Reports" for a description of the different tax reports you can create.

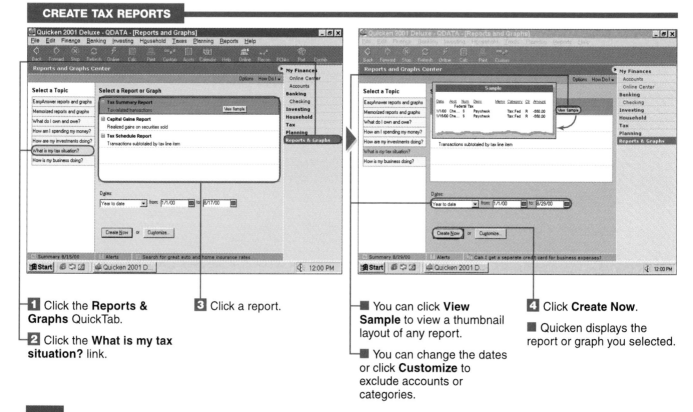

1 Click the **Reports & Graphs** QuickTab.

2 Click the **What is my tax situation?** link.

3 Click a report.

■ You can click **View Sample** to view a thumbnail layout of any report.

■ You can change the dates or click **Customize** to exclude accounts or categories.

4 Click **Create Now**.

■ Quicken displays the report or graph you selected.

VIEW TAX REPORTS

You can view your tax liability
using two different reports.
To generate a report, see the
Section "Create Tax Reports."

TYPES OF TAX REPORTS

TAX SUMMARY REPORT

This report lists each tax-related category
(first income, then expenses) and all
transactions you assigned to the category.
By default, the report includes transactions
from all accounts except tax-deferred
accounts.

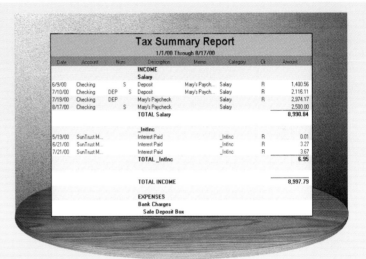

TAX SCHEDULE REPORT

You can use the Tax Schedule Report to
complete Form 1040 and its schedules
because the report lists, by tax form,
transactions you assigned to tax-related
categories. Be sure to check the report for
IRS-imposed limits (like the maximum
deduction allowed for IRA contributions).

To learn how to assign categories to
transactions, see Chapter 1. To link
categories to tax forms, see the Section
"Assign Categories to Tax Forms."

CHAPTER 9

Plan for the Future

Did you know that Quicken can help you plan for future expenses, such as your retirement, college, or even a new home purchase? Learn how in this chapter.

REVIEW THE PLANNING CENTER

Planning Services

Click these links to perform some common planning tasks or see the Quicken Services Directory.

Alerts

This section displays alerts that you have set that affect your plans.

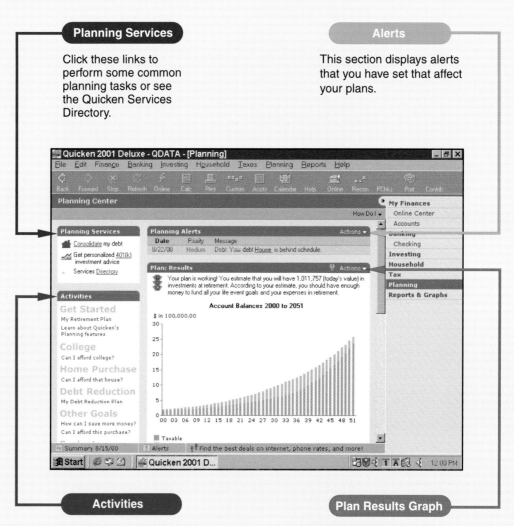

Activities

Quicken helps you set up plans to meet several life goals: retirement, college costs, purchasing a home, reducing your debt, or planning for a special occasion. You can track each goal separately or unified in one plan. Quicken uses the assumptions you supply for each goal to produce an overall plan.

Plan Results Graph

The Plan Results graph shows you how well your plan is working. The graph appears after you answer Plan Assumption questions.

Plan Assumptions

In this section, you see a recap of the information you provided about yourself while answering Plan Assumption questions. You answer these questions before you create any plan or while creating a particular plan.

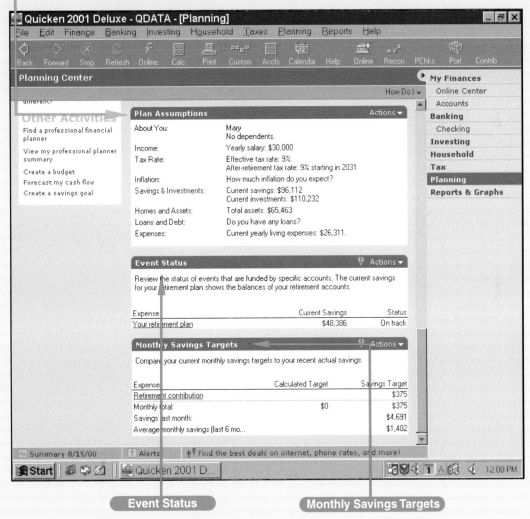

Event Status

You can see a snapshot of the progress you are making toward each life goal you create.

Monthly Savings Targets

This section shows you how you are doing with respect to your savings targets.

CATEGORY GROUPS

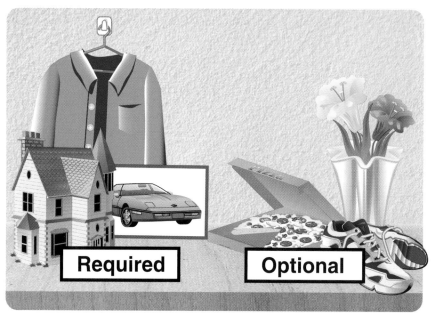

While budgeting, you can assign categories to groups (see Chapter 1 to learn how to assign transactions to categories). For example, you can divide your expenses into "Required" and "Optional" while preparing a budget.

Required

Optional

Using Category Groups in budgeting is optional.

CATEGORY GROUPS

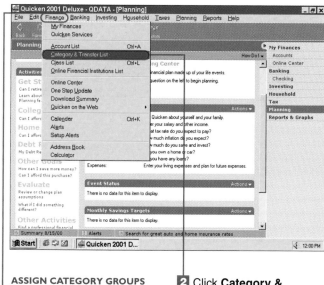

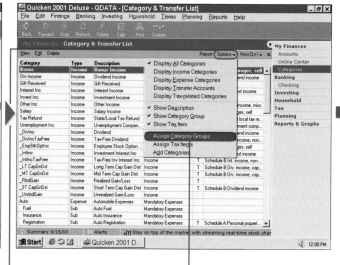

ASSIGN CATEGORY GROUPS

1 Click **Finance**.

2 Click **Category & Transfer List**.

■ Quicken displays the Category & Transfer List.

3 Click **Options**.

4 Click **Assign Category Groups** in the drop-down menu.

■ The Assign Category Groups dialog box appears.

How do I create a new category group or delete an old one?

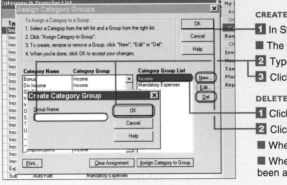

CREATE A NEW CATEGORY GROUP

1 In Step 10 of this section, click **New**.

■ The Create Category Group dialog box appears.

2 Type a name.

3 Click **OK**.

DELETE A CATEGORY GROUP

1 Click the item in the Category Group List.

2 Click **Del**.

■ When Quicken asks you to confirm the action; click **Yes**.

■ When you delete a category group, all categories that had been assigned to the deleted group simply become unassigned.

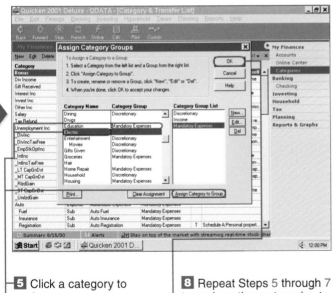

5 Click a category to assign.

6 Click a category group.

7 Click **Assign Category to Group**.

8 Repeat Steps 5 through 7 to assign other categories to groups.

9 Click **OK** to save your changes.

■ Categories are assigned.

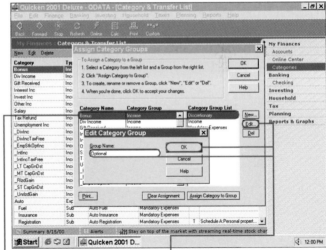

EDIT A CATEGORY GROUP

1 Perform Steps 1 through 4 in "Assign Category Groups."

2 Click a category group to change.

3 Click **Edit**.

■ The Edit Category Group dialog box appears.

4 Type the new group name.

5 Click **OK**. The Group name changes.

SET UP THE BUDGET WINDOW

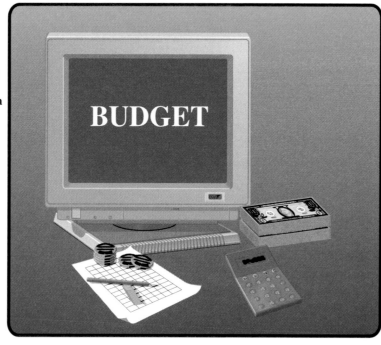

You can establish a budget in the Quicken Budget window. You can change the view in a variety of ways to make the window support the way you work. You can budget by either category or by category group. Categories appear under the folder of their category group.

To understand and set up categories, see Chapter 1. To understand and set up category groups, see the Section "Category Groups."

SET UP THE BUDGET WINDOW

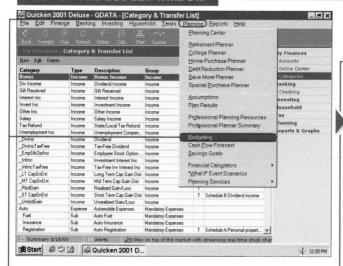

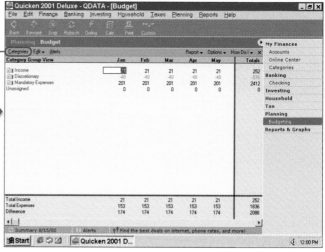

■1 Click **Planning**.

■2 Click **Budgeting**.

*Note: The first time you open the Budget window, Quicken states that it will create a budget from existing data. Click **OK**.*

■ Quicken displays the Budget window in Category Group View.

■3 To display categories, click **Categories**.

■ Quicken displays the Select Categories to Include dialog box.

When I displayed the Budget window, I saw numbers already in it. Why?

If you have been using Quicken for awhile, you might see numbers that are based on your actual transactions. You can use these numbers or start over and set up a new budget. To start over and set up a new budget, see the Section "Establish Budget Figures."

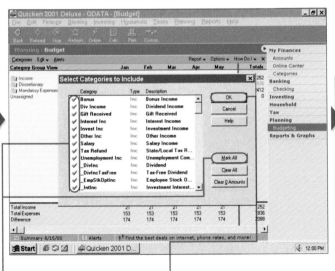

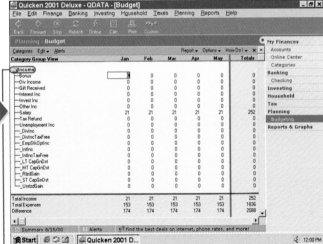

4 Click items to include in the budget (☐ changes to ☑).

■ You can click **Mark All** to select every category.

■ Alternately, you can check selected categories for which you want to budget.

5 Click **OK**.

6 Click the folder of any category group.

■ You see the Budget window showing all selected categories in that category group.

■ You can hide categories and display only the category group by clicking the category group folder.

ESTABLISH BUDGET FIGURES

When you budget, you establish dollar amounts for each category or category group and use the amounts to avoid overspending. Quicken automatically saves budget information you enter.

You might find budgeting by category easier than by category groups because categories represent specific expenses. For example, you can estimate expenses for Electricity and Rent easier than for the entire Mandatory category group of which they are a part.

ESTABLISH BUDGET FIGURES

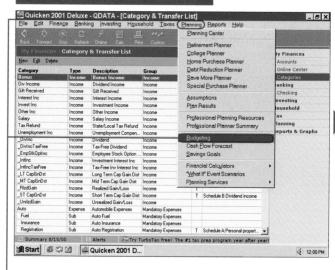

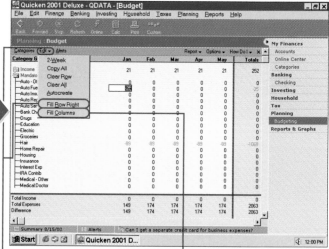

FILL IN THE BUDGET WINDOW

1 Click **Planning**.

2 Click **Budgeting**.

■ Quicken displays the Budget window.

■ You can click a category group folder to open it and budget by category.

3 Type budget amounts or click **Edit** to accelerate data entry.

■ You can click **Fill Row Right** to copy the number in one row to the same row in all columns.

■ You can click **Fill Columns** to copy all numbers in a particular column to the corresponding spot in all other columns.

Plan for
the Future **9**

How do I know what amounts to type in the Budget window?

You guess. If you already have information in Quicken, you can start with the amounts Quicken displays in the budget it creates the first time you open the window. If you have not entered information in Quicken, start by listing the amounts you know, such as your salary and your rent. Then, type guesses for the other expenses. As you incur and enter "real" expenses, Quicken will compare them to your budgeted amounts and help you adjust your budget to reflect your actual

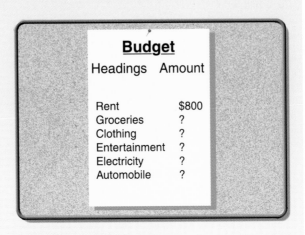

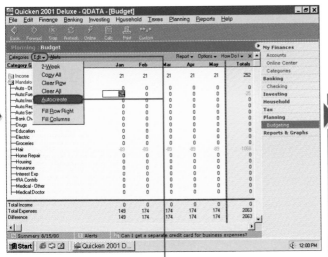

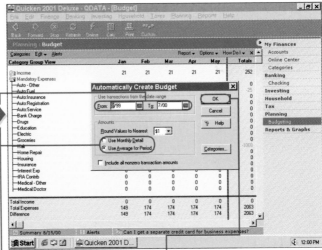

AUTOMATICALLY CREATE A BUDGET

1 Perform Steps 1 and 2 in "Fill In The Budget Window."

2 Click **Edit**.

3 Click **Autocreate**.

■ Quicken displays the Automatically Create Budget dialog box.

4 Type the date range that you want Quicken to use.

5 Select a budget option (○ changes to ◉).

■ To budget actual amounts for each month, click **Use Monthly Detail**.

■ To budget the same amount for each month in the period, click **Use Average for Period**.

6 Click **OK**.

■ Quicken creates a budget.

CONTINUED

You can use the annual view of the budget window to quickly create a budget. You supply annualized figures, and Quicken allocates the correct portion of each amount to each month. If you are unsatisfied with your budget attempt, you can start over at any time.

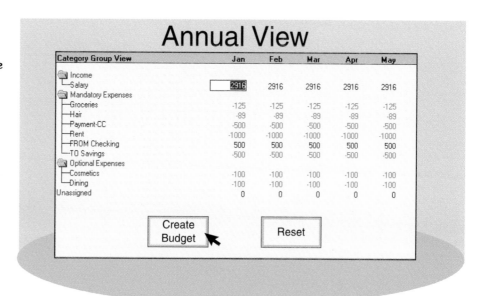

ESTABLISH BUDGET FIGURES (CONTINUED)

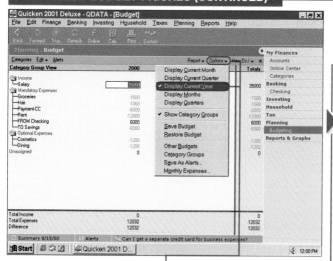

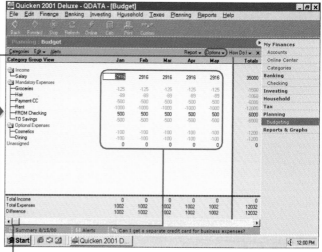

USE THE ANNUAL VIEW

1 To budget the same amount in each category every month, perform Steps 1 and 2 in "Fill In The Budget Window."

2 Click **Options**.

3 Click **Display Current Year** in the drop-down menu.

■ Quicken displays budget numbers, one month per column, for the year.

4 Type annual amounts.

5 Click **Options**.

6 Click **Display Months**.

■ Quicken divides the annual amounts equally among months in the monthly view.

How do I budget by Category Group?

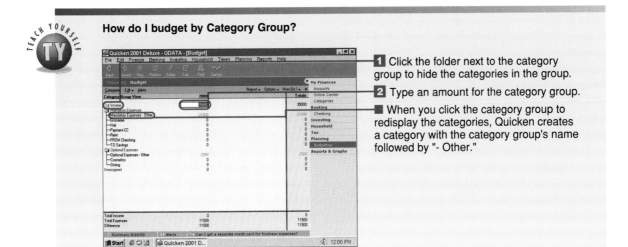

1 Click the folder next to the category group to hide the categories in the group.

2 Type an amount for the category group.

■ When you click the category group to redisplay the categories, Quicken creates a category with the category group's name followed by "- Other."

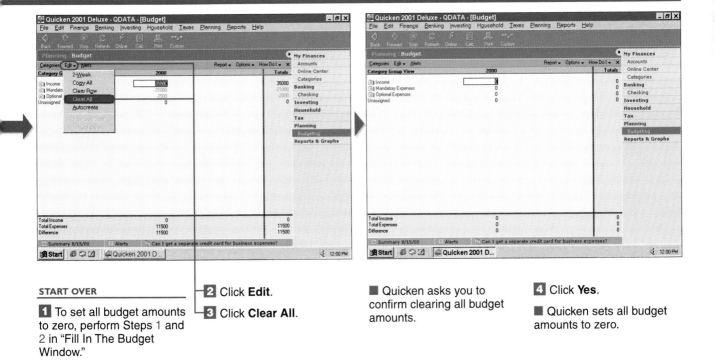

START OVER

1 To set all budget amounts to zero, perform Steps 1 and 2 in "Fill In The Budget Window."

2 Click **Edit**.

3 Click **Clear All**.

■ Quicken asks you to confirm clearing all budget amounts.

4 Click **Yes**.

■ Quicken sets all budget amounts to zero.

Quicken can help you plan for "life events" such as retirement, college education, buying a home, a special event (like a wedding), or simply to save more. Quicken uses a standard set of assumptions about you whenever you create these plans. To save time, you can fill in the assumptions before creating a plan rather than as you create a plan.

This section illustrates how to supply assumptions about yourself. You must provide assumptions for all the links that pertain to you for your plan to work.

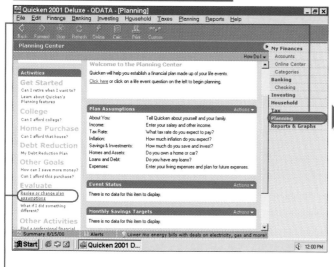

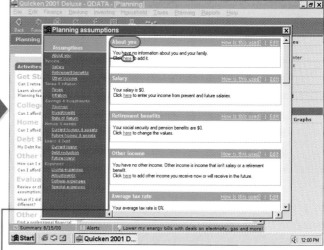

1 Click the **Planning** QuickTab.

2 Click the **Review or change plan assumptions** link.

■ Quicken displays the Planning Assumptions window.

■ For accurate assumptions, Quicken needs information for areas that apply to you.

3 Click either the **About you** or the **here** link.

■ Quicken displays a window with questions.

What if I have no idea how to answer a question?

Quicken often supplies buttons that help you estimate information. For example, if you click **Calculate** in the About You window, Quicken displays the Calculate Life Expectancy window to help you estimate your life expectancy.

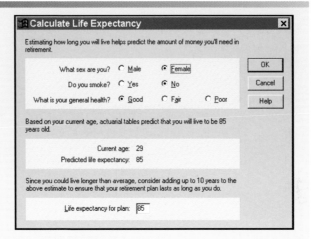

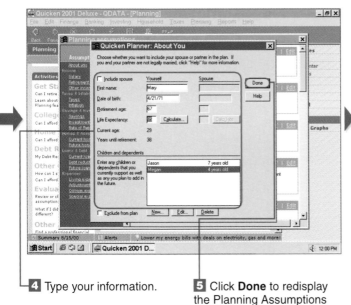

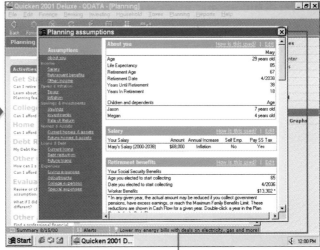

4 Type your information.

5 Click **Done** to redisplay the Planning Assumptions window.

■ Quicken updates the Planning Assumptions window as you complete sections.

6 Repeat Steps 4 and 5 for each link that pertains to you.

7 Click ⊠ to close the Planning Assumptions window.

■ When you redisplay the Planning QuickTab, the Plan Results graph is based on the assumption questions you answered.

USING THE RETIREMENT PLANNER

Although retirement might be years away, Quicken can help you begin planning for it now. After all, you work hard now. You should be able to retire with enough money to live well without working.

To use the Retirement Planner, Quicken asks assumption questions and makes estimates based on your answers. Complete the Section "Set Up Planning Assumptions" to save time creating your plan.

USING THE RETIREMENT PLANNER

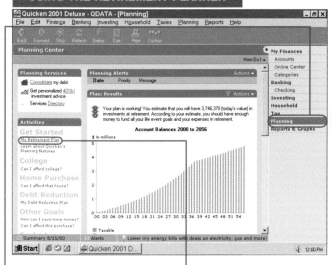

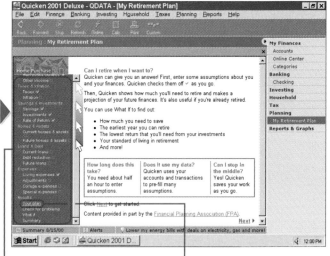

1 Click the **Planning** QuickTab.

2 Click **My Retirement Plan**.

■ Quicken displays the My Retirement Plan window.

3 Click any link on the left to display a window that you can use to complete or update Plan Assumptions.

Note: You must provide assumptions for all links that pertain to you for retirement planning to work properly.

4 When you finish updating assumption information, scroll down and click **Your Plan**.

**I want an overview of my
plan. Can I view one?**

Yes. In the My Retirement
Plan window, scroll down and
click the **Summary** link.
Quicken displays a Summary
window.

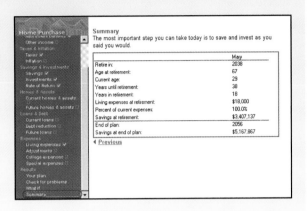

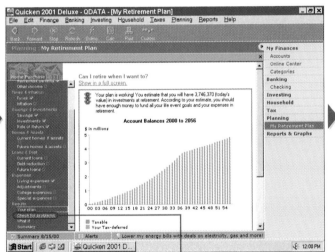

■ Your plan graph appears,
and Quicken indicates
whether your plan is
working.

■ Even though your plan
may be working, you may
need to make some
adjustments.

5 Click **Check for
problems**.

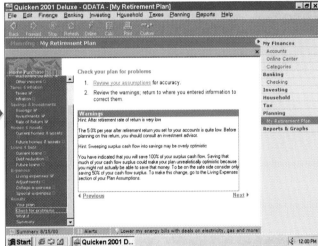

■ Quicken suggests ways
you can improve your plan. If
you think they are valid,
update the plan by clicking
the link Quicken suggests.

USING THE COLLEGE PLANNER

You can use the College Planner to help you estimate college costs, plan how much to save for college, and estimate your cash flow while making college payments.

To use the College Planner, Quicken asks assumption questions and makes estimates based on your answers. Complete the Section "Set Up Planning Assumptions" to save time creating your plan.

USING THE COLLEGE PLANNER

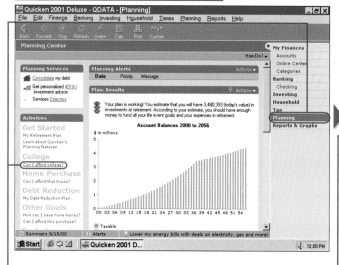

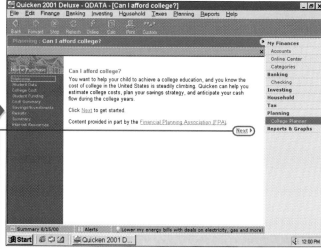

-1 Click the **Planning** QuickTab.

-2 Click **Can I afford college?**

■ Quicken displays the Welcome window of the College Planner.

-3 Click **Next** to view the Student Data window.

Note: You must provide assumptions for all links that pertain to you for college planning to work properly.

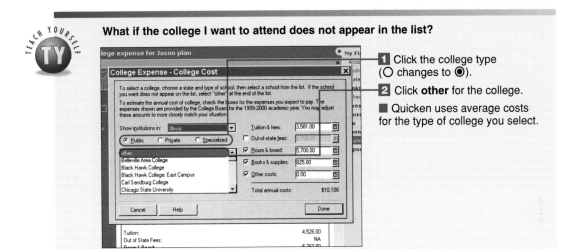

What if the college I want to attend does not appear in the list?

■ 1 Click the college type
(○ changes to ◉).

■ 2 Click **other** for the college.

■ Quicken uses average costs
for the type of college you select.

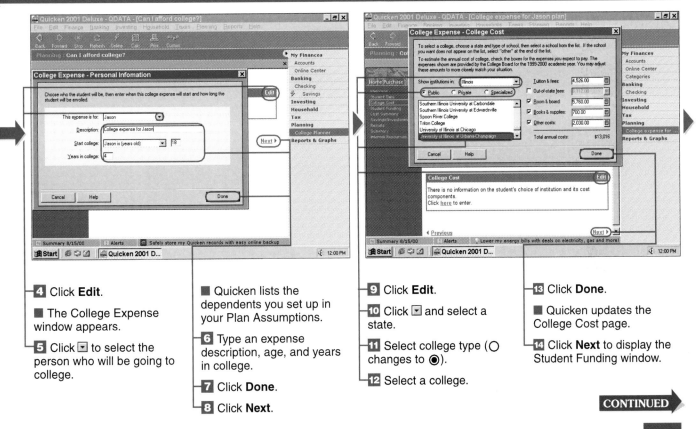

■ 4 Click **Edit**.

■ The College Expense
window appears.

■ 5 Click ▼ to select the
person who will be going to
college.

■ Quicken lists the
dependents you set up in
your Plan Assumptions.

■ 6 Type an expense
description, age, and years
in college.

■ 7 Click **Done**.

■ 8 Click **Next**.

■ 9 Click **Edit**.

■ 10 Click ▼ and select a
state.

■ 11 Select college type (○
changes to ◉).

■ 12 Select a college.

■ 13 Click **Done**.

■ Quicken updates the
College Cost page.

■ 14 Click **Next** to display the
Student Funding window.

CONTINUED

USING THE COLLEGE PLANNER

What if you see financial aid does not cover the costs in the College Expense — Financial Aid box? Before you finish the College Planner, you can figure your current or future savings into the equation.

USING THE COLLEGE PLANNER (CONTINUED)

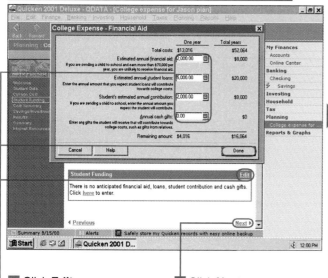

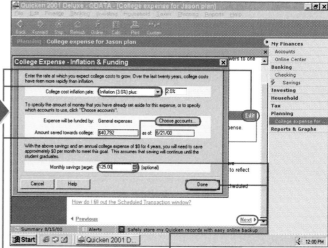

15 Click **Edit**.

16 Type in financial aid, student loans, student contributions, and gifts.

17 Click **Done** to update the Financial Aid page.

18 Click **Next**.

■ The Cost Summary window appears.

19 Click **Next** to see the Savings and Investments window.

20 Click **Edit**.

■ You can click ⯆ to change the inflation rates.

■ You can click **Choose accounts** and select Quicken accounts to apply to college costs.

21 Type a monthly savings target.

22 Click **Done**.

■ Quicken updates the window.

23 Click **Next**.

I do not want to use the balance in any of my current accounts for college. Does this mean I cannot afford college?

Not necessarily. In the final analysis, you need to be able to save the target amount that Quicken supplies to afford college. Quicken reduces that target amount if you include money from an existing account. But the remaining question is still, "Can I save the targeted amount?"

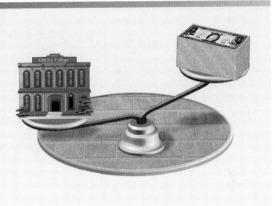

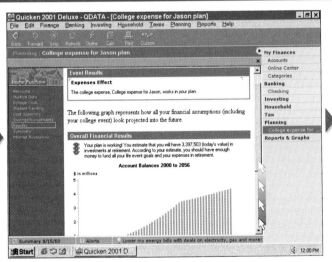

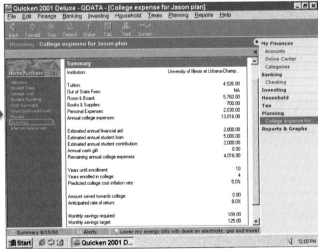

■ Quicken displays the Results page and shows whether you can afford college expenses given your total plan.

24 Scroll down and click **Next**.

■ Quicken displays a summary of your College Planner choices.

■ To change a choice, click its link.

25 Scroll down and click **Next**.

■ Quicken displays a page of Web links that provide college expense information.

USING THE HOME PURCHASE PLANNER

You can use the Home Purchase Planner to see if you can afford the home of your dreams. The Home Purchase Planner helps you determine if the home fits within your overall plan.

To use the Home Purchase Planner, Quicken asks assumption questions and makes estimates based on your answers. Complete the Section "Set Up Planning Assumptions" to save time creating your plan.

USING THE HOME PURCHASE PLANNER

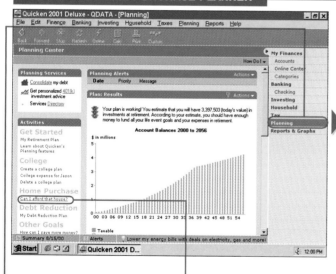

1 Click the **Planning** QuickTab.

2 Click the **Can I afford that house?** link.

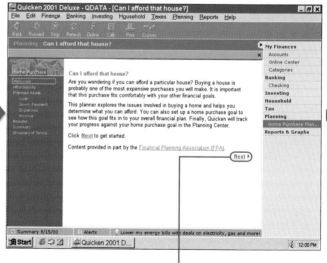

■ Quicken displays the Welcome screen of the Home Purchase Planner.

3 Click **Next**.

How do I know what amounts to type when using the calculator to find out how much a typical lender would loan me?

Use the links along the side — some of which take you to the Internet — to get more information.

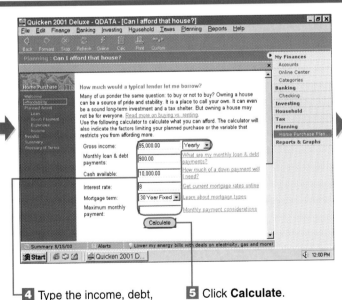

4 Type the income, debt, cash available, and mortgage information.

5 Click **Calculate**.

■ Quicken calculates an estimate of the amount you can borrow.

6 Scroll down to view the estimated amount that you can borrow.

7 Click **Next**.

CONTINUED

USING THE HOME PURCHASE PLANNER

After you estimate the amount of money you can borrow, you use the Home Purchase Planner to set up a planned asset that represents the home you want to buy and identifies its value.

A *planned asset* is not a real asset and does not affect the data in your Quicken accounts or your net worth.

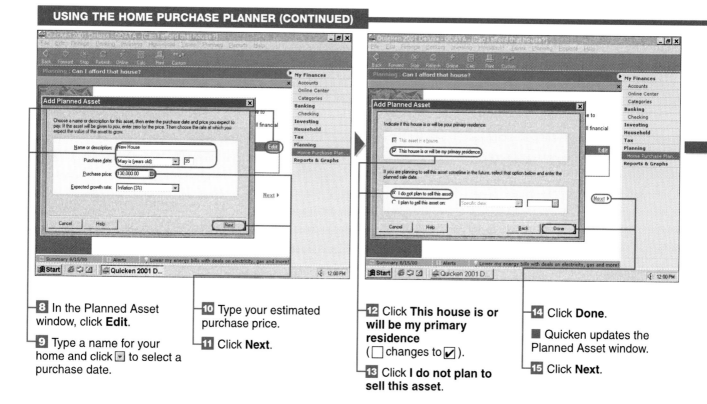

-8 In the Planned Asset window, click **Edit**.

-9 Type a name for your home and click ⏷ to select a purchase date.

-10 Type your estimated purchase price.

-11 Click **Next**.

-12 Click **This house is or will be my primary residence** (☐ changes to ☑).

-13 Click **I do not plan to sell this asset**.

-14 Click **Done**.

■ Quicken updates the Planned Asset window.

-15 Click **Next**.

When Quicken updates the Planned Asset window, what do I see?

You see a summary of the information you provided when you set up
the planned asset.

Planned Asset	Edit
Description:	New House
Purchase date:	4/2006 (Mary is 35)
Purchase price:	130,000.00
Anticipated growth rate:	3.0%
Primary residence:	Yes
Sale information:	NA

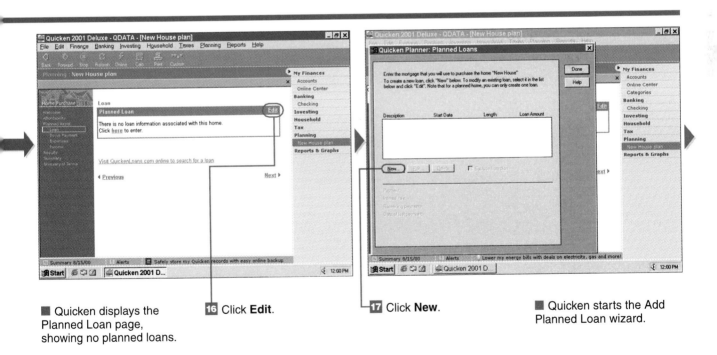

■ Quicken displays the
Planned Loan page,
showing no planned loans.

16 Click **Edit**.

17 Click **New**.

■ Quicken starts the Add
Planned Loan wizard.

CONTINUED

After you set up a planned asset for the home you want to buy, you use the Home Purchase Planner to set up a planned loan to pay for the house.

A planned loan is not a real liability and does not affect the data in your Quicken accounts or your net worth.

USING THE HOME PURCHASE PLANNER (CONTINUED)

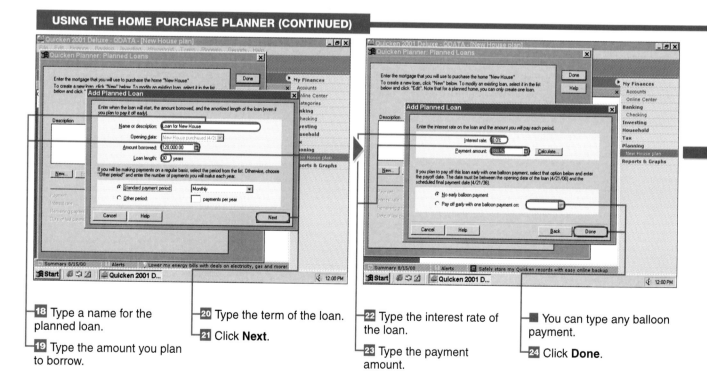

18 Type a name for the planned loan.

19 Type the amount you plan to borrow.

20 Type the term of the loan.

21 Click **Next**.

22 Type the interest rate of the loan.

23 Type the payment amount.

■ You can type any balloon payment.

24 Click **Done**.

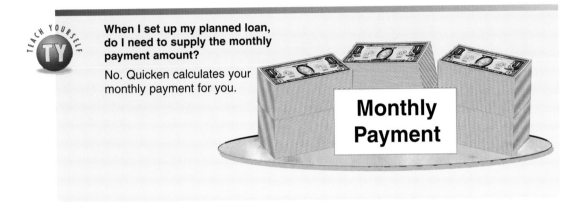

When I set up my planned loan,
do I need to supply the monthly
payment amount?

No. Quicken calculates your
monthly payment for you.

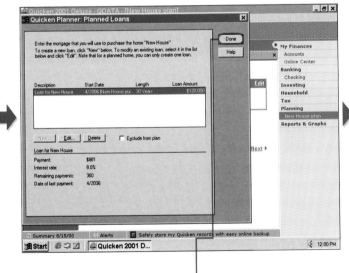

■ Quicken updates the
Planned Loans window.

25 Click **Done** to finish
setting up the planned loan.

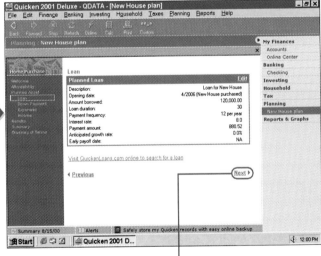

■ Quicken updates the Loan
window.

26 Click **Next**.

CONTINUED

USING THE HOME PURCHASE PLANNER

The Home Purchase Planner helps you determine how much you need to save for the down payment on your dream house. And, you identify any expenses you might incur that are associated with the house.

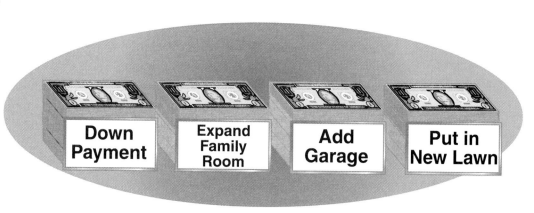

Down Payment

Expand Family Room

Add Garage

Put in New Lawn

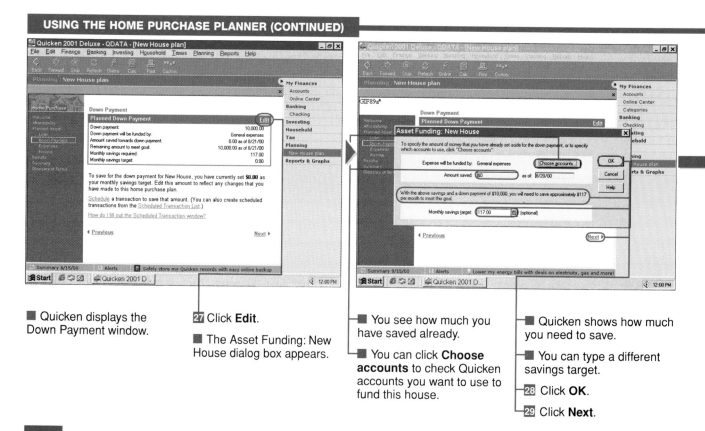

■ Quicken displays the Down Payment window.

27 Click **Edit**.

■ The Asset Funding: New House dialog box appears.

■ You see how much you have saved already.

■ You can click **Choose accounts** to check Quicken accounts you want to use to fund this house.

■ Quicken shows how much you need to save.

■ You can type a different savings target.

28 Click **OK**.

29 Click **Next**.

I am planning to remodel the home after I buy it. How do I plan for the remodeling expense?

Set up a planned expense. In the Asset Expenses box, click **New** to start a wizard. Quicken prompts you to name the expense. When you click **Next**, Quicken asks you to describe the expense. When you click **Next**, Quicken asks you how you want to fund the expense and displays windows similar to the ones you complete when you describe how you will save for your down payment.

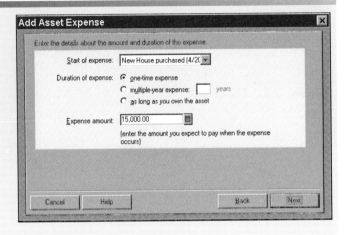

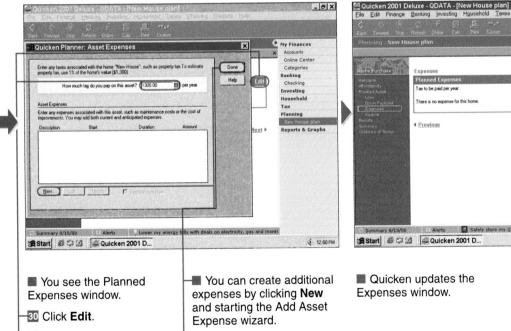

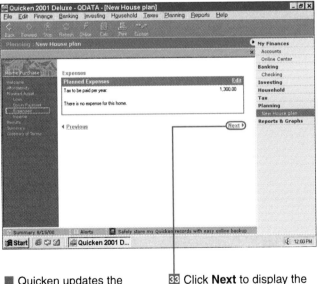

■ You see the Planned Expenses window.

30 Click **Edit**.

31 Type the estimated property taxes.

■ You can create additional expenses by clicking **New** and starting the Add Asset Expense wizard.

32 Click **Done**.

■ Quicken updates the Expenses window.

33 Click **Next** to display the Planned Income window.

CONTINUED

USING THE HOME PURCHASE PLANNER

When you complete the Home Purchase Planner, you see whether you can afford the house and how paying for it impacts your overall financial situation.

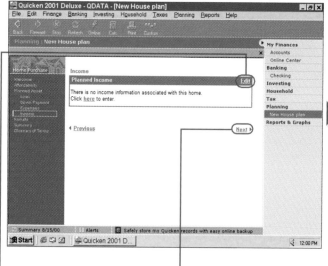

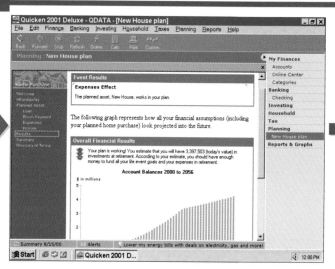

■ If you plan to rent this home to someone, you can click **Edit** to supply the income information.

34 Click **Next**.

■ Quicken updates the Overall Financial Results graph to include your planned home purchase.

What kind of information will I need to supply if I expect to generate income from the new house?

When you click **New** in the Other Income window, Quicken displays this dialog box, where you describe the expected income.

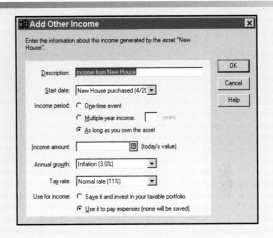

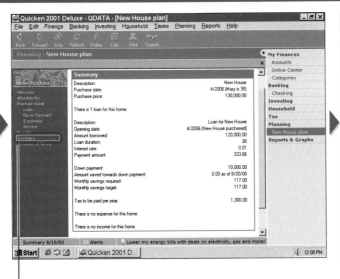

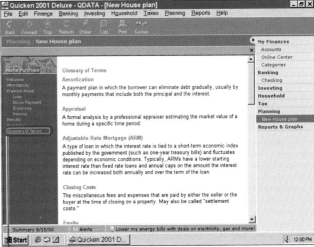

35 Click **Summary**.

■ Quicken displays a summary of your planned asset.

■ You can click **Glossary of Terms** to display a glossary of terms associated with home-buying.

USING THE SPECIAL PURCHASE PLANNER

Special events occur in life — a new car, a wedding, a bar mitzvah, a Sweet Sixteen, or that "vacation of a lifetime." You can use the Special Purchase Planner to finance them and see how they fit into your overall life plan.

To use the Special Purchase Planner, Quicken asks assumption questions and makes estimates based on your answers. Complete the Section "Set Up Planning Assumptions" to save time creating your plan.

USING THE SPECIAL PURCHASE PLANNER

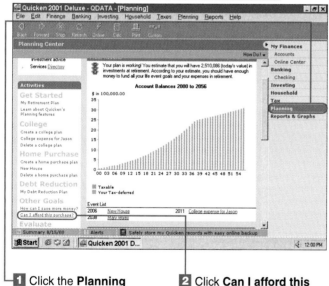

1 Click the **Planning** QuickTab.

2 Click **Can I afford this purchase?**

■ Quicken displays the first window of the Special Purchase Planner.

3 To describe the special purchase, click the **Enter** link.

■ Quicken starts the Add Special Expense wizard.

Does Quicken require that special purchases be associated with a particular person?

No. You can assign the expense to a particular person or to no person.

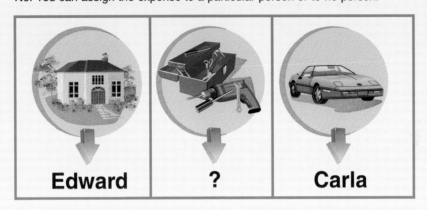

Edward   ?   Carla

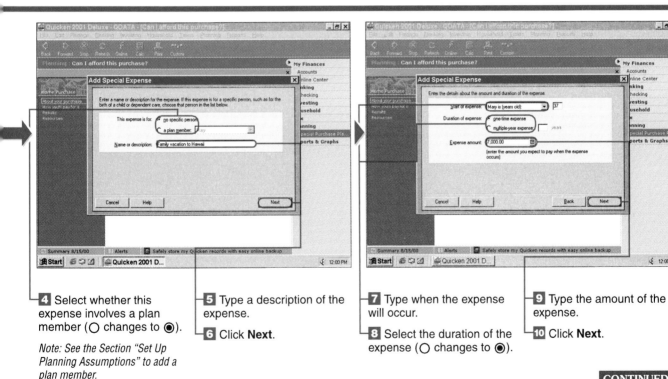

4 Select whether this expense involves a plan member (○ changes to ◉).

Note: See the Section "Set Up Planning Assumptions" to add a plan member.

5 Type a description of the expense.

6 Click **Next**.

7 Type when the expense will occur.

8 Select the duration of the expense (○ changes to ◉).

9 Type the amount of the expense.

10 Click **Next**.

CONTINUED

Loans are not the only way to finance an "unusual purchase." You can determine how to fund your purchase in the Special Purchase Planner.

Finance your next vacation?

USING THE SPECIAL PURCHASE PLANNER (CONTINUED)

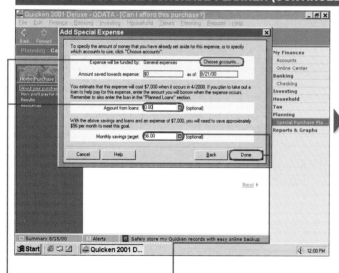

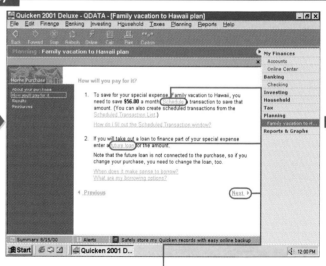

11 Click **Choose accounts** and check Quicken accounts to identify a method to pay for the expense.

■ You can type a loan amount.

■ You can type a monthly savings target.

12 Click **Done**.

■ You see the Special Purchase Planner window.

13 Click **Next**.

■ Quicken displays the **How will you pay for it?** window.

14 Select how you will pay for your purchase.

■ To set up a scheduled transaction to save for the purchase, click the **Schedule** link.

■ To set up a loan to finance the purchase, click the **future loan** link.

15 Click **Next**.

What happens if I decide to set up a scheduled payment or a loan?

If you click the link to set up a Scheduled Transaction, Quicken displays the Edit Scheduled Transaction window for you to complete. For help completing this window, see "Schedule Transactions" in Chapter 4. If you decide to set up a loan, Quicken displays the Add Planned Loans wizard. For help completing this wizard, see the Section "Using the Home Purchase Planner."

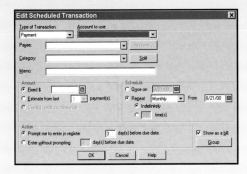

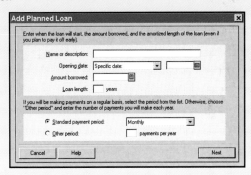

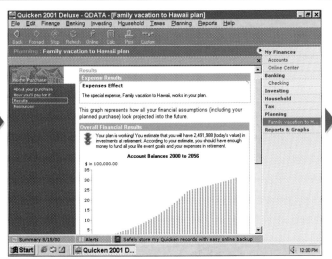

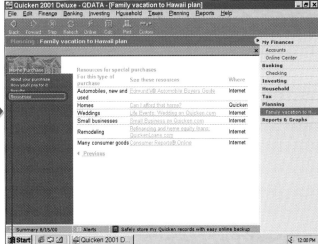

■ Quicken displays the Results window.

Note: At the top of the window, you can view Quicken's assessment of your special purchase's effect on your overall plan.

■ Quicken updates the Overall Financial Results graph to include your special purchase.

16 Click **Resources**.

■ Quicken displays a list of Web links that provide information on financing a variety of special purchases.

USING THE SAVE MORE PLANNER

Are you saving as much as you want? The Save More Planner helps you figure out how to increase the amount you save.

The Save More Planner considers your paycheck as it calculates the amount you can save. You need to complete "Set Up Your Paycheck" in Chapter 8 before you start the Save More Planner.

USING THE SAVE MORE PLANNER

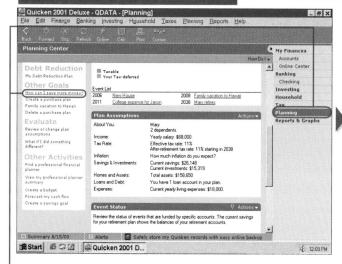

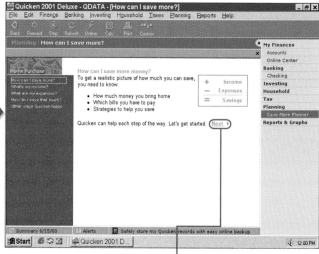

1 Click the **Planning** QuickTab.

2 Click the **How can I save more money?** link.

■ Quicken starts the Save More Planner.

■ Quicken displays an explanation of how it calculates the amount you can potentially save.

3 Click **Next**.

How do I know whether to base Quicken's analysis on my gross or net income?

Your choice determines how you tell Quicken to handle paycheck deductions when you calculate your expenses. If you are not comfortable with the way you recorded deductions — or if you want to calculate expenses starting with what you bring home — click **Net**. If you are confident that you entered paycheck deductions correctly, choose **Gross**.

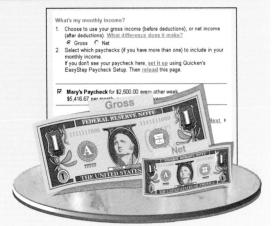

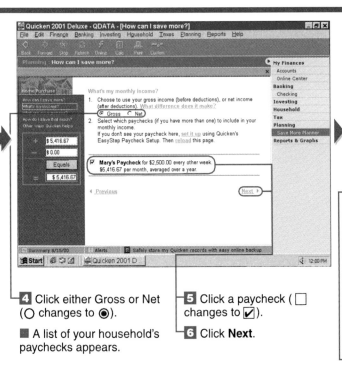

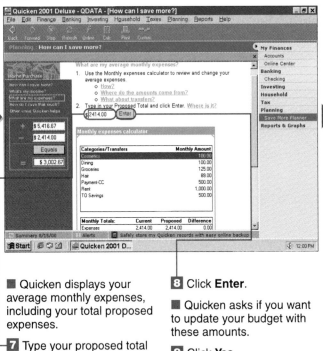

4 Click either Gross or Net (◯ changes to ◉).

■ A list of your household's paychecks appears.

5 Click a paycheck (☐ changes to ☑).

6 Click **Next**.

■ Quicken displays your average monthly expenses, including your total proposed expenses.

7 Type your proposed total expenses.

8 Click **Enter**.

■ Quicken asks if you want to update your budget with these amounts.

9 Click **Yes**.

CONTINUED

After helping you determine how much you can save, the Save More Planner identifies methods to help you save.

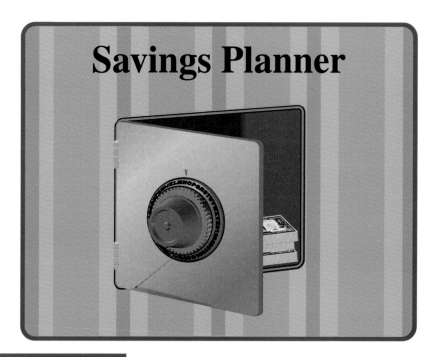

Savings Planner

USING THE SAVE MORE PLANNER (CONTINUED)

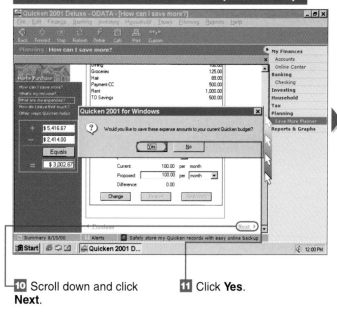

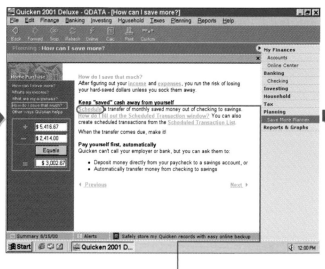

10 Scroll down and click **Next**.

■ Quicken again asks if you want to update your budget.

11 Click **Yes**.

■ Quicken displays a window, describing techniques you can use to save — such as setting up a scheduled transaction to save.

12 Click the **Schedule** link.

I do not see any expenses on the What Are My Expenses page. Why not, and what should I do?

Quicken displays last year's actual spending or budget amounts for expenses on this page. If you just started using Quicken and you have not set up a budget, you will not see any figures. You can set up a budget, or you can simply type figures on the What Are My Expenses page.

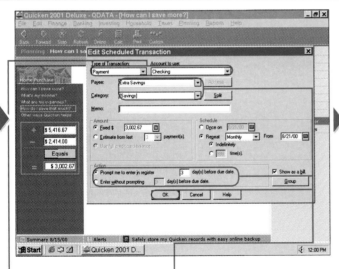

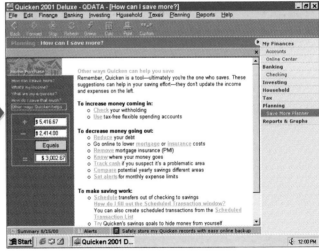

■ You see the Edit Scheduled Transaction box.

13 Click ⦁ and select Payment for the transaction type and the account from which you want to transfer the saved amount.

14 Type a payee name and an account in which to place the money.

15 Click a frequency to save (○ changes to ◉).

16 Click **OK**.

17 When Quicken redisplays the Save More Planner window, click **Next** to see this window, which describes other ways Quicken can help you save.

265

SET SAVINGS GOALS

You can use savings goal accounts to "hide" your savings, which remains in your real bank account. Your Quicken bank account decreases (and your savings goal account increases) as you near your goal.

~Savings Goals

Savings goal transactions do not affect account reconciliation. To determine how much you have available to save, see the Section "Using the Save More Planner."

SET SAVINGS GOALS

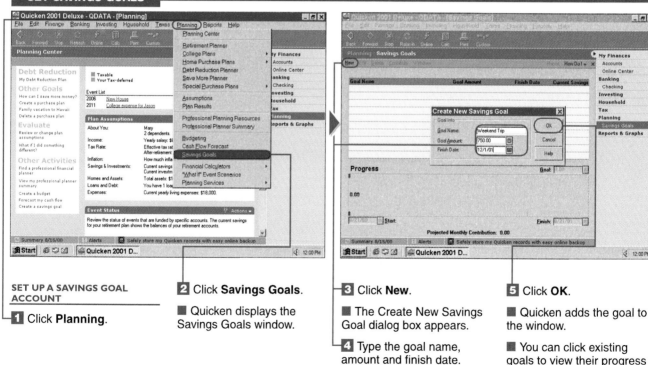

SET UP A SAVINGS GOAL ACCOUNT

1 Click **Planning**.

2 Click **Savings Goals**.

■ Quicken displays the Savings Goals window.

3 Click **New**.

■ The Create New Savings Goal dialog box appears.

4 Type the goal name, amount and finish date.

5 Click **OK**.

■ Quicken adds the goal to the window.

■ You can click existing goals to view their progress bars.

What if I need to spend some of the money hidden in my savings goal account?

You can create a "withdrawal" transaction from your savings goal account that puts money back into the account you used to hide the funds:

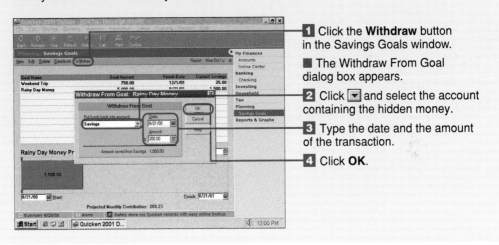

1 Click the **Withdraw** button in the Savings Goals window.

■ The Withdraw From Goal dialog box appears.

2 Click ▼ and select the account containing the hidden money.

3 Type the date and the amount of the transaction.

4 Click **OK**.

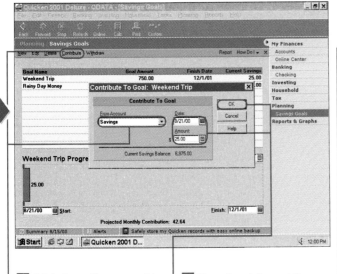

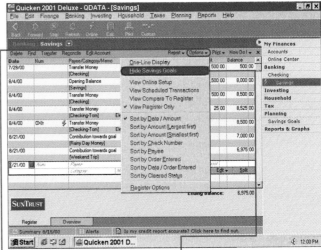

6 Click **Contribute** to add money to the savings goal account.

7 Click ▼ to select the account containing the money you want to hide.

8 Type the date and the amount.

9 Click **OK**.

■ Quicken updates the savings goal account.

VIEW YOUR "REAL" BALANCE

1 Click the register of the account in which you are hiding money.

2 Click **Options**.

3 Click **Hide Savings Goals**.

■ Quicken hides savings goal transactions and adjusts the account balance accordingly.

CREATE A CASH FLOW FORECAST

A cash flow forecast projects the balances of your accounts based on scheduled transactions and estimated average amounts. You can forecast based on actual register information or on budget amounts. The cash flow forecast does not affect any of your accounts, so you can add "what if" income and expense transactions to estimate their effect.

CREATE A CASH FLOW FORECAST

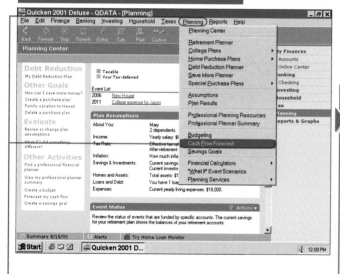

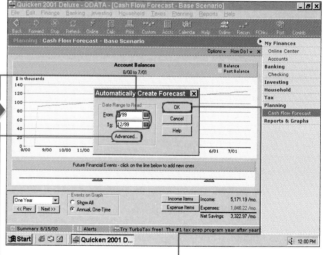

1 Click **Planning**.

2 Click **Cash Flow Forecast**.

■ Quicken displays the Automatically Create Forecast window and asks for a date range to forecast.

3 Type a date range to forecast.

■ You can click **Advanced** to customize the forecast.

4 Click **OK**.

**What happens when I click the
Advanced button while setting up
the forecast?**

You see a window where you can
select the types of items to create
(scheduled transactions, estimated
items, or both) and specify
whether to create the forecast
from register or budget data. Click
Done when you finish.

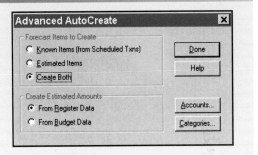

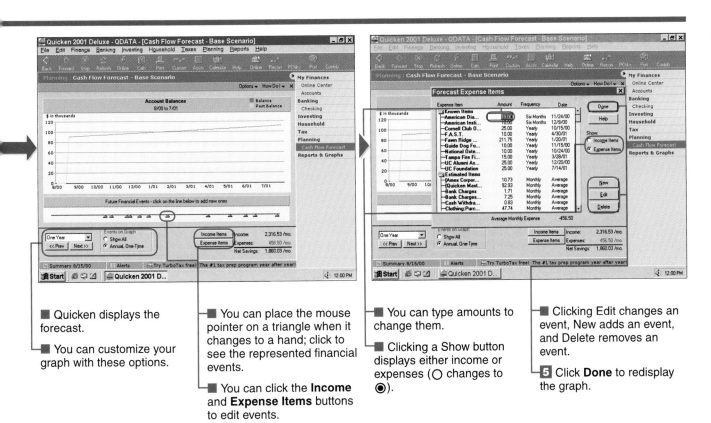

■ Quicken displays the
forecast.

■ You can customize your
graph with these options.

■ You can place the mouse
pointer on a triangle when it
changes to a hand; click to
see the represented financial
events.

■ You can click the **Income**
and **Expense Items** buttons
to edit events.

■ You can type amounts to
change them.

■ Clicking a Show button
displays either income or
expenses (○ changes to
◉).

■ Clicking Edit changes an
event, New adds an event,
and Delete removes an
event.

5 Click **Done** to redisplay
the graph.

You can create "What If" scenarios to see the effects of changes to your plan. Maybe, as you were planning, Quicken reported that your plan would not work. Or, maybe you simply want to know what would happen if you did something differently.

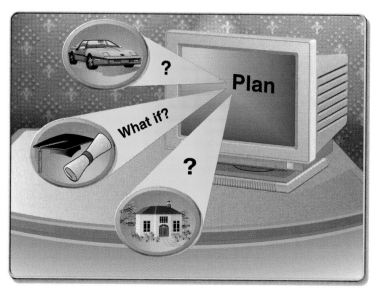

Although this example illustrates a change to a plan assumption, the steps in this section can be applied to plan goals. To create a "What-If" scenario, you must first complete the Section "Set Up Planning Assumptions."

GENERATE "WHAT IF" SCENARIOS

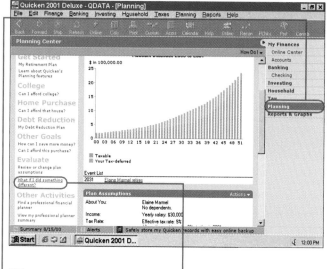

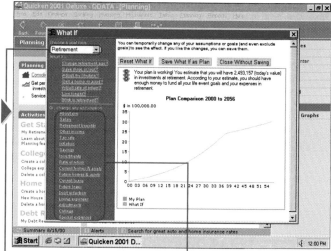

1 Click the **Planning** QuickTab.

2 Click the **What if I did something different?** link.

■ Quicken displays the What If window.

■ You can click 🔽 to change a goal.

Note: These "What if I" links and assumptions depend on the goal you choose.

3 Click a link.

Note: When you click any link in either of these sections, Quicken displays the corresponding window.

■ Quicken displays the appropriate window.

Can I create more than one "What If" scenario simultaneously?

Each time you click a link and make a change, Quicken updates your plan in the What If window. The changes become "cumulative" if you do not reset the window after each change you make. So, you can make several changes to your plan. If you prefer to see the individual effect of each change, reset the What If window after making a change by clicking **Reset What If**.

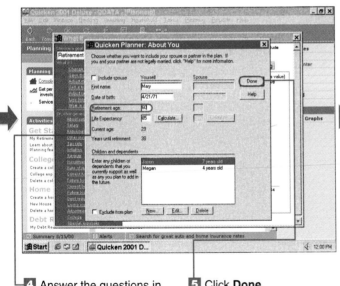

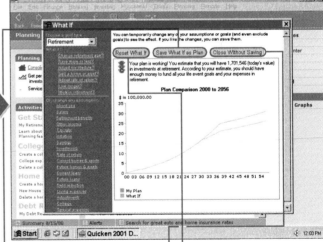

4 Answer the questions in the window.

■ This example changes the retirement age.

5 Click **Done**.

■ Quicken redisplays the What If window.

■ The line graph compares your original plan to the "What If" scenario.

■ To save your changes, click **Save What If as Plan**.

■ To try something else, click **Reset What If** and repeat Steps 3 through 5.

■ To ignore the effects of the "What If" scenario on your plan, click **Close Without Saving**.

USING THE LOAN CALCULATOR

You can use the Loan Calculator tool to calculate either a loan amount or a loan payment for a loan of one year or more.

Remember that the Loan Calculator does not integrate any plan information or assumptions.

USING THE LOAN CALCULATOR

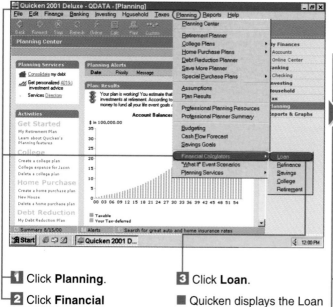

1 Click **Planning**.

2 Click **Financial Calculators**.

3 Click **Loan**.

■ Quicken displays the Loan Calculator.

4 Click a Calculate For option (○ changes to ●).

■ The available boxes for loan information change to reflect your choice.

5 Type in the Loan Information boxes.

■ When you have typed enough information, Quicken calculates the option you chose in Step 4.

■ You can click **Schedule** to see the breakdown of principal and interest on each payment.

Thinking of refinancing your mortgage solely on lower interest rates? You need to consider closing costs, upfront fees, and other expenses. Use the Refinance Calculator to determine how long it will take you to recover the refinancing costs.

Remember that the Refinance Calculator does not integrate any plan information or assumptions.

USING THE REFINANCE CALCULATOR

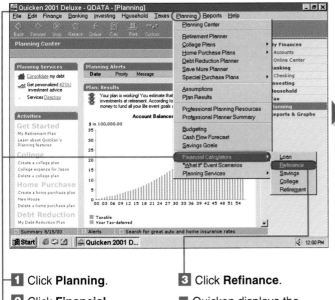

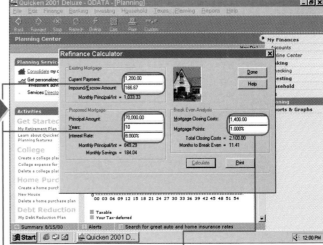

1 Click **Planning**.

2 Click **Financial Calculators**.

3 Click **Refinance**.

■ Quicken displays the Refinance Calculator.

4 Type your current payment, including escrow and the amount of your escrow and other fees.

5 Type the loan amount, the loan duration, and the interest rate.

6 Type the closing costs and points.

■ Quicken calculates your existing and new mortgage payments, closing costs, and breakeven months.

You can calculate how much you need to start or how much you need to contribute regularly to achieve an ending balance. You can also calculate how much you will have if you make a regular contribution for a specified time period.

Remember that the Savings Calculator does not integrate any plan information or assumptions.

USING THE SAVINGS CALCULATOR

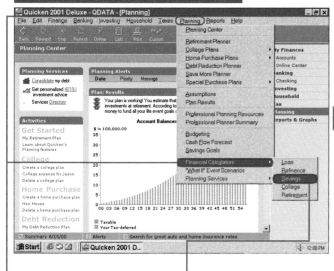

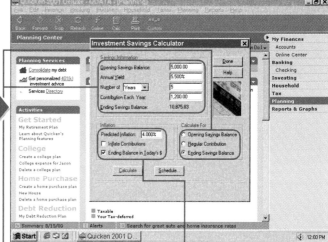

1 Click **Planning**.

2 Click **Financial Calculators**.

3 Click **Savings**.

■ Quicken displays the Investment Savings Calculator.

4 Click a Calculate For option (○ changes to ◉).

5 Type information in the Savings Information boxes.

■ You can update the inflation information in the Inflation box.

■ When you have typed enough information, Quicken calculates the option you chose in Step 4.

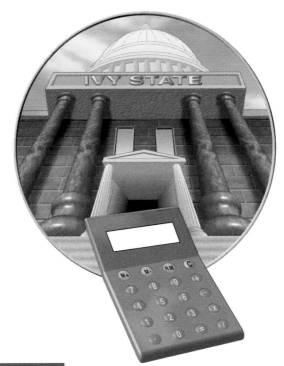

You can use the College Calculator to calculate how much you will have if you save a regular amount for a specified period. You can also calculate how much you should have now to afford a predetermined expense amount. Or, you can calculate how much you need to save to meet an expected college expense.

Remember that the College Calculator does not integrate any plan information or assumptions.

USING THE COLLEGE CALCULATOR

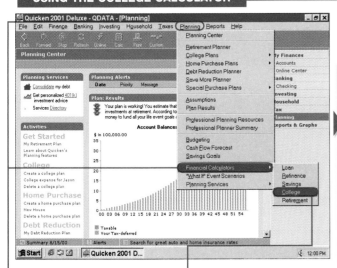

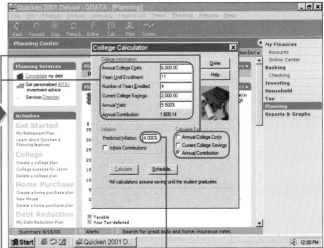

1 Click **Planning**.

2 Click **Financial Calculators**.

3 Click **College**.

■ Quicken displays the College Calculator.

4 Click a Calculate For option (○ changes to ◉).

5 Type information in the College Information boxes.

■ You can update the inflation information in the Inflation box.

■ When you have typed enough information, Quicken calculates the option you chose in Step 4.

CREATE PLANNING REPORTS

You can create a variety of reports and graphs to help you plan for life events from the Reports & Graphs Center. The steps you use to create each report are the same; the report you see when you finish depends on the report you select when you start.

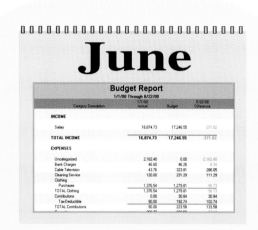

To determine which Planning Report or graph best meets your needs, see the Section, "View Planning Reports."

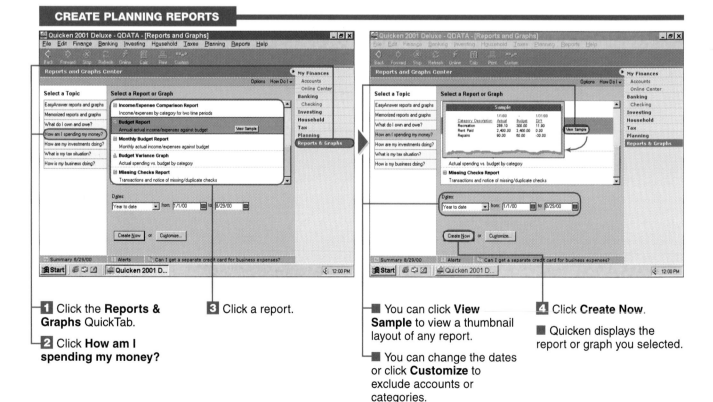

1 Click the **Reports & Graphs** QuickTab.

2 Click **How am I spending my money?**

3 Click a report.

■ You can click **View Sample** to view a thumbnail layout of any report.

■ You can change the dates or click **Customize** to exclude accounts or categories.

4 Click **Create Now**.

■ Quicken displays the report or graph you selected.

VIEW PLANNING REPORTS

Quicken allows you to view different
Investment graphs. To generate a report, *see*
the Section "Create Investment Reports".

TYPES OF REPORTS AND GRAPHS

BUDGET REPORT

You can use this report to compare the actual income and
expenses you record in each category against the amounts
you budgeted for the same category. By default, the report
shows year-to-date amounts and is organized by category
group and then broken down by category.

Budget Report
1/1/00 Through 8/22/00

Category Description	1/1/00 Actual	Budget	8/22/00 Difference
INCOME			
Salary	16,874.73	17,246.55	-371.82
TOTAL INCOME	**16,874.73**	**17,246.55**	**-371.82**
EXPENSES			
Uncategorized	2,162.40	0.00	-2,162.40
Bank Charges	46.60	46.26	-0.34
Cable Television	43.76	323.81	280.05
Cleaning Service	120.00	231.29	111.29
Clothing			
Purchases	1,376.54	1,279.81	-96.73
TOTAL Clothing	1,376.54	1,279.81	-96.73
Contributions	0.00	30.84	30.84
Tax-Deductible	90.00	192.74	102.74
TOTAL Contributions	90.00	223.58	133.58

MONTHLY BUDGET REPORT

You can use the Monthly Budget Report to make budget
comparisons on a month-by-month basis. The report is
organized, by default, by category group, and then broken
down by category.

Monthly Budget Report
1/1/00 Through 8/22/00

Category Description	1/1/00 Actual	Budget	1/31/00 Difference	2/1/00 Actual
INFLOWS				
Uncategorized	0.00	0.00	0.00	0.00
Salary	2,500.00	2,237.00	263.00	2,500.00
TOTAL INFLOWS	**2,500.00**	**2,237.00**	**263.00**	**2,500.00**
OUTFLOWS				
Uncategorized	0.00	0.00	0.00	0.00
Bank Charges	39.00	6.00	-33.00	0.00
Cable Television	0.00	42.00	42.00	0.00
Cleaning Service	0.00	30.00	30.00	0.00
Clothing				
Purchases	514.91	166.00	-348.91	74.00
TOTAL Clothing	514.91	166.00	-348.91	74.00
Contributions	0.00	4.00	4.00	0.00

BUDGET VARIANCE GRAPH

The Budget Variance Graph shows you the
difference between actual and budgeted
amounts. You can view how well you held to
your budget in the top graph. The bottom
graph shows you a comparison of budgeted
versus actual amounts by category group.

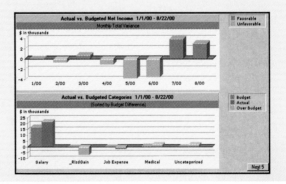

CHAPTER 10

Protect Your Information

Do you want to protect the information you have so painstakingly recorded in Quicken? In this chapter, you learn how to set passwords and back up your data.

USING AN EFFECTIVE BACKUP STRATEGY

Backing up your data can be one of the most timesaving things you do.

WHAT IS A BACKUP?

When you *back up* your data, you effectively make a copy of it. Storing the backup somewhere other than your hard drive is important because hard drives can fail. Having both your original data and your backup on your hard drive does not help you if the hard drive fails.

HOW OFTEN SHOULD YOU BACKUP?

The answer to this question relates directly to the amount of work you are willing to repeat. If you back up every Monday and discover a problem on Friday, you will have to restore your Monday backup and re-enter all information from the week. If this is acceptable to you, you can back up once each week. To avoid extra work, consider backing up each day that you use Quicken or after you reconcile an account.

HOW QUICKEN'S BACKUP WORKS

Quicken's backup program assigns your Quicken data file's name to the backup file and automatically creates five additional backups named with your data file name followed by the numbers 1 through 5. If your data file is named Elaine, and you back up Monday through Saturday, Quicken names your backup files Elaine, Elaine1, Elaine2, and so on, with Elaine5 being the latest version of your data. If you back up on Sunday, Quicken writes over the first backup file and Elaine becomes your latest backup.

BACKUP WITH DISKETTES

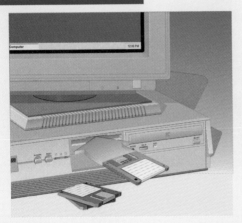

You can use 3½-inch diskettes to back up daily. Use a different diskette each day, and label each disk with the day of the week. After a week, reuse the disks. Although Quicken makes copies of your backup files, it might be easier for you to find your latest backup if you use different disks for each day of the week.

BACKUP TO LARGE MEDIA DISKS

You can back up daily with a drive that supports large media, such as a Zip or Jaz drive. When you provide a name for your backup, use the six digits that represent the month, day, and year of the backup.

BACKUP TO TAPE

You can back up your data to a tape drive, but you do not use the Backup command in Quicken; instead, use the software that runs your tape drive. Before you begin to depend on a tape backup, make sure you know how to use your tape drive software to restore your data.

STORE BACKUPS

You should not store backup disks or tapes in the same location as your computers. Consider storing your disks or tapes in a fireproof, waterproof location such as a bank vault. In the event of home or office theft, your backup disks remain safe. Similarly, if your home or office burns down or floods, you avoid destroying your back up files.

BACKUP QUICKEN INFORMATION

You can protect your data by backing it up. If you back up your data regularly, you can quickly recover from a disaster. Taking a few minutes to back up to diskettes is more desirable than starting over.

Note: If your data does not fit on one disk, Quicken enables you to back up to multiple disks.

BACKUP QUICKEN INFORMATION

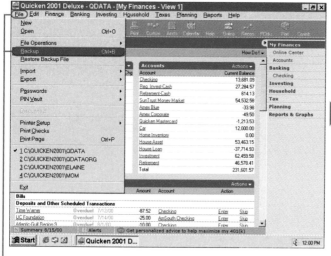

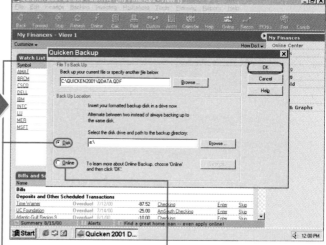

BACKUP ON ONE DISK

1 Click **File**.

2 Click **Backup**.

■ Quicken displays the Quicken Backup dialog box.

*Note: You might see an informational dialog box that tells you not to back up each time to the same floppy disk. Check the **Don't show this message again** box; then, click **OK**.*

3 Insert a disk in the floppy drive.

4 Click **Disk** (○ changes to ◉) and type your floppy drive, which is usually Drive A.

5 Click **OK**.

6 After the backup, remove the disk from the drive and store it in a safe place.

■ You can click **Online** to store your backup at Quicken's Web site for a fee.

If I choose to back up to my Zip drive, where do I supply a filename of today's date like you suggest?

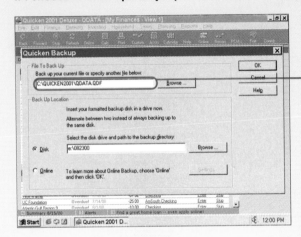

1 Follow Steps 1 through 3 in this section, inserting the disk into your Zip drive.

■ You see the Quicken Backup dialog box.

2 Type the name of the backup, setting the drive letter to your Zip drive letter.

3 Complete Steps 4 through 6 in this section.

■ Quicken creates a folder on the Zip disk with the backup name you supply and stores your backup inside the folder.

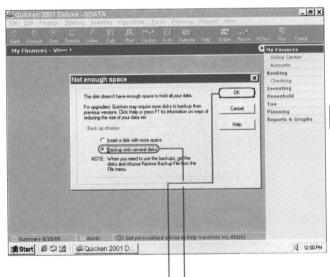

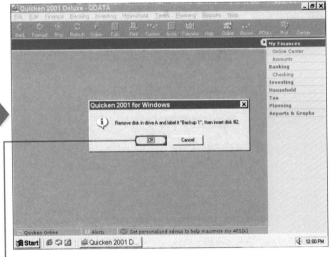

BACKUP ON MULTIPLE DISKS

1 Follow Steps 1 through 5 in the Section "Backup on One Disk."

■ If your file does not fit on one diskette, you see the Not enough space box.

2 Click **Backup onto several disks** (○ changes to ◉).

3 Click **OK**.

■ When Quicken needs another disk, it displays a message.

4 Change disks and click **OK**.

■ Quicken continues the backup.

■ When Quicken finishes, a message says the back up is successful.

5 Click **OK**.

6 Remove the disk from the drive and store all of the disks in a safe place.

283

COPY DATA FILES

You can copy some or all of your data file. Suppose that you want to start a new fiscal year and include only "new year" transactions. Or, you want to "start over," but not completely.
You can copy accounts, scheduled and memorized transactions, transaction groups, and categories to a new file without copying any transactions.

During the copy process, Quicken suggests a name for the new file. If you prefer, you can supply a more meaningful name, such as one that includes the date you made the copy in six digit format; for example, Qdata081200.qdf.

COPY DATA FILES

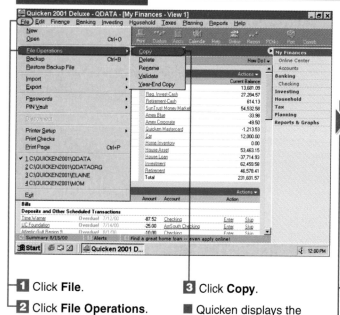

1 Click **File**.

2 Click **File Operations**.

3 Click **Copy**.

■ Quicken displays the Copy File dialog box.

4 Type the name and location of the new Quicken file.

5 Type dates for the transactions you want to include.

■ You can click to exclude uncleared or investment transactions (☑ changes to ☐).

6 Click **OK**.

■ Quicken copies your data file and then allows you to use either the original file or the new copy.

You can validate your data to correct problems if you find Quicken behaving strangely. There is no good definition of *strangely*, but think of it as Quicken behaving in unexpected ways when you take an action. If Quicken finds errors while validating, it tries to rebuild your data — and is often successful.

VALIDATE DATA FILES

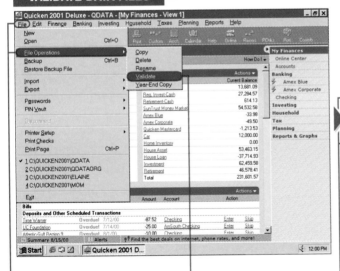

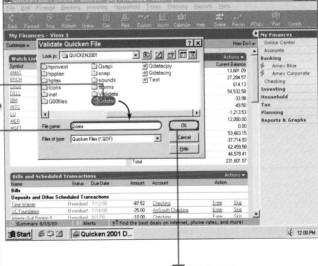

1 Click **File**.

2 Click **File Operations**.

3 Click **Validate**.

■ You see the Validate Quicken File dialog box.

4 Click a file to check.

■ The name appears in the File Name box.

5 Click **OK**.

■ Quicken validates your data file and displays a message when validation finishes.

6 Click **OK**.

RESTORE DATA

You can restore your latest
backup to solve problems,
such as a damaged data
file that you cannot open.

When you restore data, you
replace it on your hard drive
with the copy made during
backup (see the Section,
"Backup Quicken Information"
to learn how to backup data).

RESTORE DATA

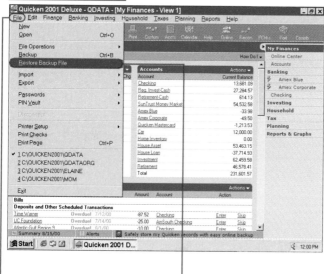

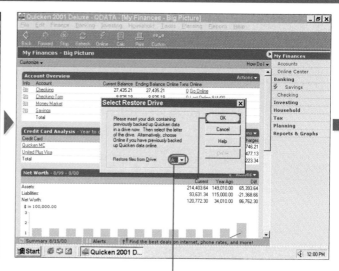

1 Click **File**.

2 Click **Restore Backup File**.

■ Quicken displays the Select Restore Drive dialog box.

3 Insert your backup disk in its drive.

4 Click 🔽 and select the drive that contains your backup disk.

5 Click **OK**.

How do I select a file to restore from my Zip disk?

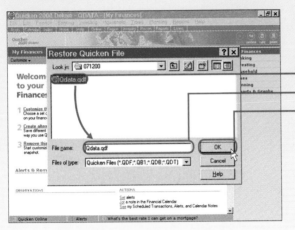

1 Follow Step 1 through 4 in the Section "Restore Data," selecting your Zip drive from the drop-down list in Step 4.

■ You see the Restore Quicken File dialog box.

2 Double-click the folder name you want to restore.

■ The file name appears in the File name box.

3 Click **OK** and complete Steps 8 and 9 in this section.

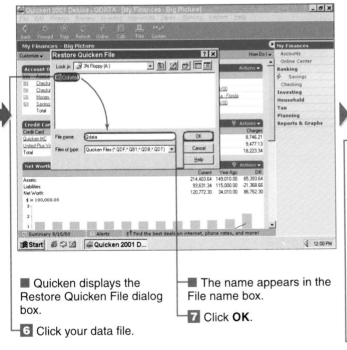

■ Quicken displays the Restore Quicken File dialog box.

6 Click your data file.

■ The name appears in the File name box.

7 Click **OK**.

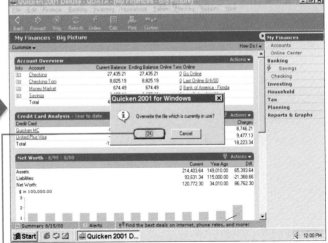

■ If you restore a backup with the same name as your data file, a warning message appears.

8 Click **OK**.

■ A message appears when the process finishes.

9 Click **OK**.

Note: If your backup is comprised of multiple disks, Quicken prompts you when it needs the next disk.

START A NEW YEAR

The more data you enter into Quicken, the slower the program runs. To reduce your data file's size, you can create a year-end copy of your data. Quicken creates a new data file that contains *all* transactions and removes transactions from your old file with a date prior to the current year.

START A NEW YEAR

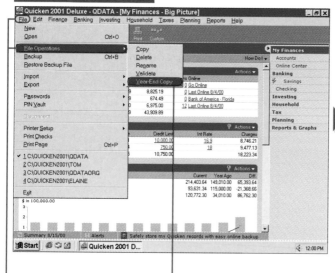

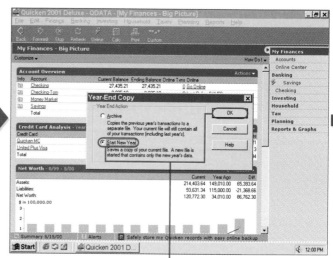

1 Click **File**.

2 Click **File Operations**.

3 Click **Year-End Copy**.

■ Quicken displays the Year-End Copy dialog box.

4 Click **Start New Year** (○ changes to ◉).

5 Click **OK**.

What happens if I choose Archive instead of Start New Year?

When you archive, the archive file only contains last year's transactions. The original file contains both last year's and this year's transactions. Archiving does not reduce the size of your data file.

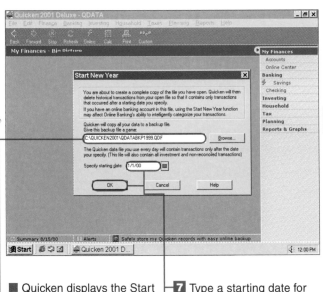

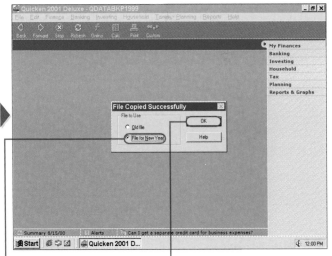

■ Quicken displays the Start New Year dialog box.

6 Type a name and location for the data file that will contain all transactions.

Note: You can name the file with the year of the transactions it will contain.

7 Type a starting date for the transactions in the file you use every day.

8 Click **OK**.

■ Quicken creates the new file and then displays the File Copied Successfully box.

9 Click **File for New Year** (○ changes to ●).

10 Click **OK**.

■ Quicken reopens your old file, which now contains only transactions with dates in the current year.

ASSIGN A FILE PASSWORD

You can protect your Quicken data from prying eyes by assigning a file password. If you assign a file password, Quicken prompts you for it every time you reopen the file. Make your password something you can easily remember but others do not know.

Passwords do not protect your file from being renamed or copied, but the password will still be in effect in the copied or renamed file.

ASSIGN A FILE PASSWORD

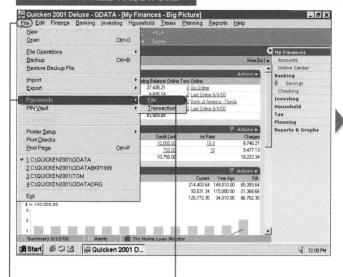

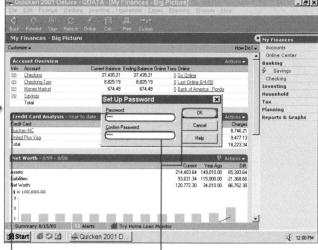

1 Click **File**.

2 Click **Passwords**.

3 Click **File**.

■ Quicken displays the Set Up Password dialog box.

4 Type a password.

■ You can create a password of up to 16 characters, including spaces. Quicken does not distinguish between uppercase and lowercase characters.

5 Type the password again.

6 Click **OK**.

■ The next time you open Quicken, you are prompted for a password.

For another layer of protection, you can assign a transaction password. With this form of security in place, no one can edit transactions dated earlier than a date you specify unless they know the transaction password.

You can assign a file password, a transaction password, or both together.

ASSIGN A TRANSACTION PASSWORD

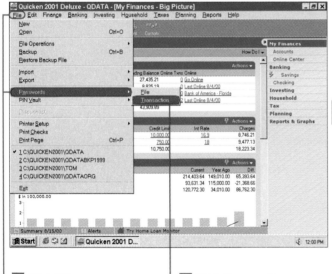

1 Click **File**.

2 Click **Passwords**.

3 Click **Transaction**.

■ Quicken displays the Password to Modify Existing Transactions dialog box.

4 Type a password.

5 Retype the password.

6 Type the last date you want the password to protect.

■ You can click ▥ to select a date.

7 Click **OK**.

■ If you try to edit a transaction dated on or before the specified date, Quicken prompts you for a password.

RENAME A DATA FILE

By default, Quicken assigns your data a name: QDATA. You can change the name of the data file to almost anything you want.

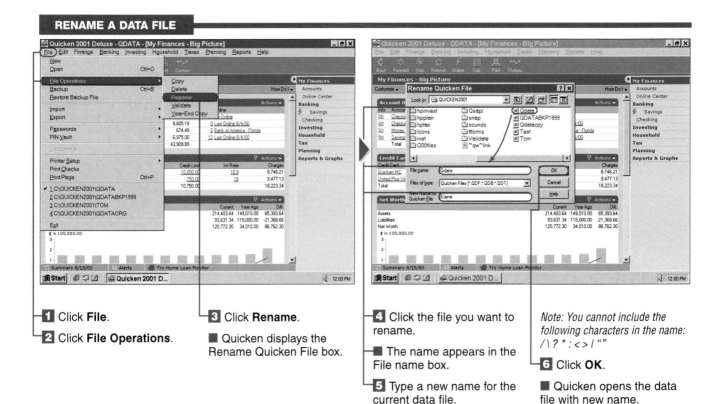

1 Click **File**.

2 Click **File Operations**.

3 Click **Rename**.

■ Quicken displays the Rename Quicken File box.

4 Click the file you want to rename.

■ The name appears in the File name box.

5 Type a new name for the current data file.

Note: You cannot include the following characters in the name:
*/ \ ? * : < > | " "*

6 Click **OK**.

■ Quicken opens the data file with new name.

As you use Quicken,
you might create data
files that you no
longer use. You can
delete them to keep
your hard drive
clean.

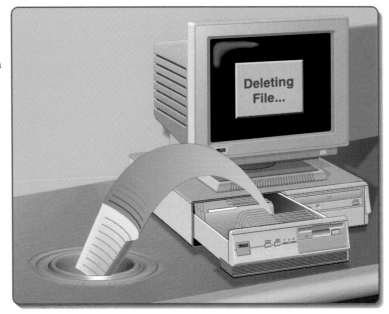

Note: You cannot
retrieve a deleted file.
To restore a deleted file
from your back up files,
see the Section
"Restore Data."

DELETE A DATA FILE

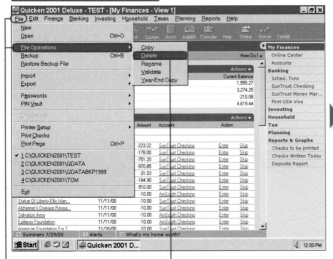

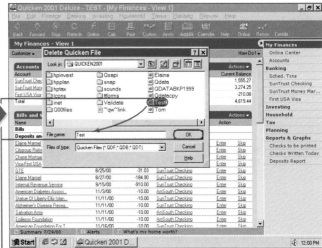

1 Click **File**.

2 Click **File Operations**.

3 Click **Delete**.

■ Quicken displays the
Delete Quicken File box.

4 Click a file to delete.

■ The name appears in the
File Name box.

5 Click **OK**.

6 When Quicken displays
the Quicken 2001 for
Windows box, type **yes** to
confirm your deletion and
click **OK**.

*Note: Case does not matter when
you type **yes**.*

■ Quicken deletes the file.

*Note: If you deleted the currently
open file, you must open another
Quicken file. Click **File**. Then click
Open.*

File Edit Finance Banking Investing Household Taxes Planning Reports H

◁ Back   ⊗ Stop   ↻ Refresh   ⚡ Online   ▦ Calc   ▥ Print   Custom

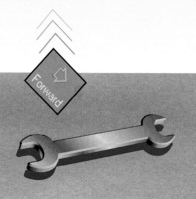
Forward

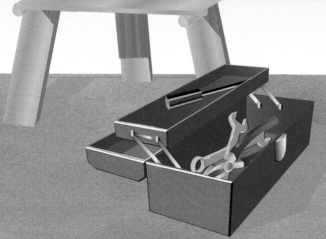

CHAPTER 11

Customize Quicken

Do you want to modify Quicken to match your working style? This chapter helps you customize Quicken to meet your needs.

ENABLE QUICKTAB OPTIONS

You can use options to control the way QuickTabs appear and operate: to choose a Quicken color scheme, to display tips if you pause your mouse pointer on a button, and view the *Action button* in the upper-right corner of the Quicken window. When you click the Action button, you see a list of commands specific to the window you are viewing.

One Step Update

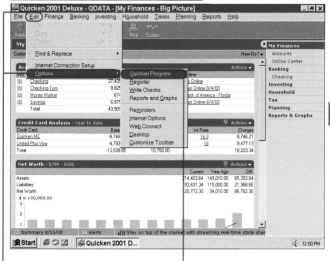

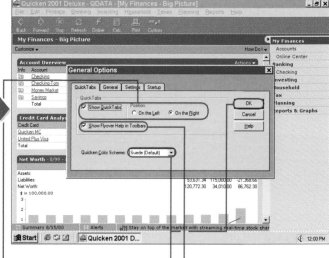

1 Click **Edit**.

2 Click **Options**.

3 Click **Quicken Program**.

■ Quicken displays the QuickTabs tab of the General Options dialog box.

4 Select the options that you want to change (☐ changes to ☑ or ◯ changes to ⦿).

■ You can click to display QuickTabs and place them on the left or right side of the screen.

■ You can click Show Flyover Help in Toolbars to see tips when you point at a button.

■ You can click ▾ and select a color scheme.

5 Click **OK** to save your changes.

Quicken's General Options let you assign categories to tax schedules, remove old memorized transactions, hide advertisements from financial institutions in the Online Financial Services Center, and enable Quicken sounds.

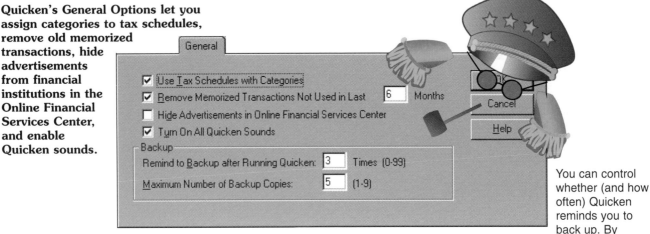

You can control whether (and how often) Quicken reminds you to back up. By default, every seventh time you exit Quicken and backup, Quicken saves a copy to your hard disk and the media you select. You can opt to keep from one to nine backup copies on your hard disk.

ENABLE GENERAL OPTIONS

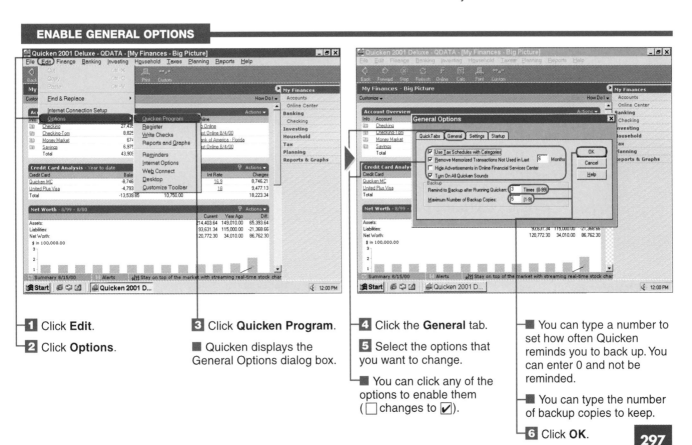

1 Click **Edit**.

2 Click **Options**.

3 Click **Quicken Program**.

■ Quicken displays the General Options dialog box.

4 Click the **General** tab.

5 Select the options that you want to change.

■ You can click any of the options to enable them (☐ changes to ☑).

■ You can type a number to set how often Quicken reminds you to back up. You can enter 0 and not be reminded.

■ You can type the number of backup copies to keep.

6 Click **OK**.

ENABLE CALENDAR AND KEYBOARD SETTINGS

You can use a fiscal or calendar year as you work in Quicken. You can also enable multicurrency support for accounts and investments in foreign currencies. And, you can opt to assign Quicken keyboard shortcuts or standard Windows keyboard shortcuts to Ctrl+X, Ctrl+C, Ctrl+V, and Ctrl+Z.

Ctrl +	Windows	Quicken
X	Cut	Edit, Transaction, Matching Transfer
C	Copy	Finance, Category & Transfer List
V	Undo	Edit, Transaction, Void
Z	Paste	QuickZoom a selected amount on a report

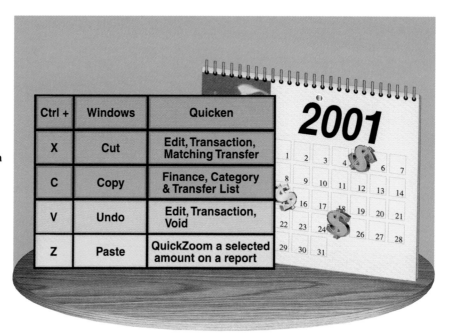

ENABLE CALENDAR AND KEYBOARD SETTINGS

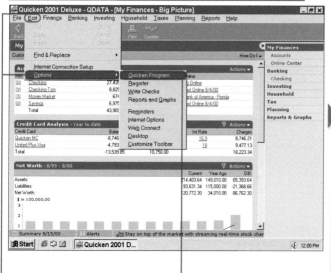

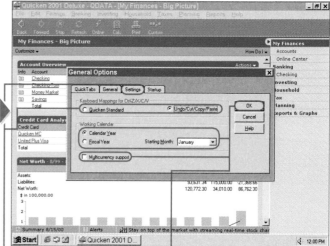

■1 Click **Edit**.

■2 Click **Options**.

■3 Click **Quicken Program**.

■ Quicken displays the General Options dialog box.

■4 Click the **Settings** tab.

■5 Select the options that you want to change (☐ changes to ☑ or ○ changes to ◉).

■ You can click an option for keyboard shortcuts.

■ You can click Calendar Year or Fiscal Year, and select the fiscal year's starting month.

■ You can click **Multicurrency** support.

■6 Click **OK** to save your changes.

You can select the screen
you view when you start
Quicken: the My Finances
page, Reminders, or the
window you were using
when you closed Quicken.

ENABLE STARTUP OPTIONS

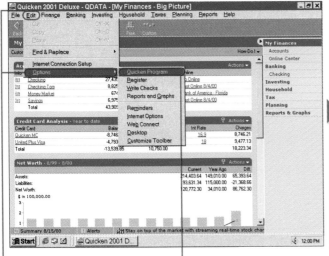

1 Click **Edit**.

2 Click **Options**.

3 Click **Quicken Program**.

■ Quicken displays the
General Options dialog box.

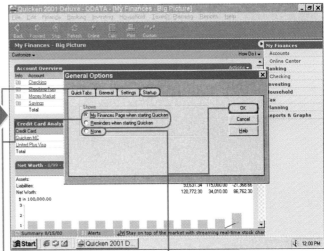

4 Click the **Startup** tab.

5 Click an option to select a
startup window (○ changes
to ⊙).

■ You can opt to see the My
Finances page or the
Quicken Reminders window.

■ If you click None, Quicken
displays, as it opens, the
window you were viewing
when you last closed
Quicken.

6 Click **OK** to save your
changes.

ENABLE REGISTER DISPLAY OPTIONS

In registers, Quicken displays by default the Date field before the number field, and the Category field before the Memo field. You can switch the order of appearance for these fields. You also can control whether buttons appear on fields that use QuickFill. And, you can choose to assign different color shadings to different registers.

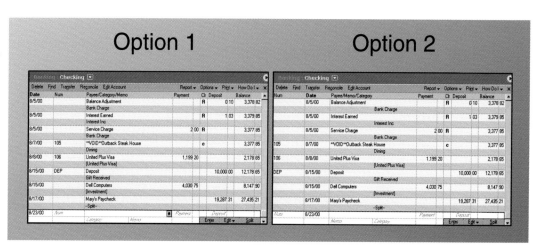

Option 1   Option 2

ENABLE REGISTER DISPLAY OPTIONS

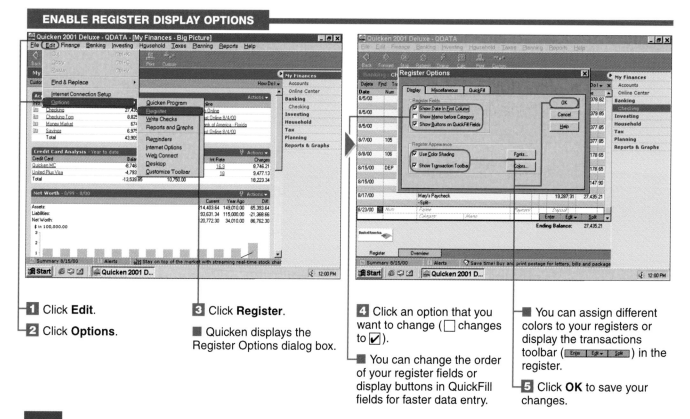

1 Click **Edit**.

2 Click **Options**.

3 Click **Register**.

■ Quicken displays the Register Options dialog box.

4 Click an option that you want to change (☐ changes to ☑).

■ You can change the order of your register fields or display buttons in QuickFill fields for faster data entry.

■ You can assign different colors to your registers or display the transactions toolbar (Enter | Edit ▾ | Split) in the register.

5 Click **OK** to save your changes.

ENABLE MISCELLANEOUS REGISTER OPTIONS

You can opt to display a message when you record transactions outside the current year, save a transaction without assigning a category, or fail to save a transaction before switching to another one.

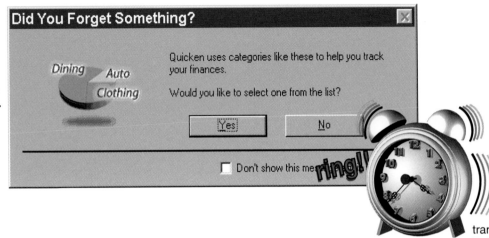

Did You Forget Something?

Quicken uses categories like these to help you track your finances.

Dining Auto Clothing

Would you like to select one from the list?

[Yes]   [No]

☐ Don't show this message again

ring!!

You can also set data entry behavior options. For example, you can display all transactions in both QuickEntry and Quicken Automatically.

ENABLE MISCELLANEOUS REGISTER OPTIONS

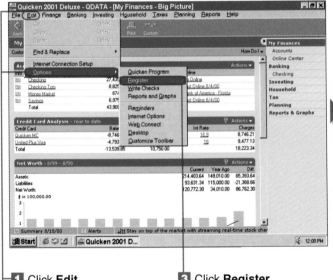

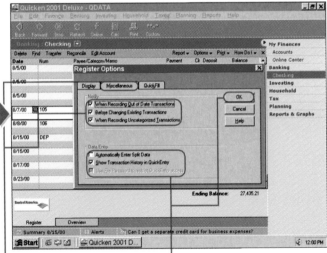

1 Click **Edit**.

2 Click **Options**.

3 Click **Register**.

■ Quicken displays the Register Options dialog box.

4 Click the **Miscellaneous** tab.

5 Click an option that you want to change (☐ changes to ✔).

■ You can opt to see messages when you click the Notify selections.

■ You can opt to record transactions from the Split window, show all transactions in QuickEntry, or enable your file password for both Quicken and QuickenEntry.

6 Click **OK** to save your changes.

301

ENABLE REGISTER QUICKFILL OPTIONS

You can change QuickFill data entry and automatic list updating. For example, by default, you move the insertion point to a new field by pressing Tab. You can change the behavior so that you press the Enter key instead of the Tab key. You also can automatically include names from the Address Book in the QuickFill list.

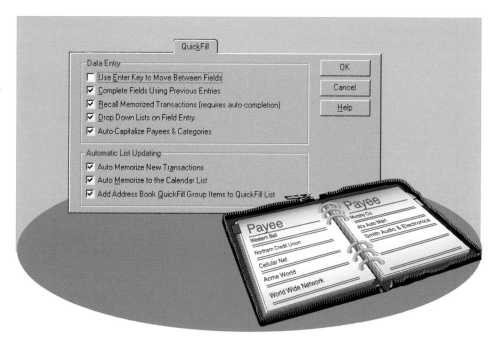

ENABLE REGISTER QUICKFILL OPTIONS

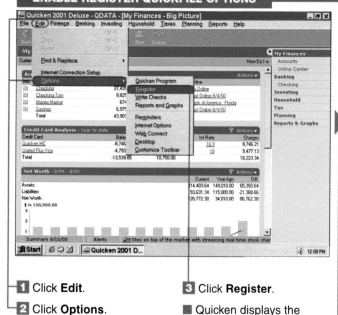

-1 Click **Edit**.

-2 Click **Options**.

3 Click **Register**.

■ Quicken displays the Register Options dialog box.

-4 Click the **QuickFill** tab.

5 Click an option that you want to change (□ changes to ☑).

■ You can change the way QuickFill behaves during data entry.

■ You can memorize new transactions, add memorized transactions to the Financial Calendar, or include Address Book names in the QuickFill list.

-6 Click **OK** to save your changes.

You can control Quicken's behavior when printing checks. Options include: adding a message box on the face of the check that does not appear in a window envelope, printing category information on the check (with splits up to sixteen lines) and storing checks by print date

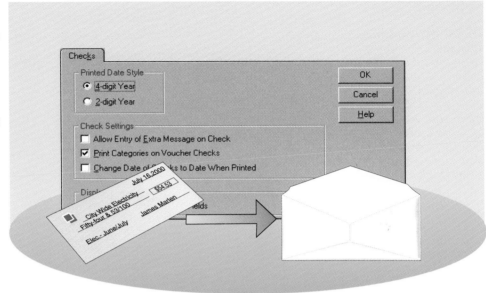

ENABLE CHECK OPTIONS

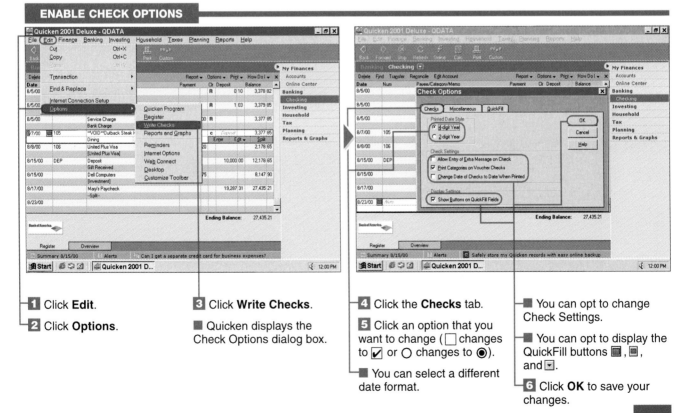

1 Click **Edit**.

2 Click **Options**.

3 Click **Write Checks**.

■ Quicken displays the Check Options dialog box.

4 Click the **Checks** tab.

5 Click an option that you want to change (☐ changes to ☑ or ○ changes to ◉).

■ You can select a different date format.

■ You can opt to change Check Settings.

■ You can opt to display the QuickFill buttons ▦, ▣, and ▾.

6 Click **OK** to save your changes.

ENABLE MISCELLANEOUS CHECK OPTIONS

You can opt to display messages while you work in the Write Checks window. Quicken displays messages when you record transactions outside the current year, try to save a transaction without assigning a category, or reuse an existing check number.

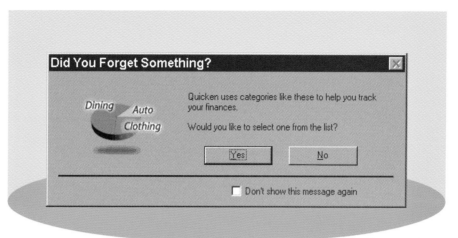

You can also opt to display a message that prompts you to save a transaction you changed before switching to another transaction.

ENABLE MISCELLANEOUS CHECK OPTIONS

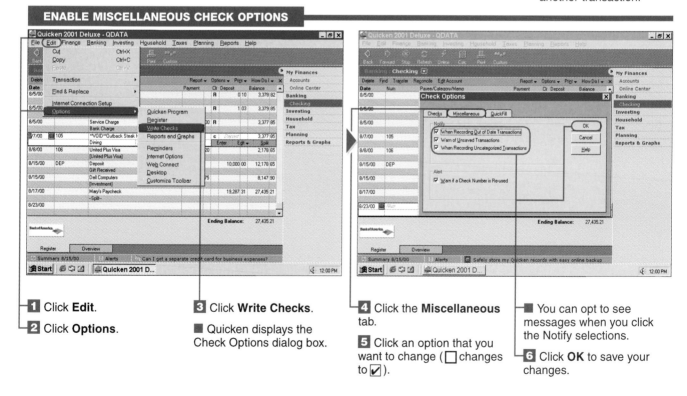

-1 Click **Edit**.

-2 Click **Options**.

3 Click **Write Checks**.

■ Quicken displays the Check Options dialog box.

4 Click the **Miscellaneous** tab.

5 Click an option that you want to change (☐ changes to ☑).

■ You can opt to see messages when you click the Notify selections.

6 Click **OK** to save your changes.

You can control QuickFill
data entry and automatic
list updating. For example,
by default, the insertion
point moves to a new field
when you press Tab. You
can change that behavior
so that you press the
Enter key instead of the
Tab key. You also can
automatically include
names from the Address
Book in the QuickFill list.

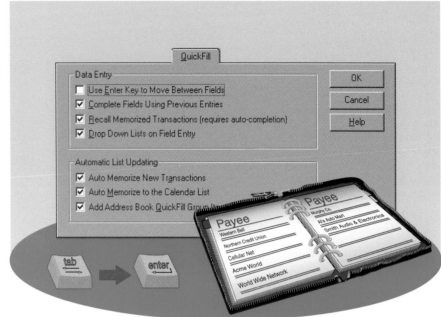

ENABLE CHECK QUICKFILL OPTIONS

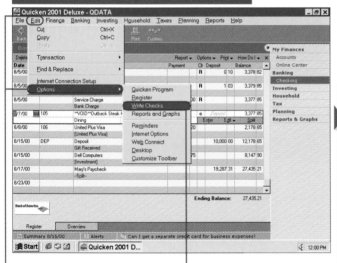

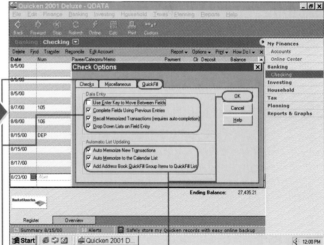

1 Click **Edit**.

2 Click **Options**.

3 Click **Write Checks**.

■ Quicken displays the
Check Options dialog box.

4 Click the **QuickFill** tab.

5 Click an option that you
want to change (☐ changes
to ☑).

■ You can change the way
QuickFill behaves during
data entry.

■ You can memorize new
transactions, add memorized
transactions to the Financial
Calendar, or include Address
Book names in the QuickFill
list.

6 Click **OK** to save your
changes.

ENABLE REPORT AND GRAPH OPTIONS

You can control the behavior of Quicken's reports and graphs. You can set default date ranges and comparison date ranges for reports and graphs. You can select color reports. You can also QuickZoom from a report to an investment form rather than to a transaction in the investment register.

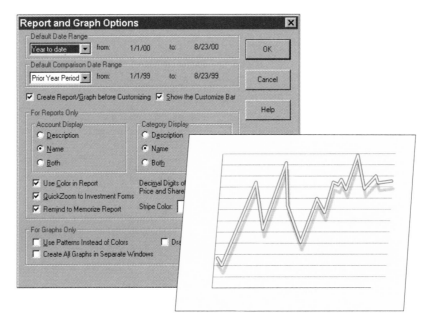

ENABLE REPORT AND GRAPH OPTIONS

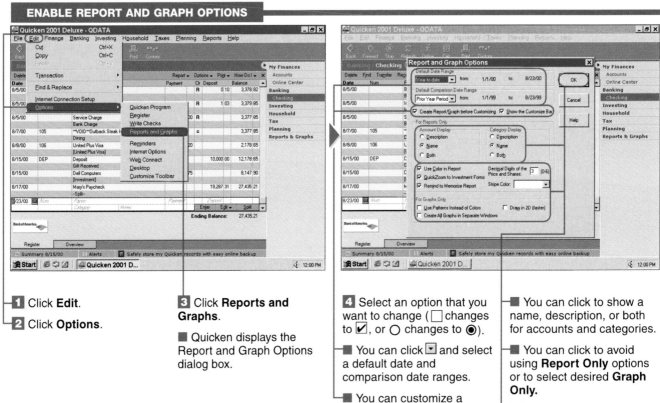

1 Click **Edit**.

2 Click **Options**.

3 Click **Reports and Graphs**.

■ Quicken displays the Report and Graph Options dialog box.

4 Select an option that you want to change (□ changes to ☑, or ○ changes to ◉).

■ You can click ▾ and select a default date and comparison date ranges.

■ You can customize a report before preparing it.

■ You can click to show a name, description, or both for accounts and categories.

■ You can click to avoid using **Report Only** options or to select desired **Graph Only**.

5 Click **OK** to save your changes.

You can specify the bank accounts that you store at Quicken.com, change downloading options, and set miscellaneous downloading behavior options.

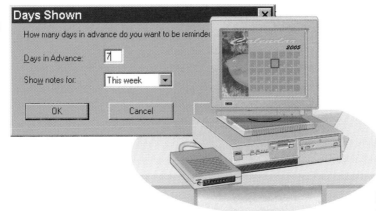

For further information on the Quotes tab or the Investment Accounts tab, see Chapter 7.

ENABLE REMINDER OPTIONS

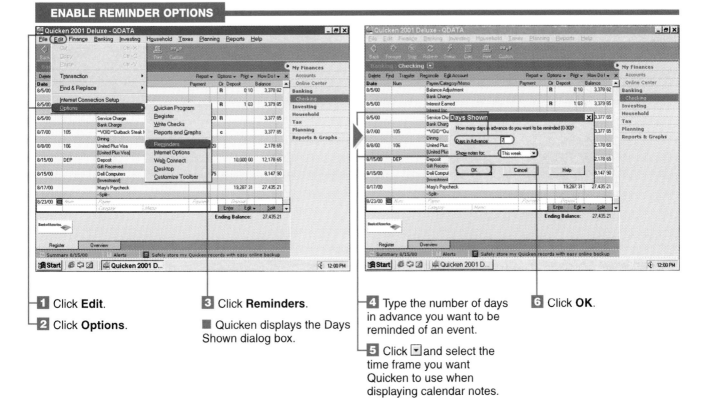

1 Click **Edit**.

2 Click **Options**.

3 Click **Reminders**.

■ Quicken displays the Days Shown dialog box.

4 Type the number of days in advance you want to be reminded of an event.

5 Click ▾ and select the time frame you want Quicken to use when displaying calendar notes.

6 Click **OK**.

ENABLE INTERNET OPTIONS

You can specify the bank accounts that you store at Quicken.com, change downloading options, and set miscellaneous downloading behavior options.

For further information on the Quotes tab or the Investment Accounts tab, see Chapter 7.

ENABLE INTERNET OPTIONS

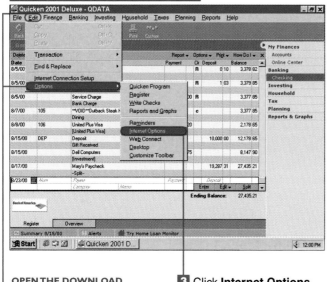

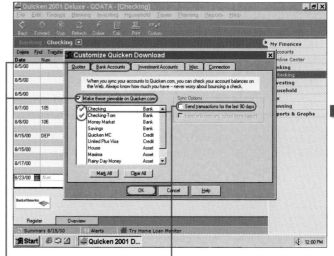

OPEN THE DOWNLOAD DIALOG BOX

1 Click **Edit**.

2 Click **Options**.

3 Click **Internet Options**.

■ Quicken displays the Customize Quicken Download dialog box.

IDENTIFY BANK ACCOUNTS

4 Click the **Bank Accounts** tab.

5 Click **Make these viewable on www.Quicken.com** (☐ changes to ✓).

6 Click each account you want available at www.Quicken.com (☐ changes to ✓).

■ You can limit the transactions you send.

7 Click **OK**.

What is the Quicken Background Download Manager and how do I run it?

You do not need to take any action; this program loads every time your computer starts.

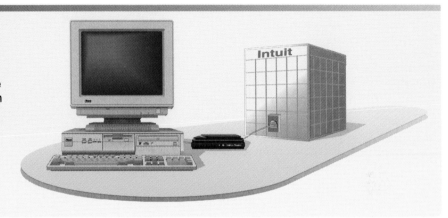

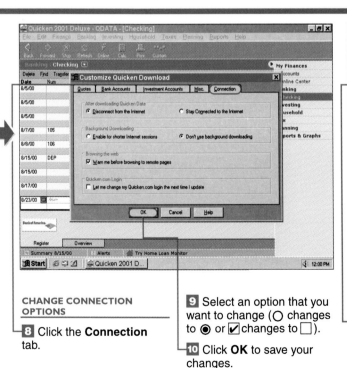

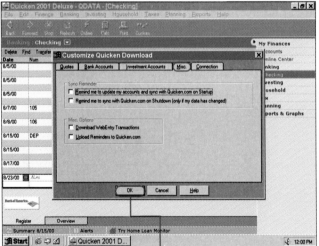

CHANGE CONNECTION OPTIONS

■8 Click the **Connection** tab.

■9 Select an option that you want to change (○ changes to ◉ or ☑ changes to ☐).

■10 Click **OK** to save your changes.

SET MISCELLANEOUS OPTIONS

■11 Click the **Misc.** tab.

■12 Select an option that you want to change (☐ changes to ☑).

■ You can set options for synchronizing with www.Quicken.com and identify information to upload and download.

■13 Click **OK** to save your changes.

You can change the way Quicken uses Web Connect data it receives from your financial institution. By default, Quicken uses information from financial institutions to update your Quicken data without saving the information to a file that you can use again. Quicken also closes after a Web Connect session. You can change these behaviors.

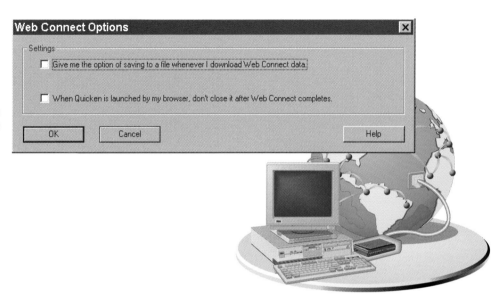

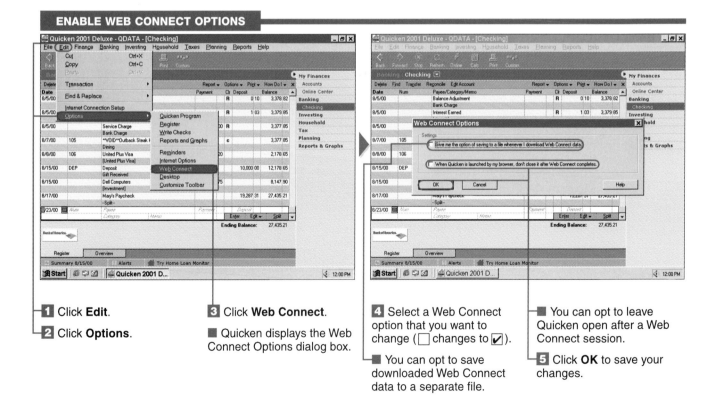

ENABLE WEB CONNECT OPTIONS

1 Click **Edit**.

2 Click **Options**.

3 Click **Web Connect**.

■ Quicken displays the Web Connect Options dialog box.

4 Select a Web Connect option that you want to change (☐ changes to ☑).

■ You can opt to save downloaded Web Connect data to a separate file.

■ You can opt to leave Quicken open after a Web Connect session.

5 Click **OK** to save your changes.

You can control the
QuickTabs that appear
each time you open
Quicken. You can choose
to "pick up where you
left off" or to display the
exact same set up of
QuickTabs each time you
open Quicken. If you
select the second option,
be sure to set up the
QuickTabs you want to
see before you exit
Quicken.

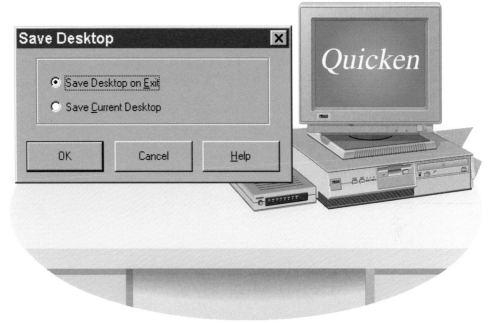

ENABLE DESKTOP OPTIONS

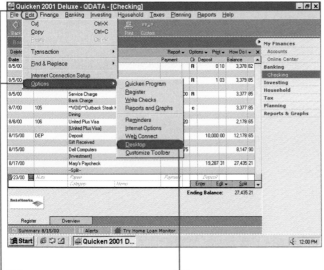

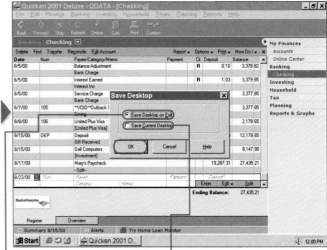

■1 Click **Edit**.

■2 Click **Options**.

■3 Click **Desktop**.

■ Quicken displays the Save
Desktop dialog box.

■4 Select an option that you
want to change (○ changes
to ●).

■ You can click **Save
Desktop on Exit** if you want
to see the same QuickTabs
you are currently viewing the
next time you open Quicken.

■ You can click **Save
Current Desktop** to see the
same set of QuickTabs every
time you open Quicken.

■5 Click **OK** to save your
changes.

CUSTOMIZE THE TOOLBAR

You can change the buttons that appear on Quicken's Toolbar to make the Toolbar support the way you work.

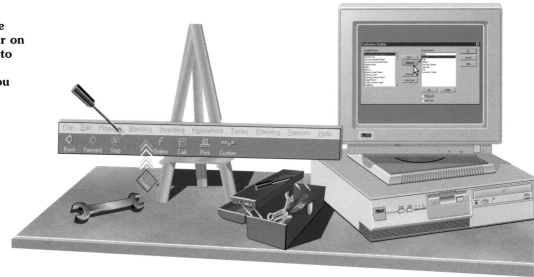

CUSTOMIZE THE TOOLBAR

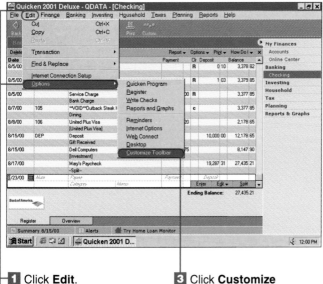

1 Click **Edit**.

2 Click **Options**.

3 Click **Customize Toolbar**.

■ Quicken displays the Customize Toolbar dialog box.

4 Select the options that you want to change.

■ To add buttons, click one in the Available Buttons list and then click **Add**.

■ To remove a button, click one in the Chosen Buttons list and click **Remove**.

■ To reorder buttons click one in the Chosen Buttons list and click **Move Up** or **Move Down.**

What happens if I hide both icons and text?

The toolbar disappears.

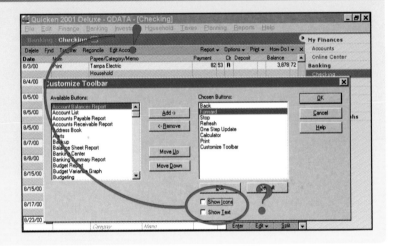

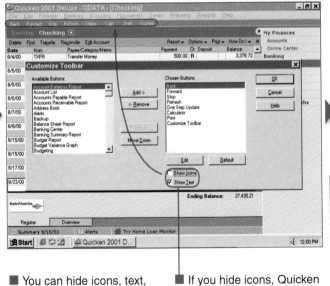

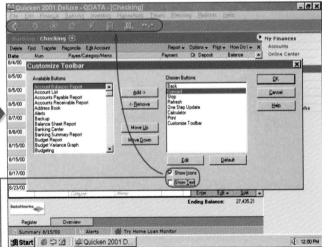

■ You can hide icons, text, or both (□ changes to ☑).

■ If you hide icons, Quicken displays text-only buttons.

■ If you hide text, Quicken displays icons as buttons.

INDEX

INDEX

INDEX

INDEX

Read Less, Learn More™

Visual

Simplified®

Simply the Easiest Way to Learn

For visual learners who are brand-new to a topic and want to be shown, not told, how to solve a problem in a friendly, approachable way.

All *Simplified*® books feature friendly Disk characters who demonstrate and explain the purpose of each task.

Title	ISBN	Price
America Online® Simplified®, 2nd Ed.	0-7645-3433-5	$24.99
Computers Simplified®, 4th Ed.	0-7645-6042-5	$24.99
Creating Web Pages with HTML Simplified®, 2nd Ed.	0-7645-6067-0	$24.99
Excel 97 Simplified®	0-7645-6022-0	$24.99
Excel for Windows® 95 Simplified®	1-56884-682-7	$19.99
FrontPage® 2000® Simplified®	0-7645-3450-5	$24.99
Internet and World Wide Web Simplified®, 3rd Ed.	0-7645-3409-2	$24.99
Lotus® 1-2-3® Release 5 for Windows® Simplified®	1-56884-670-3	$19.99
Microsoft® Access 2000 Simplified®	0-7645-6058-1	$24.99
Microsoft® Excel 2000 Simplified®	0-7645-6053-0	$24.99
Microsoft® Office 2000 Simplified®	0-7645-6052-2	$29.99
Microsoft® Word 2000 Simplified®	0-7645-6054-9	$24.99
More Windows® 95 Simplified®	1-56884-689-4	$19.99
More Windows® 98 Simplified®	0-7645-6037-9	$24.99
Office 97 Simplified®	0-7645-6009-3	$29.99
PC Upgrade and Repair Simplified®	0-7645-6049-2	$24.99
Windows® 95 Simplified®	1-56884-662-2	$19.99
Windows® 98 Simplified®	0-7645-6030-1	$24.99
Windows® 2000 Professional Simplified®	0-7645-3422-X	$24.99
Windows® Me Millennium Edition Simplified®	0-7645-3494-7	$24.99
Word 97 Simplified®	0-7645-6011-5	$24.99

Over 9 million *Visual* books in print!